TIT'HARU!

The Ten Days of Repentance

תטהרו
TIT'HARU!

The Ten Days of Repentance

by
Rav Avigdor HaLevi Nebenzahl

FELDHEIM PUBLISHERS
JERUSALEM   NEW YORK

Translated from the Hebrew *Sichos L'Yom HaKippurim*
(*Sifriat Beit El*, 5757).

The English translations of many of the Scriptural verses and Talmudic passages quoted in this book have been used with the permission of Artscroll/Mesorah Publications, Ltd.

ISBN 1-58330-718-4

First published 2004

Copyright © 2004 by Rabbi Yosef Eliyahu

All rights reserved.
No part of this publication may be translated,
reproduced, stored in a retrieval system or transmitted,
in any form or by any means, electronic, mechanical,
photocopying, recording or otherwise, without
prior permission in writing from the publishers.

FELDHEIM PUBLISHERS
POB 43163
Jerusalem, Israel

208 Airport Executive Park
Nanuet, NY 10954

10 9 8 7 6 5 4 3 2 1

www.feldheim.com

Printed in Israel

In Loving Memory of
Morris Grossman ז״ל

Husband, Father and Grandfather

He possessed the highest moral
and ethical standards.
A man of deep integrity,
whose life was a shining example
of overcoming adversity
through courage and kindness.

We will always remember him
for his inner strength, wisdom
and love of Klal Yisrael.

The world has truly lost a special person.

Richie and Anita Grossman

לזכרו האהוב של

ר' משה-מרדכי בן ישראל מענדל ז"ל

בעל, אב, וסבא אהוב

איש תם וישר
סמל להתגברות על קשיי-החיים
בנחישות, אומץ ונדיבות-הלב

לבנו ינצור לעולם את תעצומות-נפשו
חכמת-חייו, ואהבתו לכלל ישראל

בהלקחו — חסר עולמנו אדם מיוחד

"מִתְהַלֵּךְ בְּתֻמּוֹ צַדִּיק אַשְׁרֵי בָנָיו אַחֲרָיו" (משלי כ)

באהבה
ילדיו

זלמן-אליהו וחנה-רייזל גרוסמן

CONTENTS

Preface .... *ix*

Sichah One:
The Hidden Light Revealed *1*

Sichah Two:
Zochreinu LeChaim: Remember Us for Life —
      for the True Spiritual Life *17*

Sichah Three:
Ha'azinu — the Secret of the Tri-Part Code *29*

Sichah Four:
A Song of Divine Revelation *51*

Sichah Five:
Nullifying the Decrees *69*

Sichah Six:
A New Being *83*

Sichah Seven:
Joy in the Execution of Divine Justice *103*

Sichah Eight:
A Good Character — the Key to
      Heaven (and Earth) *121*

Sichah Nine:
"Chatasi LaHashem" *143*

Sichah Ten:
Taking Advantage of Heavenly Gifts *161*

Sichah Eleven:
Chukkas Olam (Turning Back the Clock) 177

Sichah Twelve:
"Selach Na al Kal Va'Chomer" 191

Sichah Thirteen:
"Before Hashem You Shall Be Purified" 205

Glossary 221

PREFACE

It is with great joy as well as fear and trepidation that I present to the English speaking public the brilliant and perceptive *sichos* on *Aseres Yemei Teshuvah* and Yom Kippur of HaRav Avigdor Nebenzahl *shlita*. The joy comes from gratitude to the Almighty for having given me the *zechus* of bringing to you HaRav Nebenzahl's insights and his elucidation of Hashem's kindness to mortal man with all his shortcomings, by giving him the opportunity to repent and come closer to Him than ever before.

In the words of Rambam:

> *How great is* teshuvah! *Yesterday he was separated from Hashem, God of Israel, as it says: "Rather, your iniquities have separated between you and your God"* (Yeshayahu *59:2*), *he cries out but is not answered...he performs mitzvos and they are thrown back in his face... Today he is beloved and pleasant...close, a friend of the Almighty...He now cleaves to the* Shechinah*...he performs mitzvos and they are eagerly and happily accepted...not only that, but Hashem yearns for them, as it says: "Then the offering of Yehudah and Yerushalayim will be pleasing to Hashem"* (Malachi *3:4*).
> (Hilchos Teshuvah *7:6–7, see* sichah *8*)

My fear and trepidation in providing this work to you stems from the great responsibility placed on my shoulders of accurately presenting to you insights and *chiddushim* that are not my own. I would like to thank Rav Nebenzahl for the trust he has placed in me by allowing me to publish this work without his prior perusal. It does, however, mean that any mistakes or concepts that are not clearly understood are my fault entirely. It has been a great honor and privilege to be associated with such a person whose entire life is devoted to the Almighty. It is my hope and prayer that after reading these *sichos*, you too will feel, as I have, that your Yom Kippur experience will never be the same.

My association with the Rav's weekly *sichos* began the week of *Parashas Shemos* 5757, when our yeshiva decided that it was time to enter the modern age and create our own website and have our own e-mail address. HaRav Aharon Bina *shlita* came up with the idea of translating HaRav Nebenzahl's weekly *sichos* into English and sending them to our alumni so that even though they were many miles away physically, they would be able to retain their spiritual attachment to the yeshiva and to the holy atmosphere of Yerushalayim. We began with a very modest list of those alumni whose e-mail addresses we had. Nobody could have imagined the success of this weekly project and today our subscription list numbers in the thousands, not to mention the many synagogues and offices who print their own copies for their members.

❑   ❑   ❑

The weekly *sichos*, as well as this book, would not have been possible without the many people who have helped and guided me throughout the years.

I would like to begin, of course, by thanking Rav Nebenzahl. His mere presence in our *beis midrash* mornings and evenings serves as an inspiration to all who come into contact with him. His all-encompassing knowledge in all areas of Torah, as well as his humility, are a shining example of what it means to be a true *eved Hashem*.

HaRav Aharon Bina *shlita*, *rosh yeshivah* of Yeshivas Netiv Aryeh, has given far more than his support for this project. The idea for this book began with a telephone call one Tammuz asking whether I would be able to translate the *sichos* for Yom Kippur and have them on our website by Yom Kippur! As formidable a task as this was, I knew that Rav Bina's devotion to *Klal Yisrael* means that when it comes to the needs of the community one can never say *no* to him. His complete dedication to his students and staff, as well as his tireless devotion to *chesed*, are renowned and are a very hard act to follow. His words of encouragement about the success of our weekly *sichos* provided me with the energy needed to complete this project.

In addition to HaRav Bina, I would like to thank the entire staff

Preface xi

of Yeshivas Netiv Aryeh for making this a great place to work. The devotion of this staff to educating the next generation and making this a *makom Torah* is unparalleled.

I would like to thank HaRav Adiel Mass for his editing of the Hebrew *sichos* during the years when the Rav spoke in Hebrew. It was his hard work and research into every source that made my own work that much easier. Now that the Rav has begun speaking to our students in English, I see just how demanding and difficult a job this is.

I would like to thank HaRav Yosef Eliyahu for his thorough and brilliant editing of the Hebrew version of *Sichos L'Yom HaKippurim*, of which this book is a translation. After all the many hours I have spent with the book, I appreciate his great efforts at clearly presenting the Rav's ideas and making sure that just the right words were chosen.

I would like to thank Mrs. Yocheved Lavon for a very professional editing job. Her choice of words, as well as her reorganizing of sentences and paragraphs, is very much appreciated. It is not for nothing that she came highly recommended by Feldheim Publishers.

I would like to thank Feldheim Publishers for giving this book a "high priority status" and doing their utmost to ensure that the book becomes available before Yom Kippur 5765.

The technical support for the weekly *sichos* is provided by Danny Schilo. His dedication cannot be described. There was a period of time when the weekly *sichah* would regularly be sent out at 2:00 AM on Thursday night, yet he always stayed awake in order to place it on our website at the first possible moment. I apologize for the *tirchah*, but the readers and I are very grateful. Danny has taken upon himself to create and to oversee the yeshiva's website as well as all of its computer operations and is always available when we need him.

Richard and Anita Grossman are the sponsors of our weekly *sichos* as well as the computer center in the yeshiva, in memory of HaRav Aryeh Bina *zt"l*. This is just one of the many acts of *tzedakah* and *chesed* they are involved in, all carried out very graciously and with great humility. May HaKadosh Baruch Hu give them the strength to continue their great service to *Klal Yisrael*.

I thank the many readers of our weekly *sichos* for their words of encouragement as well as their constructive criticism. When I push the <send> key, I cannot view the faces on the other end and this makes your letters with feedback even more important.

My own development would not have been possible without the guidance of my parents. My father Max Klein יבלחט״א and my mother Ruhama Klein ז״ל made the decision when I was a child to provide me with a Torah education, and I can honestly say that I would not be where I am without them. My father's involvement in his community throughout the years is an inspiration to all who meet him. My mother was born in Eretz Yisrael and always yearned to return. She would have been very proud to know that her grandchildren are being born and raised here.

My in-laws Sholom and Lottie Wilk of Har Nof have been a constant source of support. They have always been there when we needed them and they serve as great role models for our children, their grandchildren, showing what it means to lead a life of Torah, *avodah*, and *gemillus chasadim*.

I would like to thank my many *rebbeim* who have guided me throughout the years, beginning with my childhood in Washington, D.C., to my high school under the tutelage of HaRav Gedaliah Anemer *shlita*, and then at Yeshivas Rabbeinu Yitzchak Elchanan in New York.

Upon my arrival in Eretz Yisrael I was privileged to spend several years in *kollel*, under the leadership of HaRav Yaakov Katz *shlita*. HaRav Katz's clarity in learning, as well as in all areas of life, have been a great source of inspiration for me. He has served as a tremendous role model, demonstrating what it means to lead one's life according to the principle of תמים תהיה עם ה' אלקיך and to view the world through the lenses of אין עוד מלבדו.

No words can possibly convey the thanks that I owe to my wife Rina תחי׳. She not only encourages my growth in learning and teaching in the yeshiva, but she has been my equal partner in the weekly *sichos* as well as this book. No *sichah* is sent without her many hours of editing. There have been many weeks where there was proper justification for "skipping a week," yet she would not allow me to do so, nor to send anything that was not up to her standards. All of this is done without sacrificing her first priority to our family. I can say without a doubt, in the immortal words of R' Akiva about his righteous wife Rachel: "All my Torah and your Torah are hers." I am proud to say that she has as great, if not a greater, share in this book than I do. When it was decided to convert these *sichos* from internet to book form, it was she who took the *sichos* and edited them for publication. We spent many hours together going over nuances in language and accuracy of the text. May we merit seeing בנים ובני בנים עוסקים בתורה ובמצוות.

Last but not least, I would like to thank HaKadosh Baruch Hu not only for the *zechus* of being able to present the ideas in this book to the public, but for all the good He constantly showers upon me and my family. I am especially grateful for His having given me the privilege of teaching Torah in Yeshivas Netiv Aryeh and for being able to raise our children here in His Palace, in Eretz Yisrael.

Nehemiah D. Klein
Jerusalem
Tammuz 5764

SICHAH ONE
THE HIDDEN LIGHT REVEALED

THE SONG OF HA'AZINU —
CATALYST TO RETURN TO HASHEM

AT THE END of *Parashas Vayelech*, as Moshe Rabbeinu is preparing to take leave of the Jewish nation and pass on to the place Hashem has prepared for him in *Gan Eden*, Hashem informs him, *"Behold, you will lie with your forefathers, but this people will rise up and stray after the gods of the foreigners of the Land into whose midst they are coming, and they will forsake Me and annul My covenant that I have sealed with them"* (*Devarim* 31:16). It seems that all the sweat and toil that this loyal shepherd has invested in teaching the Jewish People will not produce perfect fruits.

This knowledge concerning the future of the Jewish nation could understandably cause Moshe Rabbeinu tremendous frustration, considering that he has literally given his life to instill in the people a strong faith in God. If all that Moshe has taught them up to this point will not deter them from abandoning Hashem, and if their witnessing all the great miracles in Egypt and the wonders in the desert has not led them to unconditional belief in Hashem, what can? Is there even a remote chance that at some point this nation will devote itself wholeheartedly to the Almighty?

Along with these harsh tidings, Hashem tells Moshe about the antidote to this problem: וְעַתָּה כִּתְבוּ לָכֶם אֶת הַשִּׁירָה הַזֹּאת וְלַמְּדָהּ אֶת בְּנֵי יִשְׂרָאֵל שִׂימָהּ בְּפִיהֶם לְמַעַן תִּהְיֶה לִּי הַשִּׁירָה הַזֹּאת לְעֵד בִּבְנֵי יִשְׂרָאֵל — *"So now, write this song for yourselves and teach it to the Children of Israel, place it in their mouth, so that this song shall be for Me a witness against the Children of Israel"* (ibid. 31:19). *Chazal* learn from here that "this song" refers to a Torah scroll, and they derive that it is a mitzvah for each person to write his own Torah scroll (see *Sanhedrin* 21b). The simple interpretation of this *pasuk*, however, refers to writing and studying the song of *Ha'azinu*, because it is that which will stand the Jews in good stead during times of trouble (see Rashi and Ramban, *Devarim* 31:19).

Hashem, *Korei HaDoros MeRosh* — *"He Who proclaimed the generations from the beginning"* (*Yeshayahu* 41:4) — reveals here that should the nation veer off the straight path and, as a result, וּמְצָאוּהוּ רָעוֹת רַבּוֹת וְצָרוֹת — *"Many evils and distresses will encounter it"* (*Devarim* 31:17), then it will be this song, describing the bitter exile that awaits those who stray off the path, which will succeed in returning those children to the bosom of their Father. Therefore, it is of utmost importance that the nation be well-versed in this song of *Ha'azinu*, so that when difficult times do arise, they will be able to recall the *girsa deyankusa* — "the text of their youth" (*"This song shall speak up before it as a witness"*) (ibid. 31:21). This is what the Omnipresent instructed, and Moshe hastened to fulfill the commandment. *"Moshe wrote this song on that day and he taught it to the Children of Israel"* (ibid.).

What elevates the song of *Ha'azinu* over the rest of the words of the Torah? For forty years, Moshe had been teaching the Jewish People the mitzvos and cautioning them that if they observed the Torah their lot would be improved, and if not, then they would, God forbid, be exiled. What, then, is so special about this last warning in the Torah — *Parashas Ha'azinu* — that it should serve as the catalyst for the Jewish People's return to Hashem?

ALL WORLD EVENTS ARE ALLUDED TO IN THIS SONG

FIRSTLY, RAMBAN TELLS us that all that is mentioned in *Ha'azinu* has actually taken place, with no exception. Furthermore, it is said in his name that all events in this world are alluded to in the song.

A story is told about a student of Ramban named Avner MiBurgus. After some time this student strayed from the righteous path, converted, and ultimately wrote hateful accusations against his brethren. Eventually he became the archenemy of the Jewish People for that era.

One day Ramban met him and asked him why he had gone astray. Avner pointed the finger of blame at Ramban himself, claiming he had taught that all the world events of the past and the future are alluded to in Parashas Ha'azinu. *Avner maintained that this was impossible — there was no way a countless number of events could be recorded in the mere forty-three* pesukim *of the song! He decided, therefore, to leave the fold.*

Ramban responded that these had indeed been his words and that, furthermore, he stood by them!

"If so," provoked Avner, "where am I and all of my actions recorded?" Ramban prayed for Divine guidance and returned to Avner with Hashem's answer: "Take the third letter of each word in the following pasuk, *and see that together they spell 'Avner'."* (אָמַרְתִּי אַפְאֵיהֶם אַשְׁבִּיתָה מֵאֱנוֹשׁ זִכְרָם) — *"(I said) I will cause their memory to cease from man" (Devarim 32:26).*

Upon hearing this, Avner was totally shocked. Trembling, he took a small sailing boat out to the depths of the ocean and drowned himself.

(Ta'amei HaMinhagim, p. 324)

THE UNIQUENESS OF HA'AZINU

INDEED, THE WORDS of Ramban hold true. Hidden among the lines of the song are countless lofty and exalted ideas. Nonetheless, since the purpose of the *parashah* is to bring about the repentance of the Jewish People, even simple contemplation of the words can reveal for us new ideas that we have not encountered before. The uniqueness of the song of *Ha'azinu* is that it condenses the world's entire history into one unit.

"Remember the days of yore, understand the years of generation after generation" (*Devarim* 32:6). The song consists of remembrance of things past, as well as an understanding of the future.

Sifri spells out that this song contains the present, the past, and the World to Come — it spans all of time. Each unit of time contributes its coloring to create a picture which is both sharp and convincing.

The song of *Ha'azinu* calls out to the Jewish People and tells them that if all that Moshe has said until now has not borne fruit, if there are still Jews who leave God because they do not fully appreciate how much Hashem is *"a God of faith without iniquity, righteous and fair is He"* (Devarim 32:4), this may stem from their having only a limited view of world events.

Jewish Nation! The events you see must be viewed in the context of world history! Do not focus only on what you see before your eyes, with your partial and truncated view of the here and now. Rather: *"Ask your father and he will relate it to you, and your elders and they will tell you"* (ibid. 32:7). Only when you view things comprehensively from the beginning of Creation until such time as *"He will bring retribution upon His foes"* (ibid. 32:43), can you derive a real understanding and lesson. Standing before the truth that will be revealed in the future, facing the past and present that will then be understood, seeing the whole picture that will then be exposed, all will acknowledge the greatness of Hashem.

Even nations that are far away will praise Hashem's conduct towards His people: *"O nations, sing the praises of His people, for He will avenge the blood of His servants"* (ibid.). Only then will it become clear how much justice Hashem demonstrates in His judging of the world. It is, therefore, wise not to wait until then, but to look now at the complete picture that is sketched for us in *Parashas Ha'azinu*.

OUR LIVES ARE LIKE A DAUB OF PAINT

SOMEONE ONCE ASKED me about the meaning of the Yom Kippur War. Without touching on all the possible answers to this question, I replied that the question itself is like looking at a large mural while standing only a few inches away from it. A person won't be able to see anything but the daub of paint directly in front of his eyes! He may even mock the artist for just splashing on blotches of various colors and calling it a painting. If, however, he views it from a distance, from a place where he can see the whole picture, he will then be able to discern trees, the sun, the moon, and so on. (Of course, painting pictures of the sun and the moon in their natural appearance is forbidden — see *Yoreh De'ah* 141:4.) Suddenly he will come to the realization that every spot of color in fact contributes marvelously to the totality of the picture.

The same applies to a wonderful tune. If one were to hear a single note, one would not enjoy it. Only a combination of many notes makes up a tune. A finished product can only be arrived at by properly combining all of the elements.

Our brief lives are like that small daub of paint in the enormous picture of world history. There are those who see but a small part, while there are those who manage to view things in a larger context. In any event, a man's life is but a miniscule segment of this multi-dimensional, eternal picture of the Creation.

Although we lack the ability to see the connections between all the events that have taken place over the thousands of years the world has been in existence, at times we manage to see Hashem's guiding hand when viewed in the context of a few hundred years. Let us look at an example of how our perception of world events changes according to the angle from which we view them.

WHAT WAS BRITAIN'S MERIT?

AROUND 300 YEARS ago, Britain was a small empire that became interested in acquiring colonies throughout the world. It succeeded to the extent that, until just after World War I, it was considered a major world power. If we were to ask, *"Through what merit did Britain manage to become such a mighty empire?"*, we would answer that it must have performed some mitzvah to deserve this.

There is no doubt that this is the correct answer — after all, Esav to this day rules in the world as his reward for the way he honored his father (see *Zohar* 1:146b).

After World War I, we would have answered that Britain became such a large empire so that it would be able to formulate the Balfour Declaration and assist in returning the Holy Land to the hands of the Jewish People. Had someone repeated this question after World War II, the answer would have had an added dimension: Hashem nurtured and developed the British Empire during this time so that it would be able to fight the dreaded German enemy and thus save the Land of Israel and the surviving remnants of the Jewish People. For example, they benefited strategically by putting military and naval bases on their colonized island of Malta and peninsula of Gibraltar, from where they could attack the Germans. However, at the end of World War II the British Empire was severely weakened — what was once a superpower was left in fragments and never recovered.

We see from here that, as each new paragraph in world history is revealed, so is another chapter in Hashem's providential management of the world. As each new chapter becomes known, the previous events become more understandable, as do the connections between these events. There is no doubt that in the distant future, new ways of viewing the British Empire will be uncovered. We will understand how exacting Hashem's judgment was, how each of Britain's protectorates had its own purpose and role in the larger picture, why each colony received its independence precisely when it did, and so on.

This broader point of view can provide the Jewish People with a truer perception of what is happening in the world, and will bring them back from their wandering in foreign fields. Today we only see things through our limited vision — it seems that one senator's vote or another's determines whether or not the United States sells arms to the Saudis, for example. However, the song of *Ha'azinu* serves to awaken us from this illusion: These decisions are not made by senators nor by the President of the United States, but by the Creator Who runs the world in accordance with His Divine plan, as sketched out for us in *Ha'azinu*. The senator is the camouflage for the realization of this plan, just as *"a high pressure system above Turkey"* is one of the ways Hashem manifests His decision to bring rain.

WHAT IS "THE HIDDEN LIGHT"?

PERHAPS WE CAN combine this thought — that *Ha'azinu* provides us with an overall view of world history — with what *Chazal* tell us regarding the light that Hashem created on the first day of Creation.

> *The light that the Holy One, Blessed is He, created on the first day, man could use it to survey everything from one end of the world to the other end. Once the Holy One, Blessed is He, looked at the Generation of the Flood and the Generation of the Dispersion and saw that their deeds were perverse, He proceeded to hide it from them. And for whom did He hide away this light? For the righteous people in the future.*
>
> (*Chagigah* 12a)

When I was younger, I understood the sentence, *"Man could use it to survey everything from one end of the world to the other end,"* to mean that, with the aid of this light, it would be possible to see over great distances. Perhaps it was even referring to circular light waves, making it possible to see beyond mountains and valleys. I now understand the essence of that ancient, hidden light on a totally different level.

This was an "intellectual light". By virtue of the illumination it provided, man was able to "survey", to discern events *"from one end of the world to the other end."* Through the illumination created on that first day, when the world was not yet run within the framework of time as we know it, world events could be viewed as one unit — as a continuum of events surrounding a central linchpin, not as fragments haphazardly occurring one after the other. Hashem, however, realized that this knowledge could be used by evil people for heresy. It is for this reason that this supreme illumination was hidden.

We find something similar in Ohr HaChaim's commentary on the *pasuk*: *"And Hashem showed him (Moshe Rabbeinu) the entire Land"* (*Devarim* 34:1). Ohr HaChaim tells us that Hashem lit up the land with the light *"that is sown for the righteous"* (*Tehillim* 97:11) — that light from Creation that is hidden away for the righteous. Through this light, says Ohr HaChaim in the name of our Sages, man can look from one end of the world to the other.

WHEN IS THE HIDDEN LIGHT REVEALED?

WHAT I WOULD like to stress today is that this light is not totally hidden! There is one day during the year when this light reappears — on Yom Kippur.

Our Yom Kippur *daven*ing begins with: אוֹר זָרוּעַ לַצַדִּיק וּלְיִשְׁרֵי לֵב שִׂמְחָה — *"Light is sown for the righteous; and for the upright of heart, gladness"* (ibid.). R' Yitzchak of Vienna wrote in his introduction to his work *Ohr Zarua* that by combining the last letter of each word in the *pasuk*, the name of R' Akiva is produced (in accordance with the Talmud *Yerushalmi*, where the last letter of the name Akiva is ה and not א, as we have it in the *Bavli*). Since R' Akiva was killed *al kiddush Hashem* on Yom Kippur (see *Midrash Shochar Tov, Mishlei* 9), our *tefillos* on this day begin with this *pasuk*.

Perhaps we can offer another reason for beginning our prayers with this *pasuk*: When *Chazal* wished to describe the Next World to us, they did so in a manner that we could comprehend. They said: *"In the World to Come, there is no eating, no drinking, no propagation, no business, no jealousy, no hatred, and no rivalry. Rather, the righteous sit with their crowns on their heads and delight in the radiance of the Divine Presence"* (*Berachos* 17a).

One who wishes to delve further will see that in this description of the World to Come we find Yom Kippur! Although refraining from eating and drinking is referred to in the Torah and colloquially as *inuy* ("affliction"), for one who strives for spirituality, who cleaves to the Torah, Yom Kippur is sweeter than honey. On this day we can finally separate ourselves from the physical compulsions of this world. We can spend a continuous twenty-four hour period immersed in spirituality. Above all, we can enjoy atonement from those sins that separate us from the *Shechinah*. It is for this reason that we begin Yom Kippur with the *pasuk*, "*Ohr zarua la'tzaddik*." When that same ancient light which was sown and hidden for the righteous of the future is revealed to us on Yom Kippur, *"the upright of heart experience gladness"* and joy — מֵעֵין עוֹלָם הַבָּא — in this preview of the Next World in which *"The righteous sit with their crowns on their heads and delight in the radiance of the Divine Presence."*

You may be tempted to ask, what is the purpose of this lofty revelation? Why do we need this hidden light that appears once a year, only to return from whence it came? In a typical Jewish manner, let us answer this question with a question. Rambam says (*Hilchos Teshuvah* 1:3) that Yom Kippur itself atones for those who repent, as it says: *"For on this day He shall provide atonement"* (*Vayikra* 16:30). By means of this day, Hashem grants atonement. For example, if one violated a negative commandment (excluding one punishable by death) and repented, his repentance would not be complete until the arrival of Yom Kippur. In other words, the *teshuvah* process would not be complete until the morning of this holy day (not the night, as it says, "for on this day"). Thus, even if the person were to sleep the entire day, the mere fact of his having been alive on that tenth day of Tishrei, combined with his repentance, would serve to atone for all the prohibitions he had transgressed.

What is the source of Yom Kippur's powers?

TESHUVAH IS BEYOND THE FRAMEWORK OF TIME

WHEN *CHAZAL* TOLD us (see *Pesachim* 54b) that *teshuvah* was one of the seven things that preceded the world, they were not trying to inform us of the chronological order of the creation, but rather, they were telling us that *teshuvah* was above and beyond the workings of this world. Under normal conditions, a person cannot perform an action today that will affect what took place yesterday, because man is bound by the framework of time. The process of *teshuvah*, however, was created before time began, and therefore the *teshuvah* one does today — which may be no more than a thought — is sufficient to erase his misdeeds from the previous day. If this repentance stems from fear (תְּשׁוּבָה מִיִּרְאָה), then whatever he did intentionally is transformed into an unintentional sin; if his repentance stems from love (תְּשׁוּבָה מֵאַהֲבָה), then his sins are transformed into merits. In other words, not only is the *lashon ha-ra* he spoke yesterday erased as if it had never been, but he even receives credit for having overcome his *yetzer ha-ra* and not slandering his fellow man anymore! (See *Yoma* 86b.)

How is it that man, who is limited and who lives in this world with all its limitations, is able to do something like that? The answer is this hidden light that comes down into our world once a year! This same illumination that is *me'ein Olam HaBa*, like a taste of the Next World, this same system that is not bound by the rules of this world, allows us on Yom Kippur to "go back in time" and act in a way that affects the past. The ability to repent the entire year derives its energy from that same light whose spark we see on Yom Kippur and that spreads throughout the entire year. The supernatural power of Yom Kippur stems from this hidden light — that same special intellectual illumination that comes down and lingers in our souls.

ADAM HARISHON DOES *TESHUVAH*

IT IS NO WONDER, therefore, that the *teshuvah* of the father of mankind — Adam HaRishon — grew from that same overall contemplation of six thousand years of history, from that same light, that same insight that sets *Ha'azinu* apart. The Midrash explains (*Bereishis Rabbah* 22) that when Adam HaRishon heard from Kayin that he had done *teshuvah* and had been forgiven, Adam HaRishon exclaimed, *"Can the power of teshuvah be so great without my knowing it?"* Adam HaRishon then stood up and recited: מִזְמוֹר שִׁיר לְיוֹם הַשַּׁבָּת — *"A psalm, a song for the Sabbath day"* (*Tehillim* 92:1).

What is the deep meaning of this Midrash, why did Adam HaRishon compose a psalm, and why specifically for Shabbos? It was the idea behind Shabbos that helped him repent! Knowing about the *tikkun* that is destined to come to the world when it reaches its seventh millennium and the accounting all of creation will be expected to give at the conclusion of six thousand years is what brought Adam HaRishon to this realization. From this more comprehensive vantage point, sin is suddenly viewed in all its worthlessness. In the context of this final accounting, the one in which each person's preparations for the "Sabbath of the World" are summed up — it becomes clear that there is no advantage to sin and that the wicked person does not emerge with any gain from his sins.

We also realize that the reasons that the British Empire grew stronger and *"blossomed like grass"* (*ibid.* 92:8) were as follows:

- ❑ In reward for a mitzvah it had performed and not due to its military strength
- ❑ Mainly in order to demonstrate Hashem's righteousness to the world: לְהַגִּיד כִּי יָשָׁר ה' — *"to declare that Hashem is just"* (ibid. 92:16), and for no other reason

It is through this understanding, as discerned in the light of *teshuvah*, that we have explained in the past how "intentional sins are transformed into merits." The sin is not only erased, it is transferred to the credit account! We have explained (*Sichos LeSefer Shemos*, Hebrew edition, p. 389) that there can be no act in this world whose outcome does not ultimately serve to glorify Hashem's Name. Even someone as evil as Pharaoh, who defied Hashem with incredible audacity, brought about a *kiddush Hashem* in the end, for Hashem smote him with ten plagues and split the Red Sea in order to drown his army. In this manner, Hashem's Name was sanctified in this world. We therefore see how even intentional sins can bring about a *kiddush Hashem* in the long run. The distinction, therefore, between sin and mitzvah lies in a person's attitude alone. The *tzaddik* wishes his actions to be part of the great *kiddush Hashem* of the future, while the evil person does not.

When the Jewish People learn the secret of this all-encompassing view, as seen in *Ha'azinu*, and are able to discern the spiritual side of every event, they will see that it is the hand of Hashem that runs things and they will understand that events in the world only occur in order to bring about changes in the lives of the Jewish People. Napoleon's victories came about in order to produce changes both for the good and for the bad in the lives of Jews in Europe and other parts of the world. Beyond this view, there is not much significance to "the Great Emperor." With such understanding, the sinner will also wish to join the ranks of the righteous! Once Hashem has been revealed as the Sole Power and the sinner recognizes that, directly or indirectly, all his deeds must ultimately sanctify Hashem's Name, he will want to sanctify the Name of Hashem directly. This will is what was previously lacking in his actions.

Teshuvah out of love is the desire to join the Godliness that is present in this world. When a sinful act is followed by a desire to repent out of love for Hashem, the act is then transformed into a complete and perfect performance of a mitzvah. We can therefore say that *Ha'azinu*'s uniqueness lies in the fact that its message will serve to awaken within the Jewish nation the desire to cleave to the Sole Driving Force in this world.

AHARON HAKOHEN IS FORBIDDEN
TO ENTER THE SANCTUARY "AT ALL TIMES"

IN HIS COMMANDMENT regarding the service of the *kohen gadol* on Yom Kippur, Hashem says to Moshe: דַּבֵּר אֶל אַהֲרֹן אָחִיךָ וְאַל יָבֹא

בְּכָל עֵת אֶל הַקֹּדֶשׁ — *"Speak to Aharon, your brother; he shall not come at all times into the Sanctuary" (Vayikra 16:2).*

בְּכָל עֵת — *"at all times"* can have two possible interpretations:

1. He shall not enter whenever he wishes, rather only on Yom Kippur and under the conditions outlined further on in the *parashah*.
2. Along the lines of what we have just said, he cannot enter בְּכָל עֵת — on any day that is bound by the limits of time.

Yom Kippur, however, whose foundation is above the general definition of time, is the one day when he is permitted to enter. Yom Kippur is made up of that special essence of the Next World, of the future, and is thus above time and not included in the word עֵת, "time". (Kli Yakar adds that just as prophecy can only exist for the sake of the Jewish nation [see Rashi on *Devarim* 2:16–17], so too the *kohen gadol*'s approaching the *Kodesh HaKodashim* can only come about through the virtue of the Jewish People. The *kohen gadol* is thus prevented from entering the *Kodesh* at any regular עֵת, when the sins of the Jewish People create a separation between them and Hashem. On Yom Kippur, when *Am Yisrael* are as angels who are above time, he is permitted to enter since this holy day does not fall into the regular category of time.)

Time, by definition, is short-lived. The world is limited by its finiteness. The day of *teshuvah*, however, which was created before the concept of time, is a day with infinite capabilities. Yom Kippur elevates us above the workings of this world, above sin, whose existence can only take place within the limited period of six thousand years known as "This World".

WHY DO WE SAY *KOL NIDREI* YOM KIPPUR EVE?

IT APPEARS TO me that this idea can provide an additional reason why *Kol Nidrei* is specifically recited the night of Yom Kippur. As we know, many reasons have been given for this *minhag*:

- *Poskim* write that this is the only time during the whole year when the entire nation is in shul (see *Tanya Rabbati* 80 in the name of Rabbeinu Tam). These *poskim* would permit reciting *Kol Nidrei* even after sunset, in order not to lose this opportunity, despite the fact that annulling vows is generally forbidden on Shabbos and Yom Tov, unless necessary for that day.
- The Rav (HaGaon HaRav Shlomo Zalman Auerbach) *zt"l* stated that there is one sin that we are able to nullify for ourselves — a vow. On *Erev Yom Kippur* we come to Hashem and say to Him, "Whatever was in our power to correct, we have corrected; now we ask You to do what is in Your power."
- Based on what we have just said, we can add an additional reason. *Hataras nedarim*, "annulling vows", is the only act with which we can correct what we have done in the past. It has a retroactive effect that actually erases the vow, as if it had never taken place. What more appropriate time to annul vows than on Yom Kippur — the day on which the hidden light is revealed?

This light contains the secret of the world above time. (From the power of this day we are able to annul vows the remainder of the year as well).

YOM KIPPUR — BEYOND TIME AND BEYOND SPACE

WE CAN NOW say that the unique attribute of this light that is revealed on Yom Kippur is that it is not bound by the restriction of what was in the past and what will be in the future — all reality is viewed as one entity. On this day, man is given the ability to view the entire world in one swoop — to understand today that what will affect the future is what we have done in the past.

This is also the secret of *Ha'azinu*. We are promised that when the Jewish People will be in a situation of *"many evils and distresses*" (*Devarim* 31:21), the message that comes from this song — that which combines past, present, and future — will elevate the Jewish People above the limited time dimensions of this world. *Teshuvah* is above time: it not only existed prior to the creation of the world with all its limitations, but will continue to exist after this world ceases. One who is able to step outside of the imaginary framework of this world and rise above the dimensions of time will find himself in the world of *teshuvah*. The infinite world of *teshuvah* surrounds time on all sides and awaits those who wish to return.

On Yom Kippur we are handed an annual pass to the endless regions of *teshuvah* — to freedom that is beyond the dimensions of this world. The physicality that drags us down (eating, drinking, etc.) is removed from us, and we are handed a ticket that brings us to what is beyond — our freedom. What is left for us to do? We are to avail ourselves of this heavenly gift and free ourselves of contrived pressures, of unnecessary worries and other insignificant matters emanating from the framework of time. On this holy day, we have the ability to easily merge with that same intellectual illumination that characterized the beginning of Creation and to utilize it for *teshuvah*, which will bring us and the Creation to its ultimate purpose.

On Yom Kippur the *kohen gadol* enters the *Kodesh HaKodashim*, a place that *Chazal* describe as "beyond space." When they measured the area of the *Kodesh HaKodashim*, it was found to be 400 square *amos*. When they measured the available space after having placed the *Aron*, "the Ark", in it — the area was the same! (See *Bava Basra* 99a and *Sichos LeSefer Shemos*, Hebrew edition, p. 178.) This means that the *Kodesh HaKodashim* had a supernatural aspect to it. When the *kohen gadol* entered this miraculous area on the tenth of Tishrei, it meant he had joined those forces which are not bound by the limits of this world.

There is a reason why the *kohen gadol* is only permitted to enter this "supernatural" space once a year, on that day which is completely above nature. The *kohen gadol* is the representative of the people; he is the person who physically enters the inner sanctum, yet the souls of the entire Jewish nation accompany him in holy awe. They are totally absorbed by the Divine benevolence that places them above the concepts of time and space.

This great day provides us with a wondrous chance to attain levels that we cannot reach the rest of the year. This is a golden opportunity to enter the portals of the world of *teshuvah*, that empire of unlimited opportunity. When this light from the ancient past which is hidden for the righteous of the future rests upon us, we are combining within ourselves the past and the future. In other words, within man suddenly resides the secret of *Ha'azinu*, the song that provides everyone with the ability to erase the undeveloped past and to begin a new future — one filled with new hope.

Even harsh decrees are confined within the limitations of time and space, while on Yom Kippur we find ourselves above time and space. We pass over the finiteness of this world to the eternity in which *"the righteous will delight in the radiance of the Divine Presence."*

As we have said, the spiritual light of this day of devotion to Hashem illuminates the entire year. As a result, the upcoming month of Marcheshvan has no need for any Yom Tov. It is called Marcheshvan because we are still under the influence of the revelation of this hidden light, and as a result our lips whisper (*merachashos*) on their own the beautiful melodies of the month of Tishrei and speak of its incredible light.

SICHAH TWO
ZOCHREINU LECHAIM: REMEMBER US FOR LIFE — FOR THE TRUE SPIRITUAL LIFE

MAP OF FAITH

Moshe spoke the words of this song into the ears of the entire congregation of Israel, until their conclusion.
(Devarim 31:30)

This song of *Ha'azinu* that Moshe taught the Jewish People was assigned a very crucial role in the history of the Jewish People in particular and the world in general. Those who explore the meaning of this song will be influenced to repent at the End of Days, as Hashem tells Moshe:

This people will rise up and stray after the gods of the foreigners of the Land, into whose midst they are coming, and they will forsake Me and annul My covenant that I have sealed with them... It shall be that when many evils and distresses come upon them, then this song shall speak up before them as a witness, for it shall not be forgotten from the mouth of their offspring.
(Devarim 31:16, 21)

Ha'azinu will be like a reliable witness who speaks such obvious truth that there is no possibility of contradicting him. What will be his testimony from the witness stand at the End of Days? The song will testify that the terrible tragedies and atrocities that befell the Jewish nation did not happen for no reason. Everything, the song will say to Israel — the sin and its associated punishment — was foreseen and foretold.

In the past we have wondered: Apart from the lofty, hidden messages in *Ha'azinu*, which we have not yet merited to understand (see Ramban 32:40), can we in any way comprehend the rare, secret power of this song? What is in it that gives it the ability to instill such a lesson into the heart of the Jewish People?

We answered that its uniqueness lies in the fact that it views all world events together, as one comprehensive whole. Perhaps we can express it as follows: A message as convincing as that of *Ha'azinu* was not available to the rebukers of Israel. The prophets went to great trouble to describe to the people the punishment that awaited them if they did not follow the words of Hashem. Yirmeyahu even walked to the outskirts of Yerushalayim with rods of wood around his neck (as described in *Yirmeyahu* 27) for this purpose — all for naught. The people did not heed the message.

Why should they believe the prophet when his forecast totally contradicted what they saw with their own eyes? Even when the prophets warned them — based on the nation's past experiences — that if they kept on sinning, the tragedies that befell their forebears would happen to them too, they had so few examples to refer to that they could not successfully motivate the people. The Jews' collective experiences were limited at the time and so they were no match for the human heart armed with the oft-quoted claim: "It will never happen to me." At the End of Days, when all the lessons derived from the events in world history accumulate, the sheer quantity of incidents will produce a qualitative lesson. Then, no argument will be able to withstand such a crushing and convincing message.

This is the meaning of the Torah's words, *"This song shall speak up before it as a witness"* — the song will speak for itself! All the warnings of the Torah and the prophets will be proven accurate beyond a shadow of doubt.

An atlas contains many maps, each pertaining to a particular topic. For example, a map of global rainfall highlights the annual rainfall in the various regions; an economic map shows the economic strengths of each area, and so on. *Ha'azinu* will eventually be revealed as the universal map of faith. It will not show changing borders or world wars. The theme that will clearly be spelled out in this map is that throughout history, Hashem has ruled the world in accordance with His will.

Despite all that we have said lauding the great impact inherent in *Parashas Ha'azinu*, we must keep in mind that it only affects those who heed its words (*ha'azinu* means to listen). Even a wonder drug only heals those who take it and follow the proper dosage! Like keeping the medication in the house and doing nothing more, just keeping *Ha'azinu* on the bookshelf will have no effect on anyone, even at the End of Days.

THE FAITH FORMULA

THE ONE THING in *Ha'azinu* that will be unquestionably convincing to the person studying it is the continuum of events throughout thousands of years of history. It will highlight the obvious connection between fulfillment of mitzvos and the condition of the nation. Understanding *Ha'azinu* will bring one to belief in Hashem.

How can this be? If we can understand the *"formula of faith"* that is found between the lines of the song, we can perhaps apply it to our own daily lives. One generally defines *emunah* as believing in that which our physical senses are not able to perceive. To define true *emunah*, however, we must add another element to our definition: Just as we must believe what our eyes cannot see, we must also suspend belief in what our eyes do see! Is faith in Hashem the main contribution of *Ha'azinu* to our lives? Not necessarily, for until 150 years ago, there was hardly a Jew who lacked this belief. Even today, a vast majority of the Jewish People believe in Hashem. Not all believers observe His mitzvos, because they attribute events in the world to external powers and forces. Through their eyes it seems that the president of a particular country decides their fate. Although they believe intellectually in the existence of a Creator, His presence is not readily apparent and there are unfortunately many casualties in this struggle between intellectual belief and what the senses perceive.

The *chiddush* of *Ha'azinu* is that through this song, the nation will understand once and for all that what occurs in this world is only in accordance with the will of the hidden Master of creation. There are no other forces at work, and we will all come to acknowledge that what our eyes saw was merely an optical illusion.

LOOKING THROUGH ROSE-COLORED GLASSES

TOTAL BELIEF IN Hashem, therefore, requires an initial understanding that our eyes are mere tools, and what they see is not reliable enough to contradict our belief in Him That Is Hidden. If we are true to this understanding and, rather than making our senses the basis for our belief, we make our belief the foundation for what our senses perceive, we will have forged a new road for ourselves. A person who uses his eyes to strengthen his belief in the spiritual, who succeeds in using them to make clear spiritual observations and distinctions, will use his vision to strengthen his belief. To use a colloquial expression: He who wears rose-colored glasses has a rosy view of the world.

This is how Rambam begins his *Mishnah Torah* (*Hilchos Yesodei HaTorah*). In the first chapter Rambam establishes the foundation for an intellectual perception of Hashem. It is not until one reaches the second chapter, after absorbing the principles of the first chapter, that he can learn to use his eyes to view the wonders of creation as a means to achieving love of Hashem. Only once there is a strong foundation of belief can we say: הַשָּׁמַיִם מְסַפְּרִים כְּבוֹד קֵל וּמַעֲשֵׂי יָדָיו מַגִּיד הָרָקִיעַ — *"The heavens declare the glory of God and the firmament tells of His handiwork"* (*Tehillim* 19:2).

THE EYES AND THE HEART WORK IN TANDEM

WE MUST EMPHASIZE that our eyes alone are not to blame for our lack of proper belief. There is another factor that causes our eyes to view what is happening purely in physical terms, devoid of any *emunah*. To use the metaphor cited above, it places "black glasses" upon the eyes — the guilty party is the heart. The heart tends to ignore the presence of the Creator, because acknowledging a Creator would necessitate suppressing its physical desires. The "boss" of the eyes, therefore, is the heart, which gives them the desire to be free of all rules and regulations and to do as they want.

Does this sound like a novel idea? You must realize that this is what we recite twice daily: וְלֹא תָתוּרוּ אַחֲרֵי לְבַבְכֶם וְאַחֲרֵי עֵינֵיכֶם — *"And you shall not explore after your heart and after your eyes, after which you stray"* (*Bemidbar* 15:39 — last paragraph of *Kerias Shema*). We usually understand this *pasuk* to be talking about watching illicit behavior. *Chazal* went further: *"And you shall not explore after your heart' — this is apostasy, 'and after your eyes, after which you stray' — this is thinking of sinning"* (*Berachos* 12b).

Why are there two derivations from this *pasuk*? If the *pasuk* had only been referring to gazing at forbidden sights, the eyes should have been mentioned before the heart, for that is the natural process — the eyes see and then the heart covets. The Torah begins by warning us about the heart, because the heart is what causes our eyes to wander and be misled! The Torah is warning us, "Take care not to follow the dictates of the heart." Why? *"So that you may remember and perform all My commandments"* (*Bemidbar* 15:40).

If the heart leads the eyes to view the world from a physical, sensory viewpoint, we should not be surprised that the information that the eyes provide is infected with heresy. Let us not forget that the section of the Torah from which we have just quoted (*Parashas Tzitzis*) which warns us against the damage our hearts and eyes can cause, comes on the heels of the Torah's narrative about the spies. This juxtaposition, *Chazal* tell us, is because their eyes saw what their hearts *told* them to see (see *Sotah* 35a).

We therefore need to have a realistic view of events — and the true reality is not what our eyes see. Our eyes view an order of reality known as nature, that Hashem gave us for our own good, so there could be some semblance of order in our lives. We need to know that to heat water we must place it on the fire, and to cool it down we must put it in the refrigerator. This in no way implies that fire has the power to heat things and that ice has the power to cool them. These are simply rules that were created for our convenience, and they can be changed at any moment according to the will of the One Who invented them (as Ramban tells us at the end of *Parashas Bo* — *Shemos* 13:16).

To summarize, we can say that the song of *Ha'azinu* can bring about a change in the life of the one who studies it, because it will bring him to the root of all things — belief in Hashem and a correct outlook on life.

WHAT IS LIFE?

THIS VIEW OF life has tremendous implications regarding our *davening* during the *Aseres Yemei Teshuvah*. What is the central focus of our prayers during these days? The word that keeps recurring is *chaim*, "life". For example, we pray: זָכְרֵנוּ לְחַיִּים מֶלֶךְ חָפֵץ בַּחַיִּים וְכָתְבֵנוּ בְּסֵפֶר הַחַיִּים לְמַעַנְךָ אֱלֹקִים חַיִּים — "Remember us for life, O King Who desires life, and inscribe us in the Book of Life — for Your sake, O living God."

We also say: מִי כָמוֹךָ אַב הָרַחֲמִים זוֹכֵר יְצוּרָיו לְחַיִּים בְּרַחֲמִים — "Who is like You, merciful Father, Who remembers His creatures mercifully for life"; וּכְתוֹב לְחַיִּים טוֹבִים כָּל בְּנֵי בְרִיתֶךָ — "And inscribe all the children of Your covenant for a good life"; and בְּסֵפֶר חַיִּים בְּרָכָה וְשָׁלוֹם — "In the book of life, blessing, and peace..." We must stop and ask ourselves, what type of life are we referring to? Are we referring to a life that is guided by our eyes or by our minds? Have we ever stopped to think what this type of life we are asking for looks like? Or do we have implanted in our hearts the childish thought, "First give us life and then we will see what we can do with it"?

Here we can determine whether we really do have the proper outlook on life. Imagine for yourselves that a person is offered a fabulous proposal. He is told that if he agrees to simply lie on the grass outside his home his entire life, all his needs will be provided for — food, clothing, everything. He will never have to work again! I would think that any intelligent person would respond, "Thanks, but no thanks." Why? Is this not the ultimate in luxury — the worry-free life people dream of? The answer is *yes* — for a cow! There can be no better life for a cow; let her lie every day in the pasture and chew the best grass. But a human being who is emotionally healthy cannot simply lie in a pasture all day. We can now say that not every kind of life is considered a true life by human standards. A person possessing his full intellect and emotions understands full well that a life centered only around food and shelter is not a real life.

This is exactly what a Jew should feel. Life that only includes food, work, raising a family, and an interest in the news, is a good life for other people, but not for a Jew with a Godly soul! Considering the potential within us and the purpose for which we were brought into this world, this type of life is like sitting idly in the pasture. The main focus of our lives should be the spiritual, the hidden, not that element which is easily perceived by our eyes. To live in light of this truth is the main challenge for those who enter this world.

THE ASHES OF YITZCHAK

LET US PRESENT an example that illustrates how the spiritual aspect is the root of physical life. In the end of the *tochachos* section of *Parashas Bechukosai*, Hashem tells us: *"I will remember My covenant with Yaakov and also My covenant with Yitzchak, and also My covenant with Avraham will I remember, and I will remember the*

Land" (*Vayikra* 26:42). The verb "to remember" is mentioned three times in the *pasuk*: once in relation to Yaakov, once in relation to Avraham, and once in relation to the Land. It is not used in conjunction with Yitzchak. Why? The Midrash explains: HaKadosh Baruch Hu *says, "I do not need to renew the remembrance of Yitzchak because his ashes are constantly gathered before Me on the* mizbe'ach *upon which he was bound'"* (*Vayikra Rabbah* 36:5).

How can this be? Yitzchak, after all, was not burned at all! The Torah explicitly tells us that he stepped down from the *mizbe'ach* and accompanied his father to Be'er Sheva. Their two attendants who were with them could testify to this (see *Bereishis* 22:19). What ashes are we then referring to?

The answer is that the *real* Yitzchak was indeed burned upon the *mizbe'ach*! The two young men could only testify that Yitzchak's body went with them to Be'er Sheva, but the body that is visible to the eyes is not the true one. The essential Yitzchak is the spiritual one; his spiritual ashes indeed remain gathered atop the *mizbe'ach* even after his body stepped down. From the perspective of his inner volition, that Yitzchak was unconditionally ready to be sacrificed. This will, that is not visible to us, is revealed before the Creator, and it is this merit that brings redemption for his descendants to this day.

FILLING OUR LIVES WITH SPIRITUAL CONTENT

A JEW'S TRUE life is entirely spiritual. We must use the physical life Hashem gives us for the sake of our spiritual side. When we beseech Hashem, זָכְרֵנוּ לְחַיִּים — "remember us for life," this is the life we mean.

We ask for physical longevity only in order to live as Avraham did. The Torah tells us: וְאַבְרָהָם זָקֵן בָּא בַּיָּמִים — *"Now Avraham was old, well on in years"* (*Bereishis* 24:1). The expression בָּא בַּיָּמִים can also mean that he "arrived (בָּא) (in the Next World) (בְּיָמִים) with days" — accompanied by all the days Hashem had given him. Avraham returned the empty vessels he had been given — his days — filled to their capacity with good.

On this point, I would like to say that Einstein was correct: time is relative — but from a spiritual perspective! The number of years of our lives, the time allocated to us from heaven, only has value according to what we do with it. It is quite possible that an old man lived the true life for only a few hours while the other eighty years of his life were wasted on "pasture" for his body.

If we desire longevity in order to fill our lives with spiritual content: to encourage Torah study, to perform more acts of *chesed*, to settle *Eretz Yisrael*, and to bring our distant brothers to Torah lifestyles, then our request for life is justified. If, however, we desire life for worldly matters, for passing moments of pleasure, we have contradicted our very prayers: זָכְרֵנוּ לְחַיִּים מֶלֶךְ חָפֵץ בַּחַיִּים — *"Remember us for life, O King Who desires life."* That is not the "life" that Hashem desires!

Some years ago at a rabbinical conference, one of the participating *rabbanim* declared that the Torah is as essential to us as air for breathing. R' Baruch Ber Leibowitz *zt"l* (author of *Birkas Shemuel* on *Shas*), who was also present at the gathering, got up and opposed this definition. He said that air is only a means through which we live; if someone were to invent a substitute for oxygen, we would be able to forego breathing air. Torah, on the other hand, is life itself! The Jewish nation has no life other than observance of Torah and mitzvos.

INVESTING WISELY

I AM AFRAID that one who asks for additional life without planning to use it for greater spirituality can be compared to the man in the following parable:

> *A person once wished to start a company, but did not have the means with which to finance it. Upon investigating the matter, he was told of a rich, charitable individual. He approached him, requesting a generous grant to lay the foundation for his business. To his great joy, the rich man immediately agreed.*

> A year later, the same person again came knocking at the door of the wealthy philanthropist. He explained to him that the business had fallen upon some difficult times and requested an even more generous donation than he had the first time.
> The donor asked, "What did you do with the initial sum of money?"
> The man produced the necessary papers and began to read: "Twenty thousand shekels went for advertising, fifty thousand shekels were used for cars for employees, sixty thousand for refresher courses in America that also included sightseeing trips, forty thousand for weekends for the employees and their families..."

One could assume that even though he was very good-hearted, it would be very difficult for the wealthy man to give such a fool even one additional penny!

Every year we ask "the Wealthy Benefactor" for an additional grant — we ask for a larger budget of life. Each year our material needs grow: we are in need of more money, more health, because the family is growing or, God forbid, there are many problems. We come before Him and it is only natural that we make this request for the upcoming year. Where shall we hide our faces when the Wealthy One asks what we did with the grant we were given last year?

Let us not even discuss the past — what will we do now with this new grant we hope to receive? Will we once again invest it in weekends? This is the ultimate in chutzpah — to come back and ask for a loan of life for these purposes! Such a person can, without a doubt, be found beating hard on his chest during Yom Kippur, reciting: עַל חֵטְא שֶׁחָטָאנוּ לְפָנֶיךָ בְּעַזּוּת מֵצַח — "For the sin we have sinned before You with brazenness."

AN INVESTMENT PROPOSAL

HOW CAN WE advise the businessman in our story? With a very simple suggestion: When he puts in his request to his benefactor, he should also include a proposal for improving his efficiency in the coming year. We must promise Him in Whose hands are life and wealth that at least from here on, there will be a drastic cutback in excesses and that this time all the money will be plowed back into rehabilitating the business and making it prosper.

In our case, the rich man is also the owner and founder of the business! If we can prove that His business will follow the right path and become productive and successful, He will gladly approve the request for a new loan. After all, the success of the business is first and foremost His concern.

זָכְרֵנוּ לְחַיִּים מֶלֶךְ חָפֵץ בַּחַיִּים. What should our intentions be when we recite this prayer? Shlomo HaMelech says: *"The end of a matter is better than its beginning"* (*Koheles* 7:8). When the beginning of a sentence is thought out, then the end of the sentence is understood. Positive end results come about when the beginning is planned well. If at the outset of our supplication we have the proper intent, then the end will also turn out well.

When we say, זָכְרֵנוּ לְחַיִּים מֶלֶךְ חָפֵץ בַּחַיִּים וְכָתְבֵנוּ בְּסֵפֶר הַחַיִּים — *"Remember us for life, O King Who desires life, and inscribe us in the Book of Life,"* if we mean the true life, the spiritual life, then we have properly understood the latter half of this sentence as well: לְמַעַנְךָ אֱלֹקִים חַיִּים — *"for Your sake, O living God."*

SICHAH THREE
HA'AZINU — THE SECRET OF THE TRI-PART CODE

"O VILE AND UNWISE PEOPLE"

AT THE ALMIGHTY'S command, Moshe Rabbeinu assembles the Jewish People and reads before them the song of *Ha'azinu*. This song can be divided into two main sections:

1. An introduction — the first seven *pesukim*
2. The history of the world, from its beginning until the end of our redemption

Rashi, in his commentary, cites Sifri's opinion that the last two *pesukim* of this introduction are a call to the Jewish People to listen closely to the words of the song and to extract from it the appropriate lessons: הֲלַה' תִּגְמְלוּ זֹאת עַם נָבָל וְלֹא חָכָם — *"Is it to Hashem that you do this, O vile and unwise people?"* (*Devarim* 32:6). Rashi comments:

> *Is it to Hashem that you do this?* — an expression of astonishment: is it before Him that you cause anguish? He Who has in His power to take His due from you and Who benefited you with all manner of goodness?!
>
> "*O people who are vile*"— for they forgot what had been done for them; "*and unwise*" — in having failed to understand the consequences of their conduct.

The description נָבָל, "vile", refers to the past, to one who repays bad for good, as was the case with Naval the Carmelite who refused to return David's *chesed*: כִּי כִשְׁמוֹ כֶּן הוּא נָבָל שְׁמוֹ וּנְבָלָה עִמּוֹ — *"For he is as his name implies — Naval is his name and* ('nevalah') *revulsion is his trait"* (*Shemuel* I 25:25). For this reason, according to Rashi's interpretation, עַם נָבָל means that the people *"forgot what had been done for them,"* in the past tense, whereas חָכָם — "wise", alludes to the future: *"Who is a wise man? One who foresees what will be"* (*Tamid* 32a), and therefore Rashi explains "unwise" as failing to understand *"the (future) consequences of"* their conduct.

This verse has two grievances against the Jewish People:

1. That they have forgotten all the good the Almighty did for them in the past
2. That they do not have the proper outlook towards the future

The next verse, therefore, instructs the Jewish People on how to right these wrongs: זְכֹר יְמוֹת עוֹלָם בִּינוּ שְׁנוֹת דֹּר וָדֹר — *"Remember the days of yore, understand the years of generation after generation"* (*Devarim* 32:7).

Rashi continues in the same vein and explains that *"Remember the days of yore"* is calling upon the nation to remember what Hashem did for them in the past, for the previous generations. זְכֹר, "remember", is the *tikkun* for *"people who are vile,"* who in the words of Rashi: *"forgot what had been done for them."*

The latter part of the *pasuk*, *"understand the years of generation after generation,"* is a call to contemplate the reward that Hashem has in His power to bestow in the future. If we follow in His path, He will reward us with the days of the *Mashiach* and life in the Next World. בִּינוּ — "understand": It is incumbent upon us to thoroughly study all that we are told, lest we remain "unwise" — and, in the words of Rashi, not sufficiently able to understand the *"consequences of our conduct."*

UNDERSTANDING THE PAST IMPACTS ON THE FUTURE

EACH OF THESE verses from the song's introduction presents two viewpoints: remembering the past on the one hand and looking ahead to the future on the other. The truth is that these are not two contradictory stances: looking to the past is strongly connected to anticipating the future. There is a strong correlation between *"O people who are vile,"* who forgot the *chesed* that had been done for them in the past, and the *"unwise"*, who have difficulty seeing the future. For if we know how to view our past properly, if we value all the miracles that Hashem has performed for us in the past appropriately, we will understand that He also has the power to provide for us in the future.

This applies to the negative aspects of our past as well. If we attempt to derive lessons from the Generation of the Flood and דּוֹר הַפַּלָגָה, the Generation of Dispersal, as well as from the plagues in Egypt, we will be cognizant of the bad that the Creator has the power to bring, God forbid, upon those who do not improve their ways.

Accordingly, we can say that a proper perspective on the past is in fact a view of the future. The past sheds light upon the future in two ways: Firstly, the past serves as a model for what the future holds in store, and secondly, the past determines what will happen in the future. Let us begin by clarifying this second definition — that the past determines the future.

Our Sages have said: מַעֲשֵׂה אָבוֹת סִימָן לְבָנִים — *"The actions of the forefathers are a sign for the children."* Because our forefathers acted in a particular manner in the past, an event with similar meaning will occur to their children in the future (*Bereishis Rabbah* 70:6).

Ramban elaborates on this theme in *Bereishis*: All the tribulations that Avraham Avinu suffered — being forced to go to Egypt because of famine conditions, the Egyptians taking his wife, Hashem smiting them until they were forced to send him off with much wealth — all these occurred in the lives of his descendants as well. Famine sent them to Egypt, the Egyptians tried to harm their daughters (see Ramban, *Shemos* 1:22), and Hashem smote them with ten plagues until finally the Egyptians were forced to send them out with gold and silver.

SIX DAYS OF CREATION EQUALS
SIX THOUSAND YEARS OF EXISTENCE

LET US NOW explain the first statement: In what way is the past a precise model for the future? The *Zohar* (1:28) teaches that R' Shimon bar Yochai revealed to his son that the key to knowledge about the entire future is concealed in the chapter on Creation. As it is written: מַגִּיד מֵרֵאשִׁית אַחֲרִית — *"From the beginning I foretell the outcome"* (*Yeshayahu* 46:10). *"From the beginning"* — of Creation, *"I foretell"* — the Creator is telling us what will be *"the outcome"* — at the End of Days. Based on this, Ramban explains (*Bereishis* 2:3) that the six days of Creation are analogous to the six thousand years the world is destined to exist (see *Rosh Hashanah* 31a). This is the meaning of the *midrash*: *"Hashem's day is one thousand years"* (*Bereishis Rabbah* 19:8).

Ramban then elaborates by showing how the events of the first thousand years of the history of the world bear a remarkable similarity to the first day of Creation. Similarly, the second thousand years closely resemble the second day of Creation, and so on. Ramban concludes his commentary by teaching us that the seventh day — Shabbos — is an allusion to the Next World, a world that is כֻּלּוֹ שַׁבָּת וּמְנוּחָה לְחַיֵּי הָעוֹלָמִים — *"entirely Shabbos and contentment for eternal life"* (*Tamid* 33b).

The state of the world at the end of six thousand years will be precisely as it was at the conclusion of the sixth day. Why is this so? Because the Creator creates everything at the height of its perfection. If He chose to create a world in a particular state, it follows that this is the ultimate state possible! Therefore, understanding *"the days of yore,"* the spiritual state of the past, reveals for us what is destined in the future — in *"the days of generation after generation,"* the perfected world.

What was the spiritual state of the Creation at its beginning? We recite in *Adon Olam*, לְעֵת נַעֲשָׂה בְחֶפְצוֹ כֹּל אֲזַי מֶלֶךְ שְׁמוֹ נִקְרָא — *"At the time when His will brought all into being, then as King was His Name proclaimed."* On the sixth day, after the Creation was organized in accordance with His will, the Almighty was proclaimed King — He appeared in all His glory. This was the ultimate revelation of Divine sovereignty in all its splendor. It is therefore clear that at the End of Days, the world will be renewed as in the days of old. Just as at the outset there was nothing that interfered with the revelation of His glory and the entire Creation declared in unison, ה' מָלָךְ — *"Hashem is King"* (*Tehillim* 10:16), so will be the case in the future.

A CLEANSING WIND

THE PROBLEM IS the in-between stage — from after the six days of Creation until the End of Days. Here opposition to God's sovereignty crops up. The sins of Adam HaRishon, Kayin, and the Generation of the Flood are just a few examples of the rebellion against His kingdom that seem to darken the full revelation of Hashem's light in this world. It is only through *"remembering the days of yore,"* through observing the dawn of Creation, when Hashem's glory was revealed perfectly, that we can manage to rise above these dark clouds of heresy, and בִּינוּ — "to understand" — two truths: First, that above the heavy gloom the light of Hashem's kingdom shines constantly in all its strength, even today, and the second, that a cleansing wind will eventually come and disperse these black clouds, and the world will then return to its original condition under Hashem's unopposed sovereignty.

This applies to the Creation in general. But this same cycle of "perfection-flaw-perfection" that takes place within the great body of Creation also takes place within the heart of the Creation — the Jewish People.

A SIMILAR CYCLE IN THE HEART OF THE CREATION

IN THE HISTORY of our nation, too, we see a process of initial perfection which then deteriorates. We can, in fact, differentiate between these two stages, both as applied to individuals — our holy forefathers — and as applied to the People of Israel.

On the individual level, in the days of our forefathers, the glory of heaven was illuminated by very precious lights — the greatest light of all being *Akeidas Yitzchak*, "the binding of Yitzchak." When a father and son, living in the heart of an idolatrous world, dedicate themselves wholeheartedly to fulfill Hashem's wish in so complete and perfect a fashion, without any hesitation or reservation, there can be no greater revelation of Hashem's glory! This was Hashem's will, and they therefore pushed aside all other considerations — Sarah's response, the reaction of the neighbors, the fear that the world would mock them — all was cancelled out by the word of Hashem. This was Divine sovereignty without limits, at its purest.

The same applies to the nation as a whole. Where did the individuals come together to form a cohesive nation? At that great assembly at Har Sinai! It was there, at the moment of the birth of the Jewish People, that the glory of Heaven was revealed in all its might. A nation numbering thousands upon thousands declared in unison, *Na'aseh ve'nishma* — *"We will do and we will obey"* (*Shemos* 24:7). All declared an uncompromising readiness to fulfill the will of Hashem. There was not a single protest! Whether to more or less stringent mitzvos, the response was the same: *Na'aseh ve'nishma*. Thus during *"the days of yore"* — the beginnings of the Jewish nation — the revelation of Hashem's honor, on the individual as well as on the national level, was at its peak.

DECLINE AND EVENTUAL *TIKKUN*

THEN CAME THE downfall. Just as Adam HaRishon's sin marked the beginning of the decline from the original perfection of Creation, the perfect state of the Jewish People deteriorated as well — both on the individual and on the national level. On the heels of *Akeidas Yitzchak*, the ultimate in individual perfection,

Ha'azinu — the Secret of the Tri-Part Code

came the selling of Yosef — the root of the decline of individuals. On the national level, following the assembly at Har Sinai, the ultimate in Divine Revelation, came the *Cheit HaEgel*, the Sin of the Golden Calf — the first failure of the Jewish nation. Thus, while the world is in a state of failure and deterioration, and the heart of the world, the Jewish nation, is suffering from frequent "heart attacks", along comes the song of *Ha'azinu* and gives us light and hope for the future. This song promises us that the *tikkun* of the Jewish nation will take place, that the heart of the world will once again beat regularly. Everything aspires to return to the source, to that initial period of perfection. Therefore, heralds the song, since the birth of the Jewish nation was accompanied by the grand revelation of Hashem's glory at Sinai, our nation has no other goal than to return to that supreme recognition — to the realization that ה' הוּא הָאֱלֹקִים בַּשָּׁמַיִם מִמַּעַל וְעַל הָאָרֶץ מִתָּחַת אֵין עוֹד — "*Hashem, He is the God — in Heaven above and on the earth below — there is none other*" (*Devarim* 4:39).

Knowledge of the past, as dictated in the song of *Ha'azinu* by the Creator of all, gives us complete confidence that the Jewish nation will eventually renew its days as of old, and its future will be a copy of its glorious past — with the return of the *Beis HaMikdash*, the reconvening of the Sanhedrin, and the reinstatement of the kingdom of Israel. All this, however, will just be the means with which to reach the great goal. The ultimate purpose of the Creation is that וְנִשְׂגַּב ה' לְבַדּוֹ בַּיּוֹם הַהוּא — "*Hashem alone will be exalted on that day*" (*Yeshayahu* 2:11).

THREE STAGES

A CLOSE PERUSAL of this song reveals how its verses help us to identify this cycle in Israel's history: perfection with all its glory and splendor, followed by deterioration, and then a return to the initial state of perfection. The song begins with Hashem's love for the Jewish nation, even before they existed as a people. Even when Hashem punished the דּוֹר הַפְּלָגָה, the Generation of the Dispersal, for angering Him, he did not totally destroy them. Instead, בְּהַפְרִידוֹ בְּנֵי אָדָם יַצֵּב גְּבֻלֹת עַמִּים — *"He separated the children of man, He set the borders of the peoples"* (*Devarim* 32:8), yet He retained them in this world. Why did He do so?

לְמִסְפַּר בְּנֵי יִשְׂרָאֵל — *"According to the number of the Children of Israel"* (ibid.) — for the sake of the Jewish People that were destined to descend from Shem (see Rashi). In other words, from the days of Creation, Hashem plotted, so to speak, how He was going to elevate His Chosen People from among the other nations, because they alone are His people and His inheritance, as it says: כִּי חֵלֶק ה' עַמּוֹ יַעֲקֹב חֶבֶל נַחֲלָתוֹ — *"For Hashem's portion is His people; Yaakov is the measure of His inheritance"* (ibid. 32:9).

The Jewish People returned this love for them back to their Father; they demonstrated how out of all the descendants of Shem it was they who were the most worthy of being chosen — not Yishmael or Esav. יִמְצָאֵהוּ בְּאֶרֶץ מִדְבָּר — *"He discovered him in a desert land"* (ibid. 32:10) — Hashem found that the hearts of *Am Yisrael* were loyal to Him in the desert when they accepted His Torah with joy, something Esav and Yishmael did not do (see Rashi). So too, וּבְתֹהוּ יְלֵל יְשִׁמֹן — *"in desolation, a howling wilderness"* (ibid.), their loyalty was revealed by the fact that they followed Him into the desert — a place of howling animals and desolation where millions of people placed their lives in Hashem's hands.

Because of this, יְסֹבְבֶנְהוּ יְבוֹנְנֵהוּ — *"He encircled him, He granted him discernment"* (ibid.) — Hashem surrounded them with the clouds of glory. He taught them how to understand the Torah, and יִצְּרֶנְהוּ כְּאִישׁוֹן עֵינוֹ — *"He preserved him like the pupil of his eye"* (ibid.). He protected them in the desert from all trouble (as we find: כִּי הַנֹּגֵעַ בָּכֶם נֹגֵעַ בְּבָבַת עֵינוֹ — *"for whoever touches you, touches the pupil of his own eye"* [*Zechariah* 2:12]).

The condition of the nation was so strong that they had no need for allies to offer them protection: ה' בָּדָד יַנְחֶנּוּ וְאֵין עִמּוֹ אֵל נֵכָר — *"Hashem alone guided them, and no other power was with them"* (*Devarim* 32:12).

The next step is known — Hashem brings them forth to *Eretz*

Yisrael: יַרְכִּבֵהוּ עַל בָּמֳתֵי אָרֶץ — *"He would cause him to ride on the heights of the Land"* (ibid. 32:13) — *Eretz Yisrael* is above all lands. He then feeds them חֶמְאַת בָּקָר וַחֲלֵב צֹאן — *"butter of cattle and milk of sheep with fat of lambs"* (ibid. 32:14).

Rashi explains how the *pasuk* describes the glorious periods of time in our people's history. We see that this section of the song opens with a description of the exalted state of the Jewish nation's closeness with Hashem during its fledgling days.

Then comes the difficult and painful period.

REBELLION OF YOUTH

וַיִּשְׁמַן יְשֻׁרוּן וַיִּבְעָט שָׁמַנְתָּ עָבִיתָ כָּשִׂיתָ וַיִּטֹּשׁ אֱלוֹקַ עָשָׂהוּ וַיְנַבֵּל צוּר יְשֻׁעָתוֹ.

Yeshurun became fat and kicked. You became fat, you became thick, you became corpulent — and it deserted God its maker and was contemptuous of the Rock of its salvation.

(ibid. 32:15)

Too much good brings with it contempt and abandonment of Hashem: יַקְנִאֻהוּ בְּזָרִים בְּתוֹעֵבֹת יַכְעִיסֻהוּ — *"They would provoke His jealousy with strangers, they would anger Him with abominations"* (ibid. 32:16), and the results are not long in coming:

וַיַּרְא ה' וַיִּנְאָץ מִכַּעַס בָּנָיו וּבְנֹתָיו. וַיֹּאמֶר "אַסְתִּירָה פָנַי מֵהֶם אֶרְאֶה מָה אַחֲרִיתָם כִּי דוֹר תַּהְפֻּכֹת הֵמָּה בָּנִים לֹא אֵמֻן בָּם".

Hashem will see and be provoked by the anger of His sons and daughters. And He will say, "I shall hide My face from them and see what their end will be — for they are a generation of reversals, children whose upbringing is not in them."

(ibid. 32:19)

Hashem hands them over to the nations and exiles them from their land, as is described in the subsequent verses detailing the calamities of the Jewish People.

In *pasuk* 36, the tide changes. *Am Yisrael*'s sorrowful state awakens Heavenly mercy: כִּי יִרְאֶה כִּי אָזְלַת יָד — *"When He sees that enemy power progresses"* (ibid. 32:36). The hand of the enemy is growing strong and begins to overpower the Jewish People. וְאֶפֶס עָצוּר וְעָזוּב — *"None is saved or assisted"* (ibid.). There is no one in control, no one to assist and guide the Jewish nation. We then see the mercy of Hashem on His children. He will grasp the attribute of justice, free the Jewish nation from all the forces that cause them trouble, and hold all enemies of the Jewish People accountable for what they have done in the past: אָשִׁיב נָקָם לְצָרָי וְלִמְשַׂנְאַי אֲשַׁלֵּם — *"I shall return vengeance upon My enemies and upon those who hate Me I shall bring retribution"* (ibid. 32:41).

This vengeance will not only be for a Jewish life that was taken, or a wound inflicted, it will even be for the shout of *"Jude!"* to a Jewish child in some deserted alley during the forgotten days of the Middle Ages. Not only that, Godly justice will even distinguish between two gentiles who both shouted *"Itbach el yehud* — Slaughter the Jews!", only one shouted louder than the other, or one harbored more of a burning hatred for the Jews than the other. Such people will be punished even more severely.

In other words, the main purpose of *"I shall return vengeance upon My enemies"* is to cleanse the world of rebellion against the Creator's sovereignty — to rid the world of any remaining murkiness of sin, in order that the light of His Kingdom should shine forth *"like the light of the seven days"* (*Yeshayahu* 30:36). Since it is the Jewish People who carry the banner of Hashem's Name in the world, he who harms them harms Hashem, so to speak. Hashem will therefore execute very exacting justice — a judgment of truth, which will boggle the minds of all who see it.

כִּי דַם עֲבָדָיו יִקּוֹם וְנָקָם יָשִׁיב לְצָרָיו וְכִפֶּר אַדְמָתוֹ עַמּוֹ — *"For He will avenge the blood of His servants; He will bring retribution upon His foes and He will appease His Land and His people"* (ibid. 30:43). So our song concludes with words of consolation: Hashem will appease His long-suffering nation.

We find that at the end of this obstacle-strewn road, total perfection awaits us. This *tikkun* will elevate everyone — the *tzaddik* who desired and worked toward this goal his entire life, as well as the wicked man who opposed it his whole life. Redemption will come to all of them. Even those same evil people who tried to oppose it through the power of their free choice will see fulfillment of the verse, הַרְנִינוּ גוֹיִם עַמּוֹ — *"O nations, sing the praises of His people"* (ibid.). They, too, will sing praises at the revelation of Godly justice (though for them this will be a bitter truth), and in this fashion, the Kingdom of Hashem will once again rule with no interference.

THE THIRTEEN MIDDOS — PARADIGM OF THE THREE-PART CODE

DURING THE PERIOD of *Aseres Yemei Teshuvah*, we intensify our recitation of the Thirteen Attributes of Mercy that Hashem revealed to Moshe. What is the reason for this? Moshe requested of Hashem, הוֹדִיעֵנִי נָא אֶת דְּרָכֶךָ — *"Make Your ways known to me"* (*Shemos* 33:13). Hashem responded with information more precious than gold: *"Any time that Israel sins, let them perform before Me this procedure and I shall forgive them"* (*Rosh Hashanah* 17b). The Almighty taught Moshe Rabbeinu that inherent in the recital of these Thirteen Attributes is the ability to invoke the quality of mercy necessary for atonement, and in the end, וְכִפֶּר אַדְמָתוֹ עַמּוֹ — *"He will appease His Land and His people"* (*Devarim* 32:43). This recitation will awaken the forgiveness of a Father towards his children. *"Any time that Israel sins"* — when they find themselves in that "in between" situation, the downfall that follows the initial state of perfection — these Attributes of Mercy have the ability to bring the world back to its original perfection. They hold the secret of how to rise up from the downfall! They contain the secret of לְתַקֵּן עוֹלָם בְּמַלְכוּת שַׁקַּי — *"perfecting the universe with the Almighty's sovereignty."* Although we have no understanding of hidden secrets, a perusal of these Thirteen Attributes will reveal that, even on a simple level, we find the process we have mentioned: perfection, downfall, return to perfection.

The Torah records in the Thirteen Attributes: וַיַּעֲבֹר ה' עַל פָּנָיו וַיִּקְרָא: ה' ה' קֵל רַחוּם וְחַנּוּן אֶרֶךְ אַפַּיִם וְרַב חֶסֶד וֶאֱמֶת — *"Hashem passed before him and proclaimed: 'Hashem, Hashem, God, compassionate and gracious, slow to anger, and abundant in kindness and truth'"* (*Shemos* 34:6). Why is the Name of Hashem mentioned twice? Most of the commentaries (Onkelos, Rashi, Ramban, Ibn Ezra, and Seforno) are of the opinion that the two times the name of God is mentioned constitute two separate attributes of the thirteen. The טְעָמִים (cantillation notes) in fact imply this, for וַיַּעֲבֹר ה' עַל פָּנָיו וַיִּקְרָא — *"Hashem passed before him and proclaimed"* ends with the note סֶגוֹל, a pause. After that, the Thirteen Attributes are enumerated, beginning with *"Hashem, Hashem."* If each of these attributes is unique and has a different effect, how are we to understand this seeming repetition of the same attribute?

Chazal answered this question in the following manner: *"I am He before a person sins, and I am He after the person sins and performs repentance"* (*Rosh Hashanah* 17b). There is a type of Divine benevolence, of *chesed* which exists prior to man's sinning — even then everything that man receives is an act of *chesed*. Even during the Creation, when the perfection and purity of the world was at its height, the abundance that entered the world was not due to any merit, but only to the kindness of the Almighty — His wish to do good for His creatures. This *chesed* is represented by the first mention of Hashem's Name — and it is this that sustained the Creation from the outset.

There is, however, a greater *chesed*, and this is alluded to by the second mention of Hashem's Name — the *chesed* that sustains the world even after man sins. Even after man has misused all the great gifts Hashem has given him, and used them for the wrong purposes, he is still given more benevolence. The difference is that now, a greater revelation of the honor of Heaven is called for. For *chesed* on this level, the first of the Attributes of Mercy is not sufficient, therefore a second one is needed, representing this superior level of mercy. (It should be noted that this second attribute only helps those who repent. Those who do not repent benefit from another of the Almighty's attributes, His being אֶרֶךְ אַפַּיִם — "slow to anger.")

And now let us ask, what is to be found between these two names of Hashem? The attribute of Justice! Hashem's leadership of the world through punishment of sinners is represented by the name "Elokim". *Elokim* — the Divine name representing the attribute of justice — is not mentioned in these Thirteen Attributes, for these attributes are solely those of mercy. In *Parashas Ha'azinu*, however, the attribute of justice appears elaborately — the destruction of the *Beis HaMikdash*, the exile and all the associated calamities mentioned in this song, all stem from "*Elokim*," which is hidden between the first mention of "Hashem" and the last.

THE THREE-PART CODE — ON HAR SINAI

ONE LAST POINT: We have a tradition that there is a strong correlation between an event and the time in which it takes place. When were these Attributes given to mankind? It is known that Moshe ascended Har Sinai three times — each time for forty days. The Thirteen *Middos* were given to Moshe during his third sojourn on the mountain, to be more specific, on the last of the forty days of mercy that began on the first of Elul — i.e. on Yom Kippur (see *Pirkei d'Rabi Eliezer* 46). What was the nature of these three ascents? Rashi explains: *"Just as the first ones were in a state of Divine favor, so too the latter ones were in a state of Divine favor, hence you may say now that the middle forty days were in a state of Divine anger"* (Rashi, *Shemos* 33:11).

Incredibly, once again we find this tri-part formula — Moshe's initial ascent in a state of perfection (to receive the Torah), the second one following a downfall (to atone for the *Cheit HaEgel*, the Sin of the Golden Calf), and the last ascent ending with forgiveness and perfection (receiving the second tablets on Yom Kippur). In other words, the secret of these Thirteen Attributes, encapsulated in "mercy, judgment, mercy," came down to the world on the same day that it was actually put into effect — the tenth of Tishrei 2449 — the same day that the Jewish People were forgiven for the *Cheit HaEgel*. That day marked the first completion of this cycle by which Hashem guides the Jewish nation. On that day came appeasement and forgiveness for His dear children.

We can add another interesting angle: Just as the last forty days are associated with these Thirteen Attributes of mercy, so are the first forty days in which the Torah was given associated with thirteen attributes. The difference is that prior to the sin, the Thirteen *Middos* were the *middos she-haTorah nidreshes ba-hen* — "the rules by which the Torah is elucidated." After Hashem taught him a mitzvah, Moshe Rabbeinu would analyze it from all angles with the aid of these Thirteen *Middos*.

These two types of Thirteen *Middos* represent two ways in which Hashem guides the world: 1) through the path of the Torah and its mitzvos, and 2) through the path of *teshuvah*. When the Torah is not observed, the world has a need for the second route of forgiveness and mercy. The Name of Hashem, *Yud Kay Vav Kay*, which is all-encompassing and sustains all the worlds, has the numerical value of twenty-six. This alludes to the above two approaches, each consisting of Thirteen Attributes — which together total twenty-six.

THE "HA'AZINU CODE" IN THE SHOFAR BLASTS

THIS THEME IS similarly seen regarding the sounding of the shofar on Rosh Hashanah. The Torah commands us: יוֹם תְּרוּעָה יִהְיֶה לָכֶם — "*It shall be a day of shofar-sounding for you*" (*Bemidbar* 29:1). Onkelos translates יוֹם תְּרוּעָה as meaning יוֹם יַבָּבָא — "a day of crying," an expression similar to the one describing Sisra's mother: בְּעַד הַחַלּוֹן נִשְׁקְפָה וַתְּיַבֵּב — "*Through the window she gazed and she cried*" (*Shoftim* 5:28). We learn from these two *pesukim* that the *teru'ah* is a crying sound — a broken, sighing sound. There are differing opinions regarding what constitutes a broken sound —

whether it consists of sounds of a medium length (*shevarim*), or whether it is made up of many short sounds (*teru'ah*), or a combination thereof. We therefore sound all three possible *teru'ah* sounds: *shevarim*, *teru'ah*, and the combination of *shevarim-teru'ah* to remove all doubt as to whether we have sounded the correct *teru'ah* (see *Rosh Hashanah* 33b–34a).

Chazal derived from various *pesukim* that this *teru'ah* must have a *peshutah* — "a simple sound" — before it and following it. In other words, before and after this broken sound we blow the long, smooth, uninterrupted sound we call a *teki'ah*. Why did the Torah require us to sound this as well? Because the *peshutah* is the *tikkun*! This smooth sound, without any complications, alludes to that initial state of perfection of the universe that was discussed earlier. It is followed by the *teru'ah*, which represents the downfall and the breaking of this perfection. It is for this reason that the *pasuk* tells us, עָלָה אֱלֹקִים בִּתְרוּעָה — "*Elokim has ascended with the blast (teru'ah)*" (*Tehillim* 47:6). The broken *teru'ah* refers to the downfall that is found between the beginning and the end, and to the name *Elokim*, denoting the attribute of judgment that sin draws along with it.

The Torah requirement to sound these shofar blasts comes to emphasize Hashem's promise to His people: Just as there was a simple *teki'ah* at the beginning, so too will the simple *teki'ah* return and be sounded in the end, and all the broken sounds of sobbing that were in the *teru'ah* will be smoothed out.

The Torah wants to stress the following nuances:

- עָלָה אֱלֹקִים בִּתְרוּעָה — "*Elokim has ascended with the* teru'ah," is followed by
- ה' בְּקוֹל שׁוֹפָר — "*Hashem with the sound of the shofar*" (ibid.)

The Name of Hashem — *Yud Kay Vav Kay* — the attribute of mercy, will once again appear. This is alluded to by the simple sound of the shofar. וְהָיָה בַּיּוֹם הַהוּא יִתָּקַע בְּשׁוֹפָר גָּדוֹל — "*It shall be on that day that a great shofar will be blown*" (*Yeshayahu* 27:13). That same sound that will bring us back to *matan Torah* — our original peak of perfection where קוֹל שׁוֹפָר חָזָק מְאֹד — "the sound of the shofar was very powerful" (Shemos 19:16).

THE ESSENCE OF ROSH HASHANAH — YOM TERU'AH

THIS BRINGS US to a question here regarding one of the names of the day, *Yom Teru'ah*. If each *teru'ah* must have the simple sound of the *teki'ah* before it as well as after it, this means that the number of *teki'os* is double the number of *teru'os*. If so, would it not have been more appropriate for Rosh Hashanah to be referred to as *Yom Teki'ah* rather than *Yom Teru'ah*? Instead of the Torah having written *Yom Teru'ah* and *Chazal* having to derive the requirement of blowing a *teki'ah* before and after (see *Rosh Hashanah* 33b), the Torah could have called it a *Yom Teki'ah*, and *Chazal* would have similarly derived the need to add on *teru'os* — which are fewer in number than the *teki'os* and thus, perhaps, subordinate in importance.

Yom Teru'ah, however, defines the very essence of Rosh Hashanah — a day of shaking and breaking, a day of deciding מִי יִחְיֶה וּמִי יָמוּת — "who will live and who will die." During these *Aseres Yemei Teshuvah*, Hashem's sovereignty is manifested primarily through justice, to the extent that even His attribute of love, as in the verse we recite in the *Shemoneh Esrei* prayer, מֶלֶךְ אוֹהֵב צְדָקָה וּמִשְׁפָּט — "the King Who loves righteousness and judgment," is hidden from us and replaced with הַמֶּלֶךְ הַמִּשְׁפָּט — "the King of judgment."

The name *Yom Teru'ah* is fitting because it is a day on which we should groan and wail — like that broken sound of the *teru'ah*. This is a day on which we bow down before the *Melech HaMishpat*, like that curved shofar which symbolizes how man must bend and subordinate himself when he prays before Hashem, as it says in the Gemara: *"On Rosh Hashanah, the more a person bows (his mind), the better it is"* (*Rosh Hashanah* 26b). Our Sages dispute whether one must actually shed tears on Rosh Hashanah, for Ezra said: וְאַל תֵּעָצֵבוּ כִּי חֶדְוַת ה' הִיא מָעֻזְּכֶם — *"Do not* be sad; the enjoyment of Hashem is your strength" (Nechemiah 8:10). The Gaon of Vilna in *Ma'aseh Rav* (*siman* 207) ruled that one should not cry. The heart, however, must cry! After seeing all those killed on the Israeli roads and in the fight for our security, how can we not be afraid and wail?

Our great consolation is that eventually there will be a פְּשׁוּטָה לְאַחֲרֶיהָ, a "simple sound" after the broken, crying sound. The day will come in which Hashem's great *chesed* will be revealed, as in the second mention of Hashem's Name in the Thirteen Attributes, and all will return to that state of perfection. There is no doubt about this! Therefore, despite everything, our hearts are joyous during these holy days. The source of our joy is that the revelation of the Almighty's glory in the past serves as a promise for the future. This serves to sweeten the current revelation of His glory — that of justice, which is so highly apparent in our times.

MAN MUST DESIRE THE REVELATION OF GOD'S GLORY

THE REALIZATION OF this hope for the *tikkun* of the world is dependent upon one necessary condition: that man must truly desire that Hashem's glory be revealed, that his main objective in life should be the fulfillment of the verse: וְהָיָה ה' לְמֶלֶךְ עַל כָּל הָאָרֶץ — "Hashem will be King over all the land" (Zechariah 14:9). Hashem will be King over all the land no matter what — only the will and desire for it depend upon man: Does he regard this occurrence happily or will it be against his will? This same idea is expressed in the *Kaddish*. The reality of יִתְגַּדַּל וְיִתְקַדַּשׁ שְׁמֵיהּ רַבָּא — "May His great name be exalted and sanctified" will occur in any event — of this there is no doubt. It is incumbent upon man, however, to desire that it take place בַּעֲגָלָא וּבִזְמַן קָרִיב — "swiftly and soon." He must feel an intense longing for that day to arrive, and exclaim out loud אָמֵן יְהֵא שְׁמֵהּ רַבָּא — "Amen, may His great name be blessed" with all his might and with deep *kavanah* (see *Shabbos* 119b).

Chazal elucidate the *pasuk* in *Amos*: "Woe to those who desire the day of Hashem: 'Why do you seek this day of Hashem?' It is darkness and not light" (*Amos* 5:18).

Our Sages express this as *"An analogy of a rooster and a bat who were awaiting the light of dawn. Said the rooster to the bat, 'I am awaiting the light, because the light is mine (Rashi: I benefit from the light), but you, why do you want the light?'"* (*Sanhedrin* 98b). My life and my goals are realized during daylight, and it is for this reason that I await the light. You, O bat, live and work mainly in the dark — why would you await the light that will do no more than emphasize your limitations?

Many of us are awaiting the *Mashiach*, yet in reality a significant number of people will not view his arrival with gladness. The radio will report the laying of the cornerstone for Yeshivas HaShomer HaTza'ir, from Southern Lebanon we will hear the live broadcast of the inauguration of Kollel Arzei HaTorah, and those who turn on the television will see an exciting *shiur* given by the *Mashiach*! What about someone who has no interest in this? He will be truly miserable — for him it will really be "darkness and not light."

A thought occurred to me, based on this. In *Kerias Shema*, we fulfill the mitzvah of accepting the yoke of the Kingdom of Heaven (קַבָּלַת עוֹל מַלְכוּת שָׁמַיִם) when we say, "*Shema, Yisrael, Hashem Elokeinu, Hashem Echad.*" The composers of the prayer added in the middle of the *Shema* the sentence, בָּרוּךְ שֵׁם כְּבוֹד מַלְכוּתוֹ לְעוֹלָם וָעֶד — "*Blessed is the Name of His glorious Kingdom for all eternity.*" What is the connection between these two sentences?

The answer is that the verse ה' אֱלֹקֵינוּ ה' אֶחָד — "*Hashem is our God, Hashem is the One and Only*" (*Devarim* 6:4) establishes a fact: I recognize and believe that Hashem rules over all. But there are many other facts in the world whose existence I acknowledge, yet not all of them please me. I know that a particular person is President of the United States; that does not mean that I am happy about it. Thus together with the intellectual acknowledgment that Hashem is our God, we add a sentence demonstrating our emotional satisfaction. We are overjoyed and declare from our hearts, בָּרוּךְ שֵׁם כְּבוֹד מַלְכוּתוֹ לְעוֹלָם וָעֶד! We demonstrate here that this is not just one more of the endless pieces of information stored in our heads; rather it is our wish for that same Kingdom of Heaven to last for all eternity. Our Rabbis have written that this is the meaning of the word בָּרוּךְ — we desire the constant benevolence of the revelation of His sovereignty, as in the scriptural בְּרֵכָה — that pool mentioned in *Shemuel* II (2:13) from which endless water flows (see *Sichos LeRosh Hashanah*, Hebrew edition, p. 69).

ACCEPTING THE YOKE

WE ARE NOW in the midst of the *Aseres Yemei Teshuvah*, which serve as a reminder of the perfected world of the future. These days may be viewed as a model representing Hashem's sovereignty, the world under absolute dominion of the King of kings — a new reality that is coming closer and closer. Therefore, during these days our קַבָּלַת עוֹל מַלְכוּת שָׁמַיִם, our "acceptance of Hashem's sovereignty," has two additional requirements:

1. That we prepare for, and accustom ourselves to, a more spiritual life — a life in which we will not be "too busy" to finally do what we wanted to, but which our tumultuous lives do not allow for. A life in which we will develop the strength of spirit to make changes we never dared to before, even though we knew deep inside that it was time for a change. The height of this adaptation to the Next World will occur on Yom Kippur — the day in which the five major pleasures of this world are pushed aside. In their stead, we recite with devotion five *tefillos* asking that service of the Almighty should fill the earth, as the *pasuk* says: כִּי מָלְאָה הָאָרֶץ דֵּעָה אֶת ה' כַּמַּיִם לַיָּם מְכַסִּים — *"for the earth will be as filled with knowledge of Hashem as water covering the sea bed"* (*Yeshayahu* 11:9).

2. That we are each personally tested — how much do we really desire the revelation of the glory of Heaven in its totality? When we say *Baruch shem kevod malchuso le'olam va'ed*, do we really mean it? Is it really one of our main priorities or are we just reciting what they who compiled the prayerbook wrote? We must be able to answer the following question: How happy are we to live with the feeling of *me-ein Olam HaBa*, this "sense of the Next World." Perhaps our heart whispers to us that it cannot wait for these solemn, tense days to pass, so that we can breathe easier and finally return to our normal routine — enough of these *selichos* and pep talks! Let us examine today whether we truly want to integrate within us this new light that will shine over Zion.

Let us make an effort to prepare ourselves for what is to come. Let us strive to be able to comfortably fit in with it — lest we, God forbid, find ourselves like that bat who lives in the darkness, to whom the prophets directed that penetrating question: "Why do you seek this day of Hashem?"

THE "HA'AZINU CODE" IN KERIAS SHEMA

IN FACT, WE repeat this message of *Ha'azinu* each and every day: In *Kerias Shema* we recite twice daily, ה' אֱלֹקֵינוּ ה' אֶחָד — "*Hashem is our God (Elokeinu), Hashem is One.*" There is a three-part idea expressed in the song that is suggested by these words. First comes Hashem, the attribute of mercy. Then we find the downfall that brings forth the attribute of judgment, as reflected in the name *Elokim*, and finally, the verse concludes with a repetition of the Name of Hashem — this time recognized by all in the ultimate *tikkun*.

Once the first *pasuk* that we recite, *Shema Yisrael...*, has expressed the acknowledgment that the Kingdom of Heaven will return to its original glory, the next sentence attests to our joy at this fact, to our great yearning to see Hashem which is contained in the words בָּרוּךְ שֵׁם כְּבוֹד מַלְכוּתוֹ לְעוֹלָם וָעֶד — *"Blessed is the name of His glorious Kingdom for all eternity."*

We can now also understand its connection to the next *pasuk* in *Kerias Shema*. One who is not only satisfied with the knowledge that Hashem is One, but actually longs for it, one who yearns for this true revelation with his whole heart, is promised that he will also achieve fulfillment of the verse, וְאָהַבְתָּ אֵת ה' אֱלֹקֶיךָ בְּכָל לְבָבְךָ וּבְכָל נַפְשְׁךָ וּבְכָל מְאֹדֶךָ — *"You shall love Hashem, your God, with all your heart, with all your soul, and with all your resources"* (*Devarim* 6:5). As we know, *Chazal* provided a number of interpretations for this verse: *"'With all your heart' means with both your inclinations — with the good inclination and with the evil inclination, 'and with all your soul' — even if He takes your life, 'and with all your resources' means with all your wealth"* (*Berachos* 54a). The essence of all these interpretations, however, is one — that your love of Hashem not remain abstract, but be transformed into active love — where this connection influences all your actions.

Shlomo HaMelech said: וְהַחוּט הַמְשֻׁלָּשׁ לֹא בִמְהֵרָה יִנָּתֵק — *"A three-ply cord is not easily severed!"* (*Koheles* 4:12). Knowing Hashem *intellectually* and loving His sovereignty with all one's *heart* is the sole guarantee that all of our *actions* will also be illuminated with Hashem's light. In the merit of these, may we be inscribed and sealed, along with the entire nation of Israel, for a good and peaceful year.

SICHAH FOUR
A SONG OF DIVINE REVELATION

HA'AZINU — THE ULTIMATE PROSECUTION

אַשְׁכִּיר חִצַּי מִדָּם וְחַרְבִּי תֹּאכַל בָּשָׂר מִדַּם חָלָל וְשִׁבְיָה מֵרֹאשׁ פַּרְעוֹת אוֹיֵב. הַרְנִינוּ גוֹיִם עַמּוֹ כִּי דַם עֲבָדָיו יִקּוֹם וְנָקָם יָשִׁיב לְצָרָיו וְכִפֶּר אַדְמָתוֹ עַמּוֹ.

I shall intoxicate My arrows with blood and My sword shall devour flesh, because of the blood of corpse and captive, because of the earliest depredations of the enemy. O nations, sing the praises of His people, for He will avenge the blood of His servants; He will bring retribution upon His foes, and He will appease His Land and His people.

(*Devarim* 32:42–43)

These two *pesukim* form the conclusion of the song of *Ha'azinu*, which depicts world events from the time of Creation. These verses describe Hashem's upcoming revenge against the enemy. Rashi cites from the Sifri that the enemies will be judged *"from the earliest depredations of the enemy,"* from the beginning of their attacks against Israel. The deliberations will not begin with the Holocaust, nor with the Crusades, not even with the destruction of the *Beis HaMikdash* — rather they will begin with the very first assault against Jews, with Nimrod's behavior towards Avraham. There will be no "statute of limitations" for the iniquities of the enemy; thousands of years of injustices will be brought forth.

A PERPETUAL DOCUMENTARY

FURTHERMORE, OHR HACHAIM derives from the *pasuk* that not only will Hashem avenge "the blood of His servants" that was actually spilled, but *"He will bring retribution upon His foes"* even for strikes they had planned against the Jewish nation and were unable to carry out. Imagine for yourselves — every evil thought of the Egyptians, the Babylonians, the Persians, the Crusaders, the Ukrainians, the Germans, the Americans, and the Arabs — all will be projected onto a huge screen that will be standing in the valley of Yehoshafat. Since the days of Creation a documentary is perpetually being filmed, which is able to record thoughts as well as actions. On that awesome Day of Judgment, the truth will be publicized: *"I will gather all of the nations and bring them down to the Valley of Yehoshafat, and I will reckon with them there concerning My people and My possession, Israel, that they dispersed among the nations, and they divided up My land"* (*Yoel* 4:2).

All the major court cases that history has witnessed, such as the Eichmann trial, will pale in comparison with this all-encompassing trial of the entire world and in comparison with the eternal revenge that will be meted out against the nations. It is not for nothing that the *pasuk* uses the expression, *"I shall intoxicate My arrows with blood."* The arrows of the Creator will be saturated with the blood of the nations being punished, as a drunkard is intoxicated with wine.

CAN SONG AND JUDGMENT COEXIST?

IF THE FIRST *pasuk* we quoted truly describes the upcoming revenge in the future, how are we to understand the subsequent verse, *"O nations, sing the praises of His people, for He will avenge the blood of His servants; He will bring retribution upon His foes"*? Rashi elucidates here that when the other nations witness this great revenge, they will praise the Jewish People for the way they stubbornly cleaved to the true God for thousands of years.

This raises a serious question — in the midst of all this retribution, will they really feel the urge to sing praises? Can song and judgment go side by side? The *pasuk* tells us:

A Song of Divine Revelation

יַעֲלֹז שָׂדַי וְכָל אֲשֶׁר בּוֹ אָז יְרַנְּנוּ כָּל עֲצֵי יָעַר. לִפְנֵי ה' כִּי בָא כִּי בָא לִשְׁפֹּט הָאָרֶץ יִשְׁפֹּט תֵּבֵל בְּצֶדֶק וְעַמִּים בֶּאֱמוּנָתוֹ.

> ...Then all the trees of the forest will sing with joy — before Hashem, for He will have arrived, He will have arrived to judge the earth with righteousness and the nations with His faithfulness.
>
> (Tehillim 96:12–13)

How does this rejoicing fit in with Hashem's great and awesome judgment?

WHY DOES HA'AZINU CONCLUDE WITH REVENGE?

A FURTHER DIFFICULTY: Rather than concluding with tidings of the *Mashiach*'s arrival and of the good that will come to the Jewish People after the long suffering described in the song, *Ha'azinu* ends with a description of the harsh revenge that will come upon the other nations. Would it not have been more pleasing to conclude on a more honorable note, with words of consolation and salvation, or with a description of the beauty and joy of the World to Come? Retribution, with all its importance (see *Berachos* 33a), is not the ultimate purpose of Creation, nor is it the zenith of the Redemption. We can ask the same question regarding one of the prayers we recite in these Days of Awe, in which we say: אָבִינוּ מַלְכֵּנוּ נְקוֹם לְעֵינֵינוּ נִקְמַת דַּם עֲבָדֶיךָ הַשָּׁפוּךְ — *"Our Father, our King, avenge before our eyes the spilled blood of Your servants."* We have elaborated (*Sichos LeRosh Hashanah*, Hebrew edition, p. 67) that in all the other *tefillos* of Rosh Hashanah there is no request whatsoever regarding the destruction of our enemies, only

> וּבְכֵן תֵּן פַּחְדְּךָ ה' אֱלֹקֵינוּ עַל כָּל מַעֲשֶׂיךָ...
> וְיִשְׁתַּחֲווּ לְפָנֶיךָ כָּל הַבְּרוּאִים...
> וְיֵדַע כָּל פָּעוּל כִּי אַתָּה פְעַלְתּוֹ.

> *And so, too, O Hashem, our God, place Your awe upon all Your works...*

*Let all creatures prostrate themselves before You ...
And let everything that has been made know that You are its Maker.*

Our only request and hope is that the entire world come to recognize Hashem's rule. What role, then, does the *"avenging of the spilled blood of Your servants"* play?

What is the nature of this revenge and what comfort will it provide? If six million Jews were slaughtered, will six million Germans then be killed? Is this what we have been eagerly awaiting and praying for? Even if all the enemies of Israel were to be slain, is this what we would choose to represent the essence of the future Redemption at the conclusion of *Ha'azinu*?

DIVINE JUDGMENT — CATALYST TO TRUE BELIEF

WE HAVE TO understand it in the following manner: Hashem's judgments are not revenge for its own sake, God forbid. They are, rather, a means with which לְתַקֵּן עוֹלָם בְּמַלְכוּת שַׁקַּי — *"to perfect the universe through the Almighty's sovereignty."* The purpose of the judgment is to reveal in a clear manner that only one Force created this world, runs it, and will bring about its redemption. When every living being arrives at this realization, the world will reach its ultimate state of perfection. In order to bring about this revolutionary awareness, there is a need for justice — to reveal the truth in its entirety as clearly as the midday sun. When everyone sees that אֵין שִׁכְחָה לִפְנֵי כִסֵּא כְבוֹדֶךָ — *"there is no forgetfulness before Your Throne of Glory,"* and that Hashem takes them to task for every drop of blood that was spilled, every slap a Jewish child had to endure, even every discomfort that a non-Jew caused to a Jew, with this His sovereignty will be revealed and there will be no denying it.

When all of creation suddenly recognizes this pure truth, they will have to acknowledge that they spent thousands of years in the shadow of futilities and false beliefs. In light of the truth that will shine forth from Zion, all events will be understood —

the senseless wars, the meaningless hatred, why the wicked flourished and why the righteous suffered. At that very instant of Truth, the world will not be able to avoid praising the incredible Godly justice that the Jewish People have clung to all along. Divine truth, justice, and righteousness will appear with such powerful force that it will be impossible not to praise them with wonder. Finally the sequence of world events will be understood; the connection between the many incidents that occurred over thousands of years will become clear. Above all, the nations will finally reach true belief in the God of Israel. This realization will bring them to admit the error of their ways, but out of a sense of deep joy — as a person who finds what he is searching for after many hardships and grabs for it כְּמוֹצֵא שָׁלָל רָב — *"like one who finds abundant spoils"* (*Tehillim* 119:162).

For the wicked, this will not only entail great rejoicing; the revelation of the truth will cause them tremendous, never-ending embarrassment as well. But they too, at that point, will prefer to be shamed and live with the truth, rather than continue to live with falsehood their entire lives. In any event, we will understand the minute details of world events — uncovering the absolute truth, the revelation of justice. All that will be to our world of suffering like a warm and gentle hand that will envelop us with love. When we understand the truth, the magnitude of the joy that will encompass the world when all doubts are resolved, we almost want to ask, "How will it be possible not to sing and praise?"

This incredible upheaval that will take place among the nations is the only reason for the joy that will grip the Jewish nation at the end of days. It is for this reason alone that the song of *Ha'azinu* concludes with revenge, for this is what will bring about the upheaval. This means that the purpose of Hashem's judgments will not be the vengeful settling of debts at the End of Days. Rather, what we yearn for is the acceptance of the yoke of the Kingdom of Heaven that will emanate from the depths of this judgment.

Let us not belittle this great turnabout in the viewpoint of the nations. We can bear witness in our lifetime that people are willing to suffer greatly, and at times even die rather than admit they are wrong. For most people this is more difficult than anything else — the embarrassment that accompanies an admission of error. At times they are even willing to give up their lives, their people, and their birthplace, rather than acknowledge their rival's credibility. Yet the day will come when the entire world will recognize and proclaim the truth. This is what we are referring to when we say in our prayers on the *Yamim Nora'im*: וּבְכֵן תֵּן כָּבוֹד ה' לְעַמֶּךְ — תְּהִלָּה לִירֵאֶיךָ וְתִקְוָה טוֹבָה לְדוֹרְשֶׁיךָ וּפִתְחוֹן פֶּה לַמְיַחֲלִים לָךְ *"And so too, Hashem, grant honor to Your people, praise to those who revere You, good hope to those who seek You, and eloquent speech to those who hope for You."* On that day the entire universe will express with joy — not under any pressure or for reasons of political expediency — its sincere admiration for those outcast Jews who have suddenly been discovered as the sole bearers of truth in the world.

REVELATION OF DIVINE JUSTICE AS THE ULTIMATE *CHESED*

APART FROM THE elation accompanying the fact that וְיֵעָשׂוּ כֻלָּם אֲגֻדָּה אֶחָת לַעֲשׂוֹת רְצוֹנְךָ בְּלֵבָב שָׁלֵם — *"All will become a single society, to do Your will wholeheartedly,"* there will be other reasons to rejoice: the truth we were willing to die for will suddenly become apparent to us as well. Today, whenever we feel lost and unable to explain world events, we cling to the solid faith that we have inherited from our ancestors. Yet how we yearn for the day when Divine Providence will no longer have a need for human "advocates", when we will realize for ourselves that what appeared to us as the opposite of justice was in fact a great *chesed*. We will understand why so-and-so, who never did anything to harm anyone, was murdered, why the only son of a particular *tzaddik* died, why that arch-terrorist was miraculously saved from death, and why a pair of twins born to a woman who was childless for twenty years were run over by a car.

A Song of Divine Revelation

In moments of great pain, one tends to ask, did this have to happen? Was there no other way? Anyone with any feelings for his fellow man often feels that the world is sitting on a swamp in the midst of an endless forest — dark and cold. Suddenly, imagine וַיְהִי אוֹר — "There was light!" (Bereishis 1:3). A giant spotlight will shine from the heavens and in its light it will be obvious that all the bad in the world was nothing but an illusion, a dream. The reality that existed prior to His revelation will be like a deep slumber in comparison to the reality that will be revealed to all. (In *Sichos LeSefer Shemos*, Hebrew edition, pp. 96–97 we explained that there are several levels of reality — each reality is only relative to a higher and truer reality. See there regarding the comparison between our world and the Next World.) Revelation of the truth by means of judgment — this is the ultimate *kiddush Hashem*, because when it becomes clear that the Hand of God controls and judges all living creatures, it is obvious as well that וּמַלְכוּתוֹ בַּכֹּל מָשָׁלָה — "His Kingship rules over everything."

It would seem to me that the beginning of *Ha'azinu* alludes to the way we have explained its conclusion: Moshe Rabbeinu begins by telling the Jewish People כִּי שֵׁם ה' אֶקְרָא הָבוּ גֹדֶל לֵאלֹקֵינוּ — "When I call out the Name of Hashem, [the result will be that you] ascribe greatness to our God" (Devarim 32:3). The Name of Hashem will rise and be magnified from your mouth.

The song continues: Why should all acknowledge that הַצּוּר תָּמִים פָּעֳלוֹ כִּי כָל דְּרָכָיו — "The Rock! Perfect is His work" (ibid. 32:4)? מִשְׁפָּט — "Because all His paths are justice" (ibid.). This exacting justice serves to prove how pure and perfect His leadership is, and to what extent He is קֵל אֱמוּנָה וְאֵין עָוֶל צַדִּיק וְיָשָׁר הוּא — "a God of faith without iniquity, righteous and fair is He" (ibid.).

"PERFORMANCE OF JUSTICE IS A JOY TO THE RIGHTEOUS"

SHLOMO HAMELECH SAID: שִׂמְחָה לַצַּדִּיק עֲשׂוֹת מִשְׁפָּט וּמְחִתָּה לְפֹעֲלֵי עָוֶן — "Performance of justice is a joy to the righteous and destruction to workers of iniquity" (Mishlei 21:15). The commentaries explain that the joy of the righteous stems from their connection to justice. According to Rashi, the *tzaddik* rejoices that Hashem is carrying out justice with him in this world in order that he may merit life in the Next World, while Ibn Ezra explains that it means that the *tzaddik* will carry out justice among the people and that this brings him joy. In other words, the *"joy to the righteous"* comes from the fact that they are somehow or other involved with justice.

Based on what we have discussed, however, we can add another explanation. The mere fact that the Creator practices justice brings joy to the righteous — even to those who are not directly involved with justice themselves. Even to those *tzaddikim* who watch from the sidelines, this clear revelation of the שׁוֹפֵט כָּל הָאָרֶץ — *"Judge of all the earth"* (*Bereishis* 18:25) brings a smile to those yearning for a glimpse of His countenance. Finally a measure of the infinite kingdom of the world has been revealed! His ongoing silence has been interrupted — to the joy of His children. This may explain the following passage from the *piyyut VeChol Ma'aminim* (recited by *Ashkenazim* in *Mussaf* of Rosh Hashanah and Yom Kippur): הַוַּדַּאי שְׁמוֹ כֵּן תְּהִלָּתוֹ — *"Whose name is 'certainty'; such is His praise."* The more His Name appears in a certain and clear manner, so כֵּן תְּהִלָּתוֹ — the greater the praise that emanates from the mouths of human beings.

"A SONG OF DAVID — SHOULD IT NOT BE A LAMENT OF DAVID?"

PERHAPS WE CAN now explain a passage in *Chazal* that I have always found difficult with an interpretation that just occurred to me. We read: מִזְמוֹר לְדָוִד בְּבָרְחוֹ מִפְּנֵי אַבְשָׁלוֹם בְּנוֹ — *"A psalm by David as he fled from Avshalom, his son"* (*Tehillim* 3:1).

David HaMelech fled Yerushalayim, his own kingdom, mourning, weeping, and crying out. The Divine Presence had parted from him and the Sanhedrin had detached themselves from him. Achitofel, possessor of Divine wisdom, opposed him, while the great Sage Shim'i cursed and denigrated him to such an extent that it was worse than all the suffering he had undergone during his entire life. In short, his whole world was destroyed. *Chazal* therefore ask, מִזְמוֹר לְדָוִד? קִינָה לְדָוִד מִיבָּעֵי לֵיהּ! — "'A song of David'? It should rather have said 'a lament of David!'" (*Berachos* 7b). What does he have to sing about?

Chazal respond,

> By an analogy, to what is this comparable? To a person regarding whom a loan document is produced. Before he pays it, he is troubled; after he pays it, he is happy. So too David, since the Holy One, Blessed is He, had said to him: "I will raise up evil against you from your own house" (Shemuel II 12:11). David was saddened. He said, "Perhaps it will be a slave or illegitimate child who will not have pity on me. Once he saw that it was his son Avshalom, he rejoiced."

(ibid.)

David sang praises to Hashem when he fled from Avshalom because the one who rebelled against him (as punishment for his sin with Bas-sheva) was not a cruel servant, but rather one of his own offspring, whom he was certain would have mercy on him. This explanation poses two difficulties:

1. Did we not learn (*Shemuel* II 16:18) that Avshalom did not have pity on David and in fact wished to kill him? It appears that David's joy and song in this psalm were misplaced!

2. The analogy used in the Gemara does not fit in with this explanation. The analogy describes a man who wished to pay off a heavy debt (see *Midrash Shochar Tov* 79, which elaborates further). This payment cleaned out all his assets until "his hands were on his head," to use the words of the *midrash*. Despite this, he was very happy to finally rid himself of this burdensome debt. If we compare the analogy with the case in question, the debt is obviously the sin with Bas-sheva, which needs atonement. If he is rejoicing that the rebellion came from Avshalom, who

will supposedly have mercy on him and alleviate his suffering, this is tantamount to his not having repaid his entire debt! How does this relate to the analogy used of one who has paid off a very heavy debt? It would have been more fitting to explain that David found it extremely difficult that his own son had risen against him, yet nevertheless he was happy because in this way he had "paid his debt" and now had been granted atonement.

Someone showed me that Maharsha, in fact, raised these same two questions. He solved the first question (that in reality Avshalom did not have mercy on his father) by saying that although Avshalom did not have mercy on his father, David thought that he would and thus sang a song of praise. With all due respect to the Torah of Maharsha, if I can be permitted to ask: the praises of David are a part of *Kesuvim* and have a degree of prophecy. Why would the Scriptures include something that ended up being proven wrong? I therefore feel that there has to be an alternative explanation to these words of *Chazal*.

DAVID'S JOY IN THE *KIDDUSH HASHEM* INHERENT IN HIS OWN PUNISHMENT

DAVID'S ACTUAL SIN in the incident involving Bas-sheva was that he caused a *chillul Hashem* (*"against you alone did I sin"* [*Tehillim* 51:6] — see *Sichos LeSefer Bereishis* 36 for an elaboration of this idea). David therefore desired to bring a *kiddush Hashem* to the world by means of the punishment that the prophet Nasan augured: הִנְנִי מֵקִים עָלֶיךָ רָעָה מִבֵּיתֶךָ — *"I will raise up evil against you from out of your own house"* (*Shemuel* II 12:11). David thought that when an individual would arise from his house and rebel against him, people would say to each other: "If Hashem has not even shown favoritism to David and has punished him this severely, how much more care must we take not to sin."

At that point David suspected that the rebel would be a servant, as is often the case, or someone else *"who will not have pity on me" (Berachos* 7b). In other words, rebels and brazen people exist in every generation and it is the nature of these people to rebel against their master. If it turned out this way, David feared, Hashem's providence in this incident would not be apparent. Political commentators would say that what happened to David had happened many times to different kings. And so, God forbid, Hashem's Name would not be exalted for His judgment. This was why David HaMelech was sad; he feared that the glory of Heaven would not immediately be returned to its original splendor.

When he saw that the rebel was his own flesh and blood, then he rejoiced! Not because his son would show him mercy — on the contrary, because it is unnatural for a son to be so cruel to his father as to try to kill him, it was obvious that this could only be a result of Hashem's awesome judgment! This would cause His Name to be feared and sanctified by all of creation. This is the reason David rejoiced and why he recited a *mizmor,* a song rather than a lament.

We find that it was explicitly this concern for *kavod Shamayim,* the honor of Heaven, that upset him most during his flight from Yerushalayim. *Chazal* tell us that when Avshalom rebelled, *"David sought to engage in idolatry" (Sanhedrin* 107a) during his flight. What caused him to entertain such terrible thoughts? David explained: *"People would say, 'A king such as I should be killed by his own son?' It is preferable that I should engage in idolatry so that the name of Heaven should not be desecrated publicly"* (ibid.). What this means is that together with his joy at Hashem's Name being exalted through him, he also feared the contrary — that His Name would be desecrated, that people would question how a person of his stature could be killed by his son, doubting the attributes of Hashem, and the result would be that the Name of Hashem would be publicly desecrated.

Rather than being troubled by his own terrible situation and by the difficult future in store for him, David HaMelech's mind was occupied only by thoughts of how to sanctify Hashem's

Name. Perhaps people would not understand how exacting the judgment was, and the opposite would result. It was for this reason that he entertained the notion of worshiping *avodah zarah* — so people would conclude that was the reason the hand of Hashem (in the guise of Avshalom) lifted up to harm him. Therefore: *"Better I should desecrate Hashem's Name alone, rather than have the entire nation desecrate His Name"* (Rashi loc. cit.).

JOY IN DIVINE JUSTICE

MANY TIMES IN *Tehillim* we find David's joy over Hashem's justice and His revenge against evil people. For example,

Declare the guilty, O God, may they fall short in their schemes; cast them away because of their many sins, for they have rebelled against You. But all who take refuge in You will rejoice, they will sing joyously forever, You will shelter them; and those who love Your name will exult in You.

(*Tehillim* 5:11–12)

The question is: Are we all not happy at the destruction of our enemies? Why did David's prayers for the destruction of the wicked merit to be included in *Tanach*?

The difference is that when David said, *"Those who love Your name will exult in You,"* he really meant "in You" — in the sanctification of Your name. Does our joy come from the downfall of Hashem's enemies or from the fact that we are rid of our personal enemies? The way to measure that is to ask ourselves: Do we feel that same joy when Hashem's justice causes pain to us as well? The "song" David sang when he fled from his son was clear proof that *"Performance of justice is a joy to the righteous"* (*Mishlei* 21:15). Even when this justice caused David much personal suffering, he was happy and sang for the revelation of Hashem's glory that came in its wake.

Here we can find the reason why *Ha'azinu*, this song of praise for Hashem's justice, must echo in our ears before Yom Kippur.

There is a profound lesson to be derived from this song. This must be our feeling before the Day of Judgment. This special and holy day is similar to that great Day of Judgment in the future. Even had this not been the day on which our sins are forgiven, just the great and awesome Day of Judgment alone, there would be reason enough to rejoice for the revelation of the King to His creatures! There would be joy in the fact that the world is not neglected and ownerless, left to the whims of those who use it as a tool for self-fulfillment. (All this is without getting into the fact that Hashem's justice provides us with yet another reason for joy. When Hashem "touches man," it is a great *chesed* for him. Hashem punishes man in order to perfect and purify his soul — making it possible for him to derive enjoyment from the pleasantness of the *Shechinah*).

This revelation of the Judge of all the land requires preparation on our part. Proper preparation will serve as a double cause for joy. Firstly, whoever goes to the trouble of purifying himself before this Day of Judgment will in any case be judged favorably and thus find it easier to rejoice over the glory of Hashem, exalted by His justice. Secondly, the heavenly Judge himself will rejoice. Can there be a greater joy to Him than the fact that He need not exercise His justice on His creations?

IGNORANCE IS NO EXCUSE!

LET US FOCUS on one central act of preparation which has far-reaching ramifications. Even in our "free" world, where anything goes, "ignorance of the law does not absolve one from punishment." The Torah's view goes even further: Even one who mistakenly thinks that a certain action is permitted is close to being considered as having acted בְּמֵזִיד, "intentionally" (see *Makkos* 7b). Each of us, therefore, must ensure to the best of his ability that he is well aware of the *halachos* of what is permitted and what is forbidden.

How can a yeshiva student tell me that he was unaware of

the prohibition of *yichud*? The laws of *yichud* are not recorded in some obscure responsa, they are clearly spelled out in the *Shulchan Aruch* in *Even HaEzer* 52, and every person is required to learn and master them! (See *Sichos LeSefer Vayikra*, Hebrew edition, pp. 220–221, for the clarification of this severe prohibition — which applies to every man and woman — forbidding them to be secluded together, except with one's spouse or certain relatives.)

Let me give you another example: This very evening, a *ben Torah* came to me with the following question. He had borrowed money from someone, promising that he would return a greater sum. Meanwhile, he suddenly discovered that this violates the prohibition of רִבִּית, "lending with interest," and he wanted to know what he should do. Many people know that it is forbidden to take interest, but they think that if the borrower agreed on his own initiative to give more, then is not prohibited. Ignorance can lead one to violate severe prohibitions! This is the reason that R' Yochanan cried whenever he reached the concluding *pasuk* of *Koheles*: כִּי אֶת כָּל מַעֲשֶׂה הָאֱלֹקִים יָבִא בְמִשְׁפָּט עַל כָּל נֶעְלָם — *"For God will judge every deed — even everything hidden"* (*Koheles* 12:14). We will be required to give an accounting even of that which is hidden from our knowledge (see *Chagigah* 5a).

WE TOO CAN FULFILL "NA'ASEH VE'NISHMA"

IT IS NOT a simple matter to master the entire Torah in a short period of time. In order to fulfill *"Performance of justice is a joy to the righteous"* on the upcoming Yom Kippur, even though we do not know a large portion of that which is demanded of us, let us offer a practical suggestion. This suggestion is aimed at anyone who wishes to learn and observe the whole Torah, but will not be able to accomplish this prior to entering this Holy Day. *Chazal* tell us: כָּל שֶׁמַּעֲשָׂיו מְרֻבִּים מֵחָכְמָתוֹ חָכְמָתוֹ מִתְקַיֶּמֶת שֶׁנֶּאֱמַר נַעֲשֶׂה וְנִשְׁמָע — *"Anyone whose actions are greater than his wisdom, his wisdom will endure, as it says 'we will do and we will obey' (Shemos 24:7)"* (*Avos d'Rabi Nasan* 22:1).

How are we to understand this? How can it be that one's *"actions are greater than his wisdom"*? How can a person do more than what he knows? Furthermore, what is the meaning of the ending of the *mishnah*, which quotes the Jewish People's declaration at *Matan Torah*? Does the *Tanna* mean to tell us that when the Jewish People received the Torah, their "actions were greater than their wisdom"?

A HEARTFELT RESOLUTION IS TANTAMOUNT TO OBSERVING THE ENTIRE TORAH!

RABBEINU YONAH *(SHA'AREI Teshuvah* 2:10) has an innovative way of understanding this. If a person resolves in his heart to follow all that he will learn in the future, it is tantamount to already having observed the entire Torah! Rabbeinu Yonah explains that, *"In one small moment this person has emerged from darkness into a great light."* That moment is the one in which he undertook to follow the dictates of those who teach Torah, from then on. Therefore, only a person who has made the decision to observe the mitzvos — even those commandments of which he is not yet aware — can be classified as someone whose *"actions are greater than his wisdom."* This person, says Rabbeinu Yonah, is praiseworthy, for he has made his soul righteous in one short moment.

This is also the connection to *"na'aseh ve'nishma"*: the Jewish People were ready to observe every mitzvah that they were to hear from that moment on. This earned them the same reward and merit as if they had observed all the mitzvos in their entirety.

As it was then, so it is now. We too have the opportunity in one short moment to observe the Torah in its entirety! There is no better time than in these holy days. After all the preparation during the days of Elul, after we have crowned Hashem King on Rosh Hashanah, the remaining stage of preparation is to make a firm decision — to be among those who are blessed from on high: *"... those who establish all the words of the Torah."*[1] Rabbeinu Yonah (*Sha'arei Teshuvah* 1:6) points out that it does not say: *"those who do,"* rather, those who have established, i.e. those who have resolved in their hearts to fulfill all that the Torah commands.

Suddenly it becomes clear that it is all in our hands. What a great joy! In order to emerge with a favorable verdict that will determine our future, there is no need for strong economic conditions, nor for wisdom, beauty, or prestigious lineage — all that is required is our will to do the right thing. Can there be any greater joy than that?

BEWARE OF THAT PROFESSIONAL LIAR!

THERE IS ONE creature, of course, who is not happy with this whole process. Who is he? None other than the *yetzer ha-ra*! He stands next to us, on guard. He might be concerned — but he does not give up. On the contrary, God forbid that he should use such a precious weapon as despair for "his own needs." He will, rather, try to sell it to us! Even during those moments when he sees that the gates of our hearts are opening before the Ark of Hashem and we are ready to change our ways, a creature like him will not give in. Listen! We have not yet finished what we are about to say and we can already hear him whispering: "This plan has no chance!" He explains it in logical terms spiced with *divrei Torah*: "Many have tried before you… How will you be able to fulfill all that you will learn? First of all, you will see that it is not easy. Secondly, you'll be sure to fail and then you will go through a crisis — it's a waste of time even to try. Thirdly, even if this notion is true, what about your past sins? Fourthly…," and so on and on without end.

Just like when he made his initial appearance during the six

---

[1]. The *pasuk* actually states *"cursed are those who do not establish the words of the Torah..."* (*Devarim* 27:26). It is to this verse that Rabbeinu Yonah refers.

days of Creation, so here too. The central hinge on which his claims rest is the lie. His entire purpose in life is to prevent people from achieving perfection and happiness. It is for this reason that he works so hard at creating despair over attaining *teshuvah*, which is truly within reach — as we said, all that is needed is our will.

When he asks us so sarcastically, how will our decision to accept the yoke of Torah help so long as we are still full of sin, do you really think he does not know the answer? Does he not know the *Yerushalmi* that states explicitly: *"Hashem said to them (the Jewish People), 'Since you have accepted the yoke of the Torah, I will view it as if you have never sinned in your lives'"* (*Rosh Hashanah* 4:8)? As we said earlier, he is a professional liar! Therefore, even in a situation in which we have no clear proof that he is lying, we must assume that this "lifetime friend" of ours would never say a true word!

SEND THE YETZER HA-RA TO AZAZEL!

WE MUST REMEMBER that lies can penetrate and lay foundations only in places which are not filled to the rafters with truth. Where there is a breach owing to a lack in the truth of the Torah within us, there the lie can become established. Even though there are proper answers to all of the *yetzer ha-ra*'s "questions," he takes advantage of the fact that we do not know them yet, in order to cause us confusion and despair. Therefore, because he chose the profession of lying and deceit, we must choose the profession of truth and we must adopt the ways of our Creator: *"In the midst of my house shall not dwell a practitioner of deceit; one who tells lies shall not be established before my eyes"* (*Tehillim* 101:7). The *yetzer ha-ra* and his lies will not dwell in our house! We can certainly send him off to *Azazel* in the desert, in order that we should be free to study the teachings of the Torah, as we see in the Yom Kippur service (see *Yoma*, end of *perek* 6, beginning of 7 — immediately after the goat was sent off to *Azazel*, they would read from the *sefer Torah* in the *Beis HaMikdash*).

Let us hasten then, and accept upon ourselves the observance of the Torah in its entirety in order that we may merit to enter this holy day pure from all sin and filled with the 613 mitzvos in their totality!

SICHAH FIVE
NULLIFYING THE DECREES

"BE'ETZEM HAYOM HAZEH"

Hashem spoke to Moshe בְּעֶצֶם הַיּוֹם הַזֶּה — *in the middle of the day, saying: "Ascend to this mount of Avarim, Mount Nevo, which is in the land of Moav, which is before Yericho, and see the land of Canaan that I give to the Children of Israel as an inheritance. And die on the mountain where you will ascend, and be brought in to your people."*

(Devarim 32:48–50)

Rashi on this *pasuk* cites Sifri:

In three places it says בְּעֶצֶם הַיּוֹם הַזֶּה, *in the middle (literally: in the brightest part) of the day:*

1. *It says of Noach, "in the middle of that day Noach came into the ark"* (Bereishis 7:13) — *by the appearance of the light of the day. Because the people of his generation were saying: By such and such we swear, if we perceive that Noach is about to enter the ark, we will not allow him to enter... The Holy One, Blessed is He, said* — *"Behold I shall bring him into the ark at midday and whoever has the power to object, let him come and object."*
2. *Of Egypt, the verse says "in the brightest part of that day Hashem took the Children of Israel out of the land of Egypt"* (Shemos 12:51), *because the Egyptians were saying "By such and such we swear, if we perceive that the Israelites are about to depart, we will not allow them to leave." The Holy One, Blessed is He, said: "Behold, I shall take them out at midday, and whoever has the power to object, let him come and object."*

> 3. Here, too, at the death of Moshe it says: "in the middle of that day," because Israel were saying, "By such and such we swear, if we perceive that Moshe is about to die, we will not let him, a man who took us out of Egypt and parted the sea for us, and brought down the manna for us, and made the pheasants fly to us, and brought up the well for us, and gave us the Torah — we will not let him die!" The Holy One Blessed is He said: "Behold, I shall bring him in at midday and whoever has the power to object, let him come and object."

Let us begin by clarifying two points. First of all, when Sifri said, "*In three places it says* בְּעֶצֶם הַיּוֹם הַזֶּה," his meaning was not that the expression only appears three times in the entire *Tanach*. This phrase in fact appears fourteen times in *Tanach*, three of these are found in *Nevi'im* (*Yehoshua* 5:11, *Yechezkel* 24:2, 40:1) and the rest in the Torah. The eleven occurrences of בְּעֶצֶם הַיּוֹם הַזֶּה in the Torah can be divided into two categories:

1. Relating to a mitzvah that must be carried out in the future. An example of this regarding Yom Kippur is: *"You shall not do any work on this very day (another meaning of* בְּעֶצֶם הַיּוֹם הַזֶּה*)" (Vayikra 23:28).*
2. When describing events that occurred in the past.

Sifri is dealing with the latter category, of which there are three such events recorded in the Torah: Noach's entering the Ark, the Exodus from Egypt, and the death of Moshe. (We actually find this phrase three times in the Torah's description of the Exodus alone).

Now to the second point that requires clarification. We find this expression used in conjunction with another event in the Torah:

> Then Avraham took his son Yishmael and all those servants born in his household and all those he had purchased for money — all the male members of Avraham's house, and he

circumcised the flesh of their foreskin on that very day as God had spoken with him.

(Bereishis 17:23)

The phrase appears yet again regarding *bris milah* (ibid. 17:26). Rashi's commentary there is similar to the Sifri quoted here:

בְּעֶצֶם הַיּוֹם הַזֶּה — *on that very day that he was commanded, by day and not by night* — *he was not afraid of the heathens nor of the scoffers* — *and a further reason was so that his enemies and contemporaries should not say, "Had we seen him, we would not have allowed him to perform circumcision and to fulfill the commandment of the Omnipresent."*

Why did Sifri not see fit to include this event as well?

Some commentators explain that the phrase בְּעֶצֶם הַיּוֹם הַזֶּה used in conjunction with Avraham's *bris milah* differs from the others. The Torah here wished to point out to us the alacrity with which Avraham and his household members fulfilled mitzvos. Immediately following the conclusion of the commandment, they ran to carry out the mitzvah *"the very day"* that they were commanded. They did not fear any potential obstacles or comments by scoffers. Despite these being the first *brisos* ever carried out in the world, and thus performed by a novice *mohel*, Avraham managed to perform 318 circumcisions, not to mention those of the slaves, all in the course of a single day!

We see that here the expression comes to inform us of Avraham's personal level of righteousness, whereas the three places quoted by Sifri come to teach us the infinite capabilities of the Creator — He is able to carry out whatever He desires in broad daylight, without having to worry about any interference.

COULD AM YISRAEL HAVE PREVENTED THE DEATH OF MOSHE?

THIS BRINGS US to a very fundamental question that should trouble anyone reading Sifri's words. Regarding Noach's entering the Ark and the Exodus from Egypt, we can understand how it is possible for people to think they could interfere with the Divine Plan. The wicked Generation of the Flood could have attempted to prevent Noach from entering the Ark and the Egyptians could have placed a roadblock across the Jewish People's exit route. How, though, could the Jewish People say that they would not allow Moshe to die? Could they or anyone else prevent Moshe's death?

We can provide a very simple explanation as is found in *Ohr HaChaim*. Hashem told Moshe:

וַיְדַבֵּר ה' אֶל מֹשֶׁה בְּעֶצֶם הַיּוֹם הַזֶּה לֵאמֹר: עֲלֵה אֶל הַר הָעֲבָרִים הַזֶּה הַר נְבוֹ... וּמֻת בָּהָר אֲשֶׁר אַתָּה עֹלֶה שָׁמָּה.

And Hashem spoke to Moshe in the middle of the day, saying, "Ascend to this mount of Avarim, Mount Nevo... And die on the mountain where you will ascend."

(*Devarim* 32:48–50)

The Torah (which was given to the Jewish People prior to Moshe's death) was informing the nation that Moshe's passing was destined to take place on Mount Nevo. (The *Ohr HaChaim* derives this from the word לֵאמֹר, which generally means that the information is to be passed on to the people). Thus, the people could possibly have tried to bar Moshe from ascending the mountain, thereby preventing his death.

Regarding this matter, my esteemed teacher, HaGaon HaRav Chaim Shmuelevitz *zt"l* expressed a fundamental principle of Jewish thought, which is the basis for authentic *tefillah* during these auspicious days: The Jewish People could have prevented Moshe's death! How could they have done so? By praying from the depths of their hearts. Even after the decree, even if the judgment is already sealed — a Jew never gives up! True prayer, emanating from the heart, has the ability to tear up a decree, and it is never returned unanswered (see *Koheles Rabbah* 5:6).

It is for this reason, in a deviation from the norm, that Hashem stressed that even this powerful medium would be of no use here: *"Even if you intensify your prayer, I will not listen"* (*Yeshayahu* 1:15).

Nullifying the Decrees

Hashem declared that He would not heed any prayer involving an entreaty to keep Moshe Rabbeinu alive, or perhaps He would ensure that Israel would not succeed in achieving a level of *tefillah* capable of overturning the decree. Radak, in his commentary on *Yonah* (2:2), brings a similar idea there:

> It was a great miracle that occurred; Yonah was inside the whale for three days and three nights and survived. An additional miracle occurred, that he was not stunned; he was able to take hold of himself, be of sound mind, and pray.

Radak is demonstrating that it was only due to a miracle that Yonah was able to pray at all. We see that Hashem has many ways in which He can prevent man from praying.

TEFILLAH — A POWERFUL TOOL IN MAN'S HANDS

WE HAVE BEEN entrusted by Heaven with an incredible force. Prayer is so potent that when Hashem absolutely has no wish to issue a positive response, the Heavens are obliged to "overcome," so to speak, the strength of man's prayers. Otherwise, a heartfelt prayer has the ability to storm the gates of Heaven and to influence the outcome.

This principle can be derived from Moshe Rabbeinu's actions. When he beseeched Hashem to repeal the decree barring his entry into *Eretz Yisrael*, we learn that he prayed 515 prayers (corresponding to the numerical value of וָאֶתְחַנַּן in the *pasuk* וָאֶתְחַנַּן אֶל ה' בָּעֵת הַהִוא — "I implored Hashem at that time": ו = 6, א = 1, ת = 400, ח = 8, נ = 50, ן = 50). Yet Hashem responded: רַב לָךְ אַל תּוֹסֶף דַּבֵּר אֵלַי עוֹד בַּדָּבָר הַזֶּה — "You have said enough. Do not continue to speak to Me further about this matter" (*Devarim* 3:26).

According to some commentaries, this was why Hashem insisted that Moshe cease to pray, for had Moshe davened even one more time, the decree would have been rescinded and consequently Moshe would have entered *Eretz Yisrael*. A proper *tefillah* has such incredible power that even the Heavenly courts cannot stand up against it.

As we saw in the case of Moshe's passing, so too in this supplication of Moshe: It was because Hashem had a profound reason for not wanting Moshe to enter the Land that He instructed him, *"Do not continue to speak to Me further about this matter"* — My hidden will is that you not enter the Holy Land. Here we see the loyal servant, Moshe, in all his greatness. Upon hearing this, Moshe Rabbeinu immediately ceased praying — in order that he not affect the outcome of the judgment. The reasoning is very simple: Moshe's whole motive for entering *Eretz Yisrael* was in order to fulfill the will of the Almighty by performing the mitzvos associated with the Land (see *Sotah* 14a). The moment Hashem revealed that His will was that Moshe not enter, this became Moshe's desire as well. Moshe Rabbeinu was happy to fulfill the wish of his Master and remain on the other side of the Jordan. (Had Moshe continued to pray, it is possible that he would have been allowed to enter, and this might have caused damage that Hashem wanted to avoid by denying him entry. Had Moshe entered *Eretz Yisrael*, in his merit the *Beis HaMikdash* would never have been destroyed, and if the Jewish People were to sin, Hashem's anger would, God forbid, have been vented on the people, rather than on the sticks and stones of the *Beis HaMikdash*.) Such is the power of prayer!

There have been many instances in which doctors have given up on someone's life, and a prayer that erupted from the depths of the heart managed to breach the Heavens and render the doctors' prognosis insignificant. The concept of "a medical miracle" has become an official term. Many experienced doctors, even the non-religious, choose their words very carefully, and rather than say "There is no chance," will say "Only prayer can help."

NULLIFY THE DECREE BEFORE IT IS SEALED!

THE RULE IS, an edict can be rescinded. Even a person who is afraid of what has been decreed on Rosh Hashanah (and who is not afraid? — we all view ourselves at best as belonging to the middle category of *beinoni*, where judgment remains suspended until Yom Kippur), must realize that the Creator has given us an extremely powerful tool, that of *tefillah*. Anyone who does not have this engraved on his consciousness may find that the hundreds of pages of *daven*ing he leafs through during *Aseres Yemei Teshuvah* are nothing but a burden.

I would like to emphasize an important point here: It is easier to nullify the decree now (during *Aseres Yemei Teshuvah*), given that the edict has not yet been sealed. These precious few days between the writing of the decree and its sealing on the tenth of Tishrei, are the time to put in that extra effort to ensure that our prayers will be of a higher quality. One who understands the immense power of prayer will realize that we must utilize these days to prepare for the *tefillos* of Yom Kippur. One cannot simply alight from the road and meet the King of kings — preparation is essential. Before beginning the actual *tefillos*, many people set aside some time to learn from *sefarim* that serve to open up their hearts, elevate them spiritually, and put them into a suitable frame of mind. This is not so difficult; after all, we are speaking of only a limited number of critical days. A few proper *tefillos* before Yom Kippur can entirely change one's status so that when he begins the purification process afforded by the Day of Mercy, he does not enter this Day of Forgiveness on an inferior level. Although even with preparation we are no more than a poor man knocking on the door, at least we should not waste precious hours of this awesome day trying to reach the door!

It was for this reason that the custom of reciting *selichos* was instituted before *daven*ing — to enable us to begin our *daven*ing on an already elevated spiritual plane. (Unfortunately, not everyone recites *selichos* with the proper *kavanah*. I was once in a shul where the *chazan* practically swallowed the entire *selichos* in a matter of a few minutes. At the conclusion of the *daven*ing I asked him, "Should there not at least be a distinction made between *Aseres Yemei Teshuvah* and *aseres b'nei Haman* [the ten sons of Haman whose names must be said in one breath when the

Megillah is read on Purim]?"

One who has tried in the past to raise his level of *tefillah* without success would do well to take advantage of the greater potential for closeness to Hashem that these days have to offer. During these days of closeness, Hashem is likened to a king who emerges from his palace and offers his subjects the golden opportunity of a direct meeting with the ultimate authority. At the conclusion of *Ne'ilah*, the gates will be locked, *"Hashem will ascend with the sound of the shofar"* (*Tehillim* 47:6), and we will then return to our usual dealings with small clerks whose power is limited. Until then, literally everything is within our grasp.

THE PRAYERS OF A KING

WE DISCUSSED EARLIER that Hashem had a particular reason for not accepting any *tefillos* on Moshe's behalf. There are, however, many examples in the *Tanach* in which an individual was slated to die, but prayer managed to ensure him a place among the living. For instance, we find such a case with Chizkiyahu, king of Yehudah. The prophet Yeshayahu informs him: *"Thus said Hashem: Instruct your household, for you shall die, and you shall not live"* (*Melachim* II, 20:1).

Chazal tell us that when Chizkiyahu discovered that the reason he was destined to die was because he had never married, he requested more time to be able to rectify this. But Yeshayahu responded, *"It has already been thus decreed"* (*Berachos* 10a) — Hashem has commanded you to write your will. What can be done once Hashem has issued a decree?

Yet Chizkiyahu refuses to yield, saying to Yeshayahu: *"Son of Amotz, cease your prophecy and leave here! I have a tradition from my ancestors that even if a sharp sword is placed on a man's neck, he must not refrain from asking for mercy"* (*Berachos* 10a). Chizkiyahu then *davens* and starts to weep. The prophet is immediately summoned to return to the king tell him: *"I have heard your prayer; I have seen your tears"* (*Melachim* II 20:5), and the decree is, in fact, canceled.

A similar incident occurred with Yehoshafat, king of Yehudah. When he saw the army of the enemy gathering around to kill him, *"Yehoshafat cried out and Hashem came to his aid; God drew them away from him"* (*Divrei HaYamim* II, 18:31).

The *Yerushalmi* (*Berachos* 9, 1) derives from here that a sword was literally placed on his neck and at the last moment Hashem prevented him from being harmed because he cried out. Here too, the death penalty had already been issued — in fact he was considered dead, to the extent that the *pasuk* does not record the years he lived beyond that point in time, yet he was saved in the merit of his crying out to Hashem, because his *tefillos* emanated from his heart!

THE WORD OF GOD IN NEWS BULLETINS

FROM THESE TWO kings we can learn another method of achieving an exalted level of prayer: by understanding that our very lives are hanging in the balance! Even if we have no prophets like there were in the days of Chizkiyahu, we have — *lehavdil* — the news. The word of Hashem reaches us every day and every hour. His word is disguised as newspaper headlines and radio bulletins, yet when we read them, we can identify with King Yehoshafat and feel that the *"witnesses for the prosecution"* are rallying around the enemies of Israel in Heaven. And how do we know? We see their seventy earthly ambassadors constantly attempting to place a sword at our neck. Yehoshafat's cry must emanate from the throat of every thinking person, before these decrees are sealed!

DO NOT WAIT UNTIL IT IS TOO LATE!

HOW STRIKING ARE the words of Yirmeyahu, who warned the Jewish People prior to their exile: *"Give honor to Hashem, your God, before it grows dark, and before your feet stub themselves upon the mountains of night"* (*Yirmeyahu* 13:16). Honor the word of Hashem before you begin your journey into exile — for by then it will be too late!

This indeed is what took place. Yirmeyahu, who accompanied the exiled people to Bavel, heard with great pain how they were crying out. *"And he said to them: 'I testify by heaven and earth! Had you cried one time while still in Zion, you would not have been exiled!' Yirmeyahu continued to cry"* (Pesikta Rabbati 26). Crying can come too late. Once Israel was exiled, it took seventy years in exile to atone for their sins.

HOW DO WE UNDERSTAND UNHEEDED PRAYERS?

IF *TEFILLAH* IS so powerful, how do we reconcile this with the fact that at times it appears that our prayers are not fully answered? To observe this phenomenon, we need look no further than this bitter exile of ours that has been in effect for over two thousand years. We pray daily, וְלִירוּשָׁלַיִם עִירְךָ בְּרַחֲמִים תָּשׁוּב — *"And to Jerusalem Your city, You will return with mercy,"* yet this exile continues. There are several answers to this question of seemingly unheeded prayers. These answers can be divided into two categories: either our prayers need improving or our understanding of the circumstances needs improving (perhaps our *tefillos* were in fact answered, although we did not recognize it; perhaps it is not in our best interest that they be answered or it would not have been good for us, given our circumstances at the time of our *tefillah*). This is not the place to delve deeply into this question, but if we can gain another insight into the power of prayer, this will enable us to shed some light on our question.

We find in *Chazal* that the potency of *tefillah* is so great that even those prayers which are not answered produce positive results. So long as there is some positive aspect to the prayer, it has to have some effect, even if, for whatever reason, the central request of the prayer is not answered. We began this discussion by speaking of Moshe Rabbeinu. Let us then conclude with a *tefillah* offered by that loyal shepherd — a prayer that was not answered, and yet this prayer of all prayers serves to highlight the tremendous power of *tefillah*.

A PRAYER THAT WAS FOUND WANTING

AT THE END of *Parashas Shemos*, immediately after Moshe's initial, fruitless meeting with Pharaoh, Moshe came to Hashem claiming, וּמֵאָז בָּאתִי אֶל פַּרְעֹה לְדַבֵּר בִּשְׁמֶךָ הֵרַע לָעָם הַזֶּה וְהַצֵּל לֹא הִצַּלְתָּ אֶת עַמֶּךָ — "*From the time I came to Pharaoh to speak in Your name, he did evil to this people, but You did not rescue Your people*" (*Shemos* 5:23). *Chazal*, who are the only ones with the authority to say such things, state here that Hashem did not graciously accept Moshe's prayer. Moshe was defending the trampled honor of the Jewish nation, a people worn out from bondage — yet without fitting consideration for the Glory of Heaven.

The Almighty responded to this in a manner that appears gentle, but in actuality is quite harsh: *"Now you will see what I shall do to Pharaoh, for through a strong hand will he send them out, and with a strong hand will he drive them from his land"* (*Shemos* 6:1).

Chazal had difficulty understanding what new information Hashem was telling Moshe. Had He not already told him, *"I shall stretch out My hand and I shall strike Egypt with all My wonders that I shall perform in its midst, and after that he will send you out"* (*Shemos* 3:20)?

Chazal, therefore, pinpointed the exact meaning of Hashem's words: *"Now you will see what I shall do to Pharaoh, the war against Pharaoh you will see. However, you will not see the war against the thirty-one kings"* (*Sanhedrin* 111a) — because you will not enter the Land! The ultimate reason preventing Moshe from entering the Land stemmed from the incident of Mei Merivah, yet here there was already a hint to Moshe that in the future a reason would develop for his not meriting to enter the Holy Land.

In addition to this bitter allusion that appears at the end of *Parashas Shemos*, Hashem's harsh response to Moshe's supplication continues at the beginning of *Parashas Va'era*: *"Elokim spoke* to Moshe and said to him 'I am Hashem'" (Shemos 6:2). The term *Elokim* generally denotes the severe attribute of judgment. Rashi therefore tells us: *"He spoke to Moshe with words of rebuke for speaking harshly and saying, 'Why have You harmed this people'?"*

What did Hashem tell him? *"And I appeared before Avraham, Yitzchak, and Yaakov"* (Shemos 6:2) which *Chazal* explain as, *"Woe for those who are lost and are not found"* (Rashi). It is too bad that you, Moshe, in the same situation as your forefathers, did not react as they did. They endured many trials and tribulations in which, to all appearances, My promises were not being kept, and, nevertheless, they did not question My ways. According to *Chazal* there was something lacking in Moshe's prayer, and thus Hashem responded to His faithful servant in unusually harsh terms.

Let us further analyze the conclusion of Hashem's response: *"Therefore say to the Children of Israel: 'I am Hashem'"* (Shemos 6:6), to which Rashi comments: *"I can be trusted to keep My promise"* even when this is not readily apparent to flesh and blood.

Hashem continues:

וְהוֹצֵאתִי אֶתְכֶם מִתַּחַת סִבְלוֹת מִצְרַיִם וְהִצַּלְתִּי אֶתְכֶם מֵעֲבוֹדָתָם וְגָאַלְתִּי אֶתְכֶם בִּזְרוֹעַ נְטוּיָה וּבִשְׁפָטִים גְּדוֹלִים וְלָקַחְתִּי אֶתְכֶם לִי לְעָם.

I shall take you out from under the burdens of Egypt; I shall rescue you from their service, I shall redeem you with an outstretched arm ... I shall take you to Me for a people.
(Shemos 6:6–7)

Chazal derive from the four expressions of redemption used here that there is a mitzvah to drink four cups of wine at the Seder. *Chazal* saw the abundant love Hashem demonstrated to the Jewish nation by using so many different expressions describing His promise to redeem them and by recording them in the Torah for posterity. Therefore, as a remembrance of this great event, *Chazal* required every Jew to drink four cups as an expression of thanksgiving for this extra love Hashem showered upon us.

A PRAYER THAT EMANATES FROM THE HEART

HOW ARE WE to understand this? Hashem has just responded very harshly to Moshe's prayer — is this the appropriate time for such a demonstration of love for the Jewish nation? Could Hashem not have found a more auspicious time to tell these things to Moshe? Why are the expressions of love juxtaposed with those of harsh rebuke?

The answer is based on what we have just said. A proper prayer must produce positive results. Since, in essence, Moshe's prayer emanated from a heart broken over the troubles of the Jewish People, it was impossible for this particular point in his prayer not to be answered immediately. Moshe's *tefillah* went right up and breached the gates of Heaven, releasing from there all the Almighty's love for *Am Yisrael*.

Here is an example of a prayer that did not satisfy the Almighty and which did not bring salvation for the Jewish People's suffering at that moment, yet despite this, was able to bring upon the world a tremendous flow of good. So much so, that *Chazal*, who understood the importance of this love that is inscribed in the Torah forever, saw to it that this event be observed throughout the generations to come. How great is the power of *tefillah* — even a prayer that is not answered immediately.

SICHAH SIX
A NEW BEING

CREATE YOURSELF ANEW

וּבַחֹדֶשׁ הַשְּׁבִיעִי בְּאֶחָד לַחֹדֶשׁ מִקְרָא קֹדֶשׁ יִהְיֶה לָכֶם...וַעֲשִׂיתֶם עֹלָה לְרֵיחַ נִיחוֹחַ לַה'.

In the seventh month, on the first day of the month, there shall be a holy convocation for you ... וַעֲשִׂיתֶם *— you shall make a burnt offering for a satisfying aroma for Hashem.*

(Bemidbar 29:1–2)

Thus commands the Torah regarding the *Mussaf* offering of Rosh Hashanah. *Chazal* pose a question regarding this passage: In all the other festival *Mussaf* offerings, the expression וְהִקְרַבְתֶּם עֹלָה — *"you shall offer a burnt-offering"* (ibid. 29:8) is used, while on Rosh Hashanah the Torah commands us וַעֲשִׂיתֶם — "you shall make the offering."

The Midrash explains:

The Holy One, Blessed is He, said to Israel: "Repent during these ten days between Rosh Hashanah and Yom Kippur, and I will grant you a positive judgment on Yom Kippur and create you anew."

(Pesikta Rabbati 41)

Thus the expression וַעֲשִׂיתֶם — "you shall make" on Rosh Hashanah tells us that anyone who sinned against God and has now repented and changed his behavior is viewed as if he is making himself anew. *Teshuvah* transforms him into a totally new entity — into a being that has only now entered the world.

Our Sages interpreted the following verse in *Tehillim* in a similar fashion: *"Let this be recorded for the final generation, so that the newborn people will praise God" (Tehillim* 102:19). Who is this "final generation", and who is the nation that is destined to be "newborn" following the demise of this final one? *Chazal* explain, *"These are the generations who by their actions are considered as if they are dead, and on Rosh Hashanah and Yom Kippur they come and pray before You, and You create them into a new being" (Midrash Shochar Tov).*

Many generations, therefore, could have been classified as the last generation on earth, had Hashem judged them based on their actions. It is only *teshuvah* that performs this wonder — that is able to recreate, to renew the generations again and again. Therefore, concludes the *midrash*, it is fitting that these same *"newborn"* people *"praise God"* specifically on Sukkos, which follows on the heels of Yom Kippur, while holding the Four Species in their hands.

The expression *"a new being"* is not an exaggeration. The wicked person is usually not aware of the severity of his situation. He continues to live his life the way he always has — he functions at work, with his family, and smiles at everyone. Internally, spiritually, however, he is in very bad shape. He can be compared to a person who appears to be successful in everything; little do people know that a malignant illness is, God forbid, spreading its tentacles over him. Regarding one's spiritual health, a majority of the time even the person concerned is not aware of how critical his condition is.

"HIS MITZVOS ARE THROWN BACK IN HIS FACE!"

ONE OF THE greatest physical and spiritual healers of all time wrote a diagnosis of the serious condition of the sinner who knowingly violates the Torah's dictates. Rambam declares:

> *How great is* teshuvah! *Yesterday he was separated from Hashem, God of Israel, as it says: "Rather, your iniquities have separated between you and your God" (Yeshayahu 59:2), he*

cries out but is not answered ... he performs mitzvos and they are thrown back in his face.

(Rambam, *Hilchos Teshuvah* 7:7)

Not only has the sinner been ostracized and banished from the Divine Presence, teaches Rambam in this innovative interpretation, but as long as he does not try to change his ways, even his prayers and mitzvos are not accepted.

It seems, however, that we must qualify these words and explain them. In his commentary to the *pasuk*, הַצּוּר תָּמִים פָּעֳלוֹ כִּי כָל דְּרָכָיו מִשְׁפָּט — *"The Rock! Perfect is His work, for all His paths are justice"* (*Devarim* 32:4), Rashi cites from the Gemara that *"The wicked are paid in this world for even a minor mitzvah they perform"* (*Ta'anis* 11a).

It seems, therefore, that Rambam was referring to particular types of mitzvos performed by the sinner that are not accepted, whereas other mitzvos are accepted and are even rewarded.

Rambam quotes *pesukim* that discuss the specific categories of mitzvos that are not accepted: *"Who sought this from your hand, to trample My courtyards? ... Even if you were to intensify your prayer, I will not listen"* (*Yeshayahu* 1:12,15). In particular, Hashem does not desire any offerings, neither prayers nor *korbanos* brought by the sinner when he comes to the *Beis HaMikdash* on the *Shalosh Regalim*. For other mitzvos, it appears that even the wicked man receives reward.

The reward for these mitzvos, however, will be in the worst way possible — in the words of Rambam, *"He does mitzvos and they are thrown back in his face."* The sinner will indeed be repaid, but his recompense will be far less than what he could have received. Rather than receiving the reward for his mitzvah in the World to Come, which is eternal, he will receive his reward in This World, which is temporary and fleeting. Being rewarded in such a fashion is actually a tremendous punishment. Payment for a mitzvah in the physical world pales into insignificance compared to the great spiritual reward enjoyed by the soul in the upper worlds.

INFINITE REWARD VERSUS IMMEDIATE PAYMENT

THE SOURCE FOR this is an explicit verse in the Torah: *"You must know that Hashem, your God, He is the God, the faithful God, Who safeguards the covenant and the kindness for those who love Him and for those who observe His commandments, for a thousand generations"* (*Devarim* 7:9). How can we speak of payment *"for a thousand generations"* regarding an individual who does not live for more than a few generations? The meaning here is that the descendants will benefit from the reward that their ancestor, who is now in the Next World, received for performance of a mitzvah.

Another verse informs us that Hashem is נוֹצֵר חֶסֶד לָאֲלָפִים — *"Preserver of kindness for thousands of generations"* (*Shemos* 34:7), i.e. the reward for the mitzvah is spread out over a thousand generations or even more (since "thousands" is in the plural). Many commentaries, including Ibn Ezra and Ohr HaChaim, interpret these numbers as just a manner of speaking, implying that there is no limit. Therefore it stands to reason that the reward for the mitzvah is almost entirely paid out after he reaches the Next World. How does this occur?

1. Hashem protects the descendants of the one who performed the mitzvah — aiding them materially and spiritually. This is one of man's great desires: to care for his offspring — as we recite in *Shemoneh Esrei*: וְזוֹכֵר חַסְדֵּי אָבוֹת וּמֵבִיא גוֹאֵל לִבְנֵי בְנֵיהֶם לְמַעַן שְׁמוֹ בְּאַהֲבָה — *"Who recalls the kindnesses of the Patriarchs and brings a redeemer to their children's children for His Name's sake with love."*

2. The benevolence that Hashem brings to the descendants of the one who observed the mitzvah will help them to fulfill still more mitzvos — such as supporting the needy, building yeshivos, etc. The reward for these mitzvos in turn will also increase the ancestor's merit and serve to elevate his soul in the eternal world that is all good.

A New Being

With this manner of calculation, there is no end to the mitzvos added to his credit with the passing of years! We can therefore say that Hashem intentionally does not grant the reward to *"those who love Him and those who observe His commandments"* until they arrive in the Next World, for this is the ultimate way of being rewarded.

In the subsequent *pasuk*, however, we read of a reward that is immediate: *"And He repays His enemies in his lifetime to make him perish; He shall not delay for His enemy — in his lifetime He shall repay him"* (*Devarim* 7:10). Rashi explains that Hashem does not delay the reward, but He pays the wicked immediately — in This World — in order *"to make him perish"* from the Next World (so that he not attain the World to Come).

This is precisely Rambam's meaning when he said: *"It is thrown back in his face."* How can we compare any payment given us in the weak currency of This World, which only retains its value for seventy years, with the eternal reward of the Next World?

If one were to trade his reward in the World to Come for earthly wealth of mythical proportions, eating fantastic delicacies his entire life, this "transaction" would still be a terrible punishment. Imagine for yourselves: a person has enjoyed a lifetime of eating meat (on which the Mishnah comments, מַרְבֶּה בָשָׂר מַרְבֶּה רִמָּה — *"The more meat, the more worms"* [*Avos* 2:7]) instead of the good he could have received — the glory of the Divine Presence and the pleasure that the soul has yearned for, the good that Rambam describes thus: *"No man has the power to comprehend it and no one knows the size and beauty and strength of it, except Hashem Himself!"* (Rambam, *Hilchos Teshuvah* 8:7).

Have we not learned: *"Better one hour of spiritual bliss in the World to Come than the entire life of This World"* (*Avos* 4:22)?

Even a very small moment of pleasure in the Next World is worth more than all the delights of all the people during the six thousand years this world will be in existence.

HASHEM PAYS IN THE CURRENCY THAT MAN DESIRES

THE DIFFERENCE BETWEEN reward in This World and reward in the Next World is so vast that the following question is inevitable: If *"Hashem does not deprive any creature of any reward due it"* (*Bava Kamma* 38b), as it says: *"a God of faith without iniquity"* (*Devarim* 32:4), and therefore we have to say that a wicked man receives his due reward for mitzvos that he performed, how can Hashem reward him with valueless "This World currency", while the *tzaddik* receives the true reward in the Next World?

The answer to this can be found in *Tehillim:* פּוֹתֵחַ אֶת יָדֶךָ וּמַשְׂבִּיעַ לְכָל חַי רָצוֹן — *"You open Your hand and satisfy the desire of every living thing"* (*Tehillim* 145:16). Hashem pays every living thing in the currency that it desires. The sinner, who is so immersed in the physical world, would rather be paid in physical terms. That is what he values. One who presents a bill for services rendered in shekels will be paid in shekels, while one whose bill is in dollars will be paid in dollars. The sinner has managed to corrupt his soul into something so physical that payment in spiritual currency is now impossible.

Viewing the sinner's negligible reward in this way, which is the simple understanding of the verse, only highlights his sorry state. Even if, by chance, he has fulfilled some mitzvos and he comes to claim his just reward, he has built such a barricade around himself, barring any spirituality from entering, that he prohibits any spiritual recompense and receives a lesser reward for any mitzvos he does perform.

Furthermore, in light of Rambam's negative description of the sinner, *"He is despised by Hashem, contemptible and far removed"* (Rambam, *Hilchos Teshuvah* 7:6), it is clear that even the little reward Hashem gives him is granted with a lack of enthusiasm, so to speak. Hashem has no interest in the sinner nor in any of the random mitzvos he happens to perform; He only hastens the reward in order that the sinner take his leave as soon as possible. It is even conceivable that Hashem will grant him longevity, just to

A New Being

keep him from showing his face in Heaven for a while longer!

TRANSFORMING AN ANIMAL INTO AN ANGEL

AND YET, DESPITE all this, the sinner's lowly status can change instantly. It does not require gradual improvement or a "cooling off period," as is normal in human relationships. The estranged, distant relationship between the sinner and his Creator can be quickly transformed by *teshuvah* into glowing love. The sinner, who has lost the superior status of "man", and who is considered inferior even to an animal (for an animal at least follows the dictates of its Creator), can, by becoming a *ba'al teshuvah*, reach the level of an angel, if not higher.

In the words of Rambam:

אָהוּב וְנֶחְמָד... קָרוֹב וִידִיד... וְהַיּוֹם הוּא מְדֻבָּק בַּשְּׁכִינָה... וְעוֹשֶׂה מִצְוֹת וּמְקַבְּלִין אוֹתוֹ בְּנַחַת וּבְשִׂמְחָה... וְלֹא עוֹד, אֶלָּא שֶׁמִּתְאַוִּים לָהֶם, שֶׁנֶּאֱמַר "וְעָרְבָה לַה׳ מִנְחַת יְהוּדָה וִירוּשָׁלָיִם..."

[He will then be] beloved and pleasant... close, a friend of the Almighty...He now cleaves to the Shechinah...*he performs mitzvos and they are eagerly and happily accepted...not only that, but Hashem yearns for them, as it says: "Then the offering of Yehudah and Yerushalayim will be pleasing to Hashem"* (Malachi 3:4). (ibid.)

Hashem actually longs for him and awaits him — when will he come and perform mitzvos? This is the intention of the Gemara when it teaches: בְּמָקוֹם שֶׁבַּעֲלֵי תְשׁוּבָה עוֹמְדִים צַדִּיקִים גְּמוּרִים אֵינָם עוֹמְדִים — *"In the place where* ba'alei teshuvah *stand, the completely righteous do not stand"* (Berachos 34b).

The *ba'al teshuvah* took an animal and transformed it into an angel. Even a *tzaddik* cannot undergo such extreme change.

THE BA'AL TESHUVAH AND THE TZADDIK

WHAT IS THE meaning of this — are we to understand that immediately after Rosh Hashanah we have risen to a level higher than that of R' Akiva Eiger *zt"l*, greater than Abaye and Rava, and certainly greater than Avraham, Yitzchak, and Yaakov?! After all, they were not able to effect such drastic changes in their persona, they were only *tzaddikim*, and we, *baruch Hashem*, are *ba'alei teshuvah*! We can testify that this is not an accurate description. Last year, too, we did *teshuvah*, but we are still worlds apart from our holy forefathers. How, then, are we to understand these words of *Chazal* regarding the greatness of the *ba'al teshuvah*, without drawing wrong inferences?

Let us add another, similar question and, *im yirtzeh Hashem*, we will be able to provide the same answer for both questions. The Gemara in *Kesubos* lists two comparisons between people living in *Eretz Yisrael* and those who dwell in *chutz la'aretz*.

1. A resident of *Eretz Yisrael* is considered equal to two residents of *chutz la'aretz*.
2. A native of *chutz la'aretz* who makes *aliyah* to *Eretz Yisrael* is equivalent to two native residents of *Eretz Yisrael*.

If we take this at face value we can reach absurd conclusions. We, by virtue of our living in the Land of Israel, are on the combined level of Abaye and Rava, who lived in *chutz la'aretz*! Every young man who moves from America to Israel in order to study Torah is equal to R' Yochanan and Reish Lakish, who were born in *Eretz Yisrael* and lived there all their lives!

What *Chazal* meant was if two people, one living in *chutz la'aretz* and one in *Eretz Yisrael* put the same amount of effort into their spiritual pursuits, the merit of *Eretz Yisrael* will serve to raise the achievements of the one living there to the combined level of two people living in *chutz la'aretz*. The sanctity of the Land helps one accomplish twice the amount he would have been able to accomplish in Bavel. Similarly, when they say that one who immigrated to Israel is equivalent to two people who already live there, *Chazal*'s meaning is that the great effort he made in leaving his place of birth in the Diaspora and moving to Israel will yield him enough merit to reap a spiritual harvest

A New Being

equivalent to that of two lifelong residents of Israel, who put the same amount of effort into their spiritual pursuits. In each case the spiritual effort is identical, yet any additional merits one has increase the final yield.

We can now explain the comparison between the *ba'al teshuvah* and the *tzaddik*. A *ba'al teshuvah* who learns ten hours a day, due to the prodigious exertion necessary on his part to do so, attains more merit for effort than the *tzaddik* who does the same. We dare not say, however, that the *ba'al teshuvah* who may have mastered a few *mishnayos* has reached the level of the *tzaddik gamur*!

AN ACCOUNT IN THE PRESTIGIOUS BA'AL TESHUVAH DEPARTMENT

IN ANY EVENT, let us return to our main topic — the praiseworthiness of the *ba'al teshuvah*. After Rambam describes the supreme status attained by the *ba'al teshuvah* — that he is beloved, and close, and a friend to his Creator, such that his mitzvos are accepted in heaven with great joy — we obviously want to know whether we, too, have the ability to reach such a level, or whether this is only reserved for those *ba'alei teshuvah* who have altered their lifestyle in an extreme manner. *B'ezras Hashem* we will try to answer this question.

Rabbeinu Yonah, in his classic work *Sha'arei Teshuvah* (1:9), teaches us that the concept of *teshuvah* is multifaceted. At first glance, it appears that *Chazal* teach that once a person becomes a *ba'al teshuvah*, his "account" is closed. In fact, the contrary is true — one who undergoes *teshuvah* has now opened a new account! His account sits in the prestigious *"ba'al teshuvah* department." (In fact, the Israeli banking system refers to a current, liquid account as עוֹבֵר וָשָׁב — literally, "going out [or transgressing] and returning [or repenting]"!) At the same time, it is obvious that opening the account is only the first step. One who opens a new account does not immediately become the bank manager's close friend — that would require making large deposits into the account and gaining a certain amount of credibility.

GUIDE TO STAIN REMOVAL

RABBEINU YONAH COMPARES *teshuvah* to cleansing a stained garment. By rinsing it with a small amount of water, the stain will begin to fade, while pouring a larger quantity of water and scrubbing it will further remove the stain. The more effort one puts in and the more of the appropriate stain remover he uses, the more the stain will fade, until it disappears altogether. Similarly, the more one invests in doing *teshuvah*, the more one's soul is cleansed and the closer he gets to Hashem.

Every bit of *teshuvah* has forgiveness associated with it. A person may not necessarily attain the highest level of *teshuvah*, yet there is a direct correlation between the amount of sin that is erased and the person's level of *teshuvah*. The *teshuvah* process must then continue in order to wipe out the rest. A major part of the first *sha'ar* of *Sha'arei Teshuvah* is devoted to Rabbeinu Yonah's recommended twenty known and tested "cleansing agents."

We can now answer a much asked question: How is it that on Yom Kippur we are able to recite the *berachah* of: מֶלֶךְ מוֹחֵל וְסוֹלֵחַ לַעֲוֹנוֹתֵינוּ וְלַעֲוֹנוֹת עַמּוֹ בֵּית יִשְׂרָאֵל וּמַעֲבִיר אַשְׁמוֹתֵינוּ בְּכָל שָׁנָה וְשָׁנָה — *"The King Who pardons and forgives our iniquities and the iniquities of His people, the family of Israel, and removes our sins every single year"*?

If we and the entire Jewish People are cleansed and purified from all sin, how is it that the *Mashiach* has not yet arrived?

It is tremendously difficult to totally eradicate every last impression of sin, and yet this eradication is necessary for the achievement of absolute and total *teshuvah*. Each year, the Jewish nation repents on a certain level and is thus forgiven in accordance with that level, and for this we bless and thank Hashem. But the forgiveness is not absolute because the *teshuvah* is not absolute! Partial *teshuvah* and partial forgiveness can only bring about a partial redemption.

ATONEMENT OF A PROPHET

A GOOD EXAMPLE of the infinite degrees of *teshuvah* and of the serious difficulty in reaching the highest level we find regarding the prophet Yeshayahu. Yeshayahu sinned when he said, *"I dwell among a people with impure lips"* (*Yeshayahu* 6:5). For this negative remark concerning *Am Yisrael* he was punished: *"One of the Seraphim flew to me and in his hand was a coal; he had taken it with tongs from atop the mizbe'ach, he touched it to my mouth"* (ibid. 6:6–7).

My esteemed teacher, HaRav Dessler, asked the following questions about this: (1) What is the significance of this burning coal from the *mizbe'ach* — that by touching the prophet's lips it brought about atonement? and (2) *Chazal* tell us (*Yalkut Shimoni* 407) that the angel tried to pick up the coal with one tong and was burned. The angel then took a second tong, placing one inside the other, and only then was he able to lift the coal (therefore "tongs" is written in the plural). What do his getting burned and these double tongs symbolize?

Rav Dessler answers in his typically profound fashion. The prophet's sin was so minor (his words were not heard by anyone else and were not even meant to be critical), that it was impossible to even discern the sinfulness of it. The only way to see it was in the light of a heavenly fire — in the light of the supreme devotion of the *tzaddikim*'s souls, who sacrifice themselves on the heavenly *mizbe'ach* (from where the coal was taken). It is only relative to their perfection that we can comprehend what was lacking in the prophet's choice of words.

Yeshayahu's atonement therefore was that he was brought closer to that burning coal, thus achieving this same supreme level of devotion to Hashem. This level was so exalted that it even burned the angel, who was only able to approach it with double tongs — a dual barrier. When the prophet reached this ultimate level, his minor blemish disappeared (see *Michtav MeEliyahu* II, p. 282).

Once the prophet has reached this lofty state of purification, the angel declares to Yeshayahu in the name of God, *"Behold, this has touched your lips; your iniquity has gone away and your sin shall be atoned for"* (*Yeshayahu* 6:6). It would stand to reason that the prophet's sins are forgiven and his "account" is now closed, yet Yeshayahu knows that this is not the case and he must now begin the process of completely wiping out his sin. It is for this reason that he responds to Hashem's call of *"Whom shall I send?"* (*Yeshayahu* 6:8) — to be the prophet of Israel — with *"Here I am, send me!"* (ibid.).

All the other prophets, each for his own reason, tried to avoid being sent on these missions. Yeshayahu though, decided to take upon himself this arduous task, and he carried the yoke of prophecy for the next eighty years. This was a very difficult role indeed, as he himself describes: *"I submitted my body to those who smite and my cheeks to those who pluck; I did not hide my face from humiliation and spit"* (*Yeshayahu* 50:6).

During the reigns of the evil kings Achaz and Menashe, the activities of the prophet involved much suffering. During those eighty years, Yeshayahu undoubtedly continued to repent and purify himself. (Do you really think he was satisfied with mumbling *Ashamnu* a few times, as we do?) In addition, the *sa'ir hamishtale'ach*, was sent to *Azazel* eighty times, on each of the eighty Yom Kippurs during the span of his prophecy, and the Torah has said that each goat atoned for all the sins of the Jewish People (see *Vayikra* 16:22). Eighty times they saw with their own eyes how the red string turned white. What greater atonement can there be?

And yet, despite this Divine purification process and after eighty years of this laborious *teshuvah*, Menashe succeeded in killing Yeshayahu. Why? Because of his unfitting description of *Am Yisrael* (see *Yevamos* 49b)! Our feeble minds cannot understand such exacting justice, but we certainly can derive some idea here of the tremendous gap between a preliminary form of *teshuvah* that is joyfully accepted in the heavens and that of total *teshuvah* that leaves no impression whatsoever of the sin. This possibly explains why the angel told Yeshayahu *"and your sin shall be atoned for"* (in the future tense). Purifying his lips with burning coals of devotion to Hashem was only the beginning of a long process of purification.

"THE MATTER IS VERY NEAR TO YOU"

I WAS ONCE asked: If this process is so lengthy and arduous, what is to keep someone from giving up? Who has the strength to even begin? My response was that we can actually derive much encouragement from what happened to Yeshayahu. Immediately after Yeshayahu began this process of repentance, he became worthy of being a prophet of Hashem! (Of course this was only possible given the mildness of the sin, as well as the high spiritual status he had already attained.) The achievement of a partial level of *teshuvah* should therefore not be taken lightly, for one who has attained even this level is highly regarded and the strength of such *teshuvah* can produce wonders — it was this that was able to turn the red string to white on Yom Kippur. This level of repentance can even assure a person a share in the Next World — as we find regarding R' Elazar ben Durdaya[2] (see *Avodah Zarah* 17a), and also regarding the Roman who lessened the

---

2. "They said about R' Elazar ben Durdaya that there was not a single harlot in the world with whom he did not cohabit. Once he heard of a certain harlot in one of the overseas cities, who would take a purse of coins for her fee. Elazar thereupon took a purse of coins and went and crossed seven rivers along the way for her sake. At the moment of the onset of cohabitation, the harlot blew out a puff of air and said: 'Just as this current of air cannot return to its place of origin, so they will not receive Elazar ben Durdaya in repentance'... He exclaimed: 'The matter depends solely on me!' He thereupon placed his head between his knees and burst forth in crying until his soul departed his body. A Heavenly voice then issued forth and proclaimed: 'R' Elazar ben Durdaya has now been readied for the life of the World to Come.'"

suffering of R' Chanina ben Teradion[3] (ibid. 18a). We see a similar idea in connection with the Roman who gave his life in order to save Rabban Gamliel[4] (see *Ta'anis* 29a).

Our difficulty in comprehending these levels of spirituality stems from our inability to understand the infinite distance between human beings and the Creator. A child who spots an airplane flying high above him is liable to conclude that it is flying next to the sun. The level of prophecy is so much higher than where we are, so that to us it appears to be the ultimate in perfection. Yet we discover that the gap between prophecy and absolute *teshuvah* is greater than eighty years of intensive spiritual effort by a prophet of Hashem during the times of the *Beis HaMikdash*!

There is a lower level of *teshuvah* that can be attained with the aid of three basic requirements: וּמוֹדֶה וְעֹזֵב יְרֻחָם — *"He who confesses sins and forsakes them will be granted mercy"* (*Mishlei* 28:13). Rabbeinu Yonah explains that מוֹדֶה, confession, includes regret

---

3. "R' Chanina ben Teradion was sitting engaged in Torah…and a Torah scroll was resting in his lap…the Romans brought him and wrapped him in a Torah scroll, encircled him with bundles of vine shoots and set them on fire. They then brought tufts of wool, soaked them in water and placed them over R' Chanina's heart, so that his soul would not depart quickly…The Roman executioner said to R' Chanina: 'If I increase the flame and remove the tufts of wool from over your heart, will you bring me with you to the life of the World to Come?' R' Chanina answered him *yes*…The executioner increased the flame and removed the tufts of wool from over R' Chanina's heart. His soul departed quickly, then the executioner also jumped into the fire. A Heavenly voice issued forth and proclaimed: 'R' Chanina ben Teradion and the executioner have now been readied for the life of the World to Come.'"

4. "When Turnus Rufus plowed under the ruins of the Sanctuary, it was decreed upon Rabban Gamliel to be put to death. A certain Roman official came and stood in the study hall and announced: 'The one with the prominent nose is wanted, the one with the prominent nose is wanted.' Rabban Gamliel understood and went and hid from the Romans. The Roman official went secretly to Rabban Gamliel and said to him: 'If I save you, will you bring me to the World to Come?' Rabban Gamliel answered him *yes*…The official thereupon went up to the roof and fell off and died. Since there was a tradition among the Romans that if a decree is issued and one of the council members dies, they annul their decree, a Heavenly voice came forth and declared: 'This official is prepared for the life of the World to Come.'"

as well. One who has regret, confesses, and forsakes the sin will receive Hashem's mercy. This lower level is not difficult to attain, as it says: *"The matter is very near to you — in your mouth and your heart — to perform it"* (*Devarim* 30:14). One who enters these gates is defined as a *ba'al teshuvah* and a *tzaddik gamur* (*Kiddushin* 49b).

CLIMBING THE *TESHUVAH* LADDER

THEN THERE IS the ultimate level of *teshuvah*, which, as far as we understand, not even the prophets attained. We have explained in the past (*Sichos LeRosh Hashanah*, Hebrew edition, p. 31) that in order to climb to the top rungs of this ladder of *teshuvah*, we must first and foremost correct the past. For this incredible miracle to occur, that the present should serve to correct the past, we must toil ceaselessly. The returnee must constantly cry out to Hashem and distance himself from his act of sin (see Rambam, *Hilchos Teshuvah* 2:4).

Much has been said by *Chazal* with regard to this level of *teshuvah*: *"For on account of an individual who repented, he and the entire world are forgiven"* (*Yoma* 86b).

This level of *teshuvah* is obviously very far from man's reach. Between these two extremes, however, there are an infinite number of intermediate levels. One can ascend to the next level by climbing a rope interwoven with these three components: regret, confessing, and forsaking the sin.

Based on the accepted definition, we can say that the majority of people who observe mitzvos can be classified as *beinoni'im* — steering the middle course between the righteous and the wicked. Most of us manage to reach higher levels within this range at times or, God forbid, we may at times slip to a lower one. The point we would like to make today is that even ascending one rung within the intermediate level serves to transform a person into a totally new being. One step up the ladder changes a person into *"a close friend of the Almighty, beloved and pleasant"* in the words of the Rambam — and the celestial beings long for the moment that he will fulfill mitzvos.

From where do we know this? It is not possible that וַעֲשִׂיתֶם עוֹלָה — *"you shall make a burnt offering"* (which, as we have explained, alludes to creating one's self anew through *teshuvah*) refers only to one who reaches the top of the ladder, for we saw that one who reaches that level transforms the entire world into a new creation! We must therefore say that any ascent within the *beinoni* level makes the individual into something new, into a totally different being in comparison to his previous level.

There is a simple confirmation for this in the Torah. The *pasuk* relates: *"The king of Egypt died" (Shemos 2:23)*. Our Sages clarify here that he did not literally die, but developed *tzara'as* (*Shemos Rabbah* 1:34). Why, then, does it say that he died? Relative to his standing beforehand, he is considered dead — it is his previous, higher status that is actually dead. If descending to a lower level is tantamount to dying, then rising to a higher one is like a birth — creating a new life.

Similarly, *Chazal* elucidate the description in *Malachi* (3:18) of *"one who serves Hashem"* as referring to one who reviews what he has learned 101 times. On the other hand, one who has "only" reviewed his learning 100 times is called *"one who does not serve Him"* (even though he is still a *tzaddik gamur*) (see *Chagigah* 9b). The answer here too lies in relativity — relative to the superior status of the scholar who has reviewed his learning 101 times, the person one rung beneath him is considered as if he does not serve Hashem. (See *Sichos LeSefer Vayikra*, Hebrew edition, p. 161).

Within this realm of the individual's new creation, there are many levels — from the level of a microbe one can ascend to the level of a worm or one can rise to that of a ministering angel. The choice is ours! We can decide what new creature we will become during these days, how many rungs of this ladder we will climb. Now to the practical question: How do we actually climb up this ladder? How, at the end of this *sichah*, do I proceed to become a new creation? What must I do in order to bring about this impressive self-growth?

A New Being

THE JUDGMENT OF THE *BEINONI* IS SUSPENDED

IF WE ARE meritorious and can truly be classified as *beinoni* (an assumption that is not at all simple, for the holy *Amora* Rava [some say Rabba] said of himself that he was [only] a *beinoni* [see *Berachos* 61b]), let us ascend by perusing Rambam's description of a *beinoni*. The Rambam states in *Hilchos Teshuvah* (3:13):

> Each and every year, a person's sins are weighed against his merits on Rosh Hashanah. One who is found to be a tzaddik *is inscribed and sealed for life.* One who is found to be a rasha *is sealed for death. The* beinoni's *judgment is suspended until Yom Kippur. If he repents, he is sealed for life; if not, then the opposite happens, God forbid.*

Rambam provides only one route for the *beinoni* — *teshuvah*.

Our Rabbis questioned this statement — if a *beinoni* is defined as one whose scales are level — with an equal number of sins and mitzvos (as Rambam taught us in *halachah* 1), why should he not simply perform another mitzvah, thereby tipping the scales in his favor, and thus be guaranteed life? Why is *teshuvah* the only way? Rambam wrote in *halachah* 4 that a person must always view himself as half meritorious and half unworthy: *"If he does one mitzvah, he has tipped the scales for himself and for the entire world to the positive side, and brought salvation for himself and everyone else."*

My revered teacher HaGaon HaRav Chaim Shmuelevitz *zt"l* answered this question: On Rosh Hashanah, the judgment of the entire world is sealed, including that of the *beinoni*. The *beinoni* is in fact sealed for death, God forbid. The Gemara's words that the *beinoni*'s judgment is suspended (תָּלוּי — "hanging") until Yom Kippur (see *Rosh Hashanah* 16b), are to be taken literally! It is as if he is standing on a chair and the noose is already around his neck — all that is needed is.... The King Who desires life, however, in His great mercy, waits for him until Yom Kippur... perhaps he will merit getting his life back. At this point, in order to receive a new lease on life, it is not enough to have one more mitzvah than sin, as it would have been earlier. The only thing that can save him now is *teshuvah* — for only *teshuvah* uproots and nullifies his sins retroactively.

PERFORMANCE OF A MITZVAH IS THE *TESHUVAH*!

EVEN SO, IF I may dare, I would like to suggest another answer. We asked why Rambam states that a *beinoni* must do *teshuvah* in order to emerge with a positive judgment, rather than advising the person to perform another mitzvah that will tip the scales in his favor. When Rambam said that the *beinoni* must do *teshuvah*, he meant that he should do one mitzvah! Performance of any mitzvah is the *teshuvah*! Until this point, his scale was level. Now, with this additional mitzvah, he will end up on the positive side.

What support do I have for this idea? Immediately following *halachah* 3, in which Rambam wrote that the *beinoni* must repent, he writes:

> *As a result, the entire Jewish nation is accustomed during these days to increase their level of* tzedakah and good deeds, and to involve themselves in mitzvos during this period between Rosh Hashanah and Yom Kippur *more than the rest of the year.*
>
> (*Halachah* 4)

Who is Rambam referring to? Who are these people who increase their mitzvah observance between Rosh Hashanah and Yom Kippur? He cannot be referring to the *tzaddikim*, because they obviously gave *tzedakah* before as well, and are already inscribed for life. Similarly, the wicked have already been sealed for death. He must be referring to the *beinoni'im*. If so, then of what use to them are mitzvos and good deeds? Did Rambam not just tell us that only *teshuvah* can save them? This, then, is the confirmation that performance of mitzvos is their *teshuvah*, for the main part of *teshuvah* is improving one's ways.

A New Being

ASCENDING EVEN IN TINY STEPS

וַעֲשִׂיתֶם עֹלָה לְרֵיחַ נִיחֹחַ לַה'.

Va'asisem — *You shall make an "olah" — a burnt offering for a satisfying aroma to Hashem.*

(*Bemidbar* 29:2)

In their precise way of analyzing the language of the Torah, *Chazal* discovered insights into this *pasuk* that give us an important understanding of the *teshuvah* process. The way to climb up the *teshuvah* ladder is to constantly make oneself into a new being — to fulfill within oneself the commandment to *"make a burnt offering,"* to make yourself into a new entity. How does one achieve this? Let us look at the word *olah* — an offering that is completely burnt, that is entirely for Hashem, unlike other offerings which may be eaten in part by their owners or by the *kohanim*. The simplest meaning of this word *olah* is "something ascending". In order to make oneself into a new entity, a *"burnt offering"*, one must make some sort of movement upward, even if it is minor, as long as it is totally for Hashem.

A person is not expected to immediately reach the top rung of the ladder; he need not even become R' Akiva Eiger all at once. He is, however, required to improve himself slightly. For example, he can have that much more *kavanah* in his *daven*ing. Even in the way he honors his parents, he is not expected to immediately reach the highest level that the Torah demands, but he should at least talk nicely to his parents for the first ten minutes after he comes home. Perhaps the next day it will not be too difficult for him to increase the number of minutes.

In this manner, with these slight improvements, a person rises one level of the infinite number of levels within the *beinoni* category and is transformed into a *ba'al teshuvah*. Then a new being is created in the world — there is now a "newborn" who cleaves to the *Shechinah*. He becomes, in the words of Rambam, *"Beloved and pleasant and close, a friend of the Almighty."* His prayers are answered immediately and the entire Heavenly

Kingdom longs for and eagerly awaits his mitzvos. In relation to his previous standing on the ladder of *teshuvah*, there stands before us a totally different being.

A new account must be opened for this new being. His account is now free from sin, like that of a newborn baby. When many follow in this path and are written and sealed for a good life on Yom Kippur, the world is filled with new, pure beings. These *"newborn people will praise God"* during the upcoming festival of Sukkos. Amen.

SICHAH SEVEN
JOY IN THE EXECUTION OF DIVINE JUSTICE

HASHEM REGRETS HAVING CREATED THE EXILE

כִּי יָדִין ה' עַמּוֹ וְעַל עֲבָדָיו יִתְנֶחָם כִּי יִרְאֶה כִּי אָזְלַת יָד וְאֶפֶס עָצוּר וְעָזוּב.

When Hashem will have judged His people, He shall relent regarding His servants, when He sees that the hand is going (the enemy power progresses) and none is saved or assisted.

(*Devarim* 32:36)

In his commentary on this verse, Rashi explains:

Up to this point, Moshe called words of admonishment as a witness against Israel — for this song to be a witness when the punishment would come upon them, to say, "Let them know that I informed them in advance." From here on, he called words of consolation as a witness, which would come to them at the conclusion of the punishment.

(Rashi, *Devarim* 32:35)

Based on Rashi, we can divide the forty-three *pesukim* of the song of *Ha'azinu* into five groups:

1. The introduction — a call to derive lessons from what is about to be said in the song. (*pesukim* 1–7)
2. The choosing of Israel as the nation of Hashem. (*pesukim* 8–14)
3. The Jewish People's straying from the path of Hashem. (*pesukim* 15–18)

4. A description of the exile. (*pesukim* 19–35)
5. A description of the Redemption. (*pesukim* 36–43)

If we compare the last two of these groups, those that deal with the exile and those that deal with the Redemption, we will immediately notice that seventeen *pesukim* are used to describe the bitter exile, whereas the description of the Redemption consists of a mere eight *pesukim*. Without raising the issue of why the Torah places greater emphasis on warning and punishment than on reward and consolation (see *Sichos LeRosh Hashanah*, Hebrew edition, p. 100), it would have been logical to expect that this small section describing the Redemption would mention the Redemption's central themes. These *pesukim* should at least give us a glimpse of the essence of those changes for which we have been yearning for thousands of years.

Instead, these *pesukim* surprise us. They begin by describing Hashem's mercy for His nation: *"He shall relent regarding His servants."* Hashem will regret, so to speak, having exiled His children among the nations, as *Chazal* tell us (*Sukkah* 52b). The exile is one of four things Hashem regrets having created. The reason for this is that instead of the exile helping *Am Yisrael* to achieve their goals (see for example *Pesachim* 87b), it actually worsened their condition, both physically and spiritually.

> *For Hashem will judge His people... when He sees that the hand is going and none is saved or assisted.*
>
> (*Devarim* 32:36)

The expression אָזְלַת יָד — *"the hand is going"* implies a dearth. *Chazal* (*Sanhedrin* 97a) elucidate this verse in the following manner: *"The son of David will not come (a) until the students of Torah have become few."* (Rashi: "When they hold the hands of Israel [to keep them] from coming back to good." [This means a lack of spirituality.]) Or another explanation: *"(b) until the perutah (a small coin) has left the purse."* (Rashi: "The hands of Israel will be empty." [This means a lack of material things.])

IS THIS THE END OF DAYS?

AND WHEN THE time of reconciliation comes and Hashem bestows good on His people, in what way will this good manifest itself? The conclusion of the song informs us:

> *O nations, sing the praises of His people, for He will avenge the blood of His servants; He will bring retribution upon His foes and He will appease His Land and His people.*
> (*Devarim* 32:43)

The Master of All promises to avenge *Am Yisrael* and to totally destroy the other nations.

Why is there no description of the good awaiting us in the future? Why is there no mention of the arrival of the *Mashiach*, the repentance of the entire nation, the end of enslavement by other nations, and all the other wondrous events that will occur then? In *Parashas Nitzavim* we find a description of this period:

> *Then Hashem, your God, will bring back your captivity and have mercy upon you, and He will gather you in from all the peoples to which Hashem, your God, has scattered you. He will do good to you and make you more numerous than your forefathers. Hashem, your God, will circumcise your heart and the heart of your offspring to love Hashem.*
> (*Devarim* 30:3–6)

Not a single element of this account is even mentioned in *Ha'azinu*! All that we read about in the five concluding *pesukim* of the song is the great vengeance Hashem will wreak upon the nations.

This leads us to two questions: Firstly, is this the consolation we have been hoping for? Are these the ultimate tidings for the long-suffering Jewish nation? Would not it have been better for Jews not to have been killed in the first place, and thus Hashem would not have to take revenge on the other nations? The end of the song seems to focus excessively on the subject of avenging the Jewish nation, which may be important in its own right, but not so important as to form the central motif of the End of Days. Rather than ending with tidings of a new epoch in which the world will be filled with the grace of Hashem, rather than describing to the Jewish People the good that is destined to arrive when *"a new light shines over Zion,"* the song ends with an accounting of retribution for the past, the same past that other nations of the world are going to want to forget!

Secondly, according to some of the commentaries (and so it appears from the Sifri), *"O nations — sing the praises of His people"* means that the other nations will sing along with Hashem's people when they see Hashem's great retribution. This exacting judgment will prove to all in this world, says Seforno, that *"Hashem is just, my Rock, in Whom there is no wrong"* (*Tehillim* 92:16), as it says: *"Regimes will be glad and sing for joy, because You will judge the peoples fairly"* (*Tehillim* 67:5).

The Divine integrity involved in rendering a true judgment for the Jewish people will awaken joy within the other nations. (A proof for this explanation is the Torah's use of the word הַרְנִינוּ conjugated in הִפְעִיל rather than the simple imperative form רֹנוּ, as it would be conjugated in קַל. הַרְנִינוּ suggests that the other nations will initiate the song and so cause the Jewish people to sing about their redemption.)

This interpretation requires a further understanding: What reason will there be for the other nations to sing? When Hashem executes this awesome judgment it will be *"from the earliest depredations of the enemy"* (*Devarim* 32:42), from the very first trouble caused to the Jewish People, these hostile nations themselves will be the ones punished! Why then, should they sing?

The answer is: There are certainly many promises regarding the End of Days — the building of the *Beis HaMikdash* in all its glory, the return of sovereignty to Israel, and all that is described by Rambam in *Hilchos Melachim* (ch. 11). Nevertheless, Scripture did not mention any of these, because it upheld the same attitude as the *Haggadah*: דַּיֵּנוּ — "it would have sufficed." Even had we gone through the travails recorded in *Ha'azinu*,

Joy in the Execution of Divine Justice 107

only to witness Hashem's revenge against the other nations in the future — *dayenu*! Not because the other nations will finally be repaid for their wickedness and hypocrisy, but because this revenge will reveal that there is a Master in this world! When our eyes see that there is order and justice in the world, or, to be more exact, that there always was justice in this world and we just were never able to see it — this will be the greatest possible cause for joy!

"THERE IS NO GREATER JOY THAN THE REMOVAL OF DOUBTS"

THIS IS THE ultimate yearning of the Jew — to attain an awareness of the Creator at the highest possible level. Regarding this, Shlomo HaMelech said: *"Performance of justice is a joy to the righteous"* (*Mishlei* 21:15). The source of the righteous man's joy is not seeing others suffer — wicked as they may be. *Chazal* tell us that, on the contrary, we should feel the pain of Hashem's creatures when they are punished (see *Megillah* 10b). The prophets of Israel would cry over the anticipated destruction of the other nations (see *Yeshayahu* 15:5 and Rashi there). It is therefore obvious that the amazing pleasure derived by the righteous from the "performance of justice" is because *"There is no greater joy than the removal of doubts"* (*Metzudas David, Mishlei* 15:30).

Their pleasure will stem from no longer having to puzzle over צַדִּיק וְרַע לוֹ רָשָׁע וְטוֹב לוֹ — *"Misfortune that befalls the righteous, while the wicked prosper"* (*Berachos* 7a), for which we do not have a clear-cut answer. All that has been written regarding this very troubling and painful question will finally be resolved. How, then, will the heart rejoice at understanding the depth of Hashem's answer to Iyov (see *Iyov* 38:41), and knowing in no uncertain terms that Iyov was not accidentally mistaken for *oyev* — an enemy, God forbid! (See *Bava Basra* 16b.)

We can say, then, that there will be two aspects to the future joy of the nations:

1. Praise for Hashem's just verdict relating to all who caused suffering to the Jewish People. It is possible that this will be the reason that the nations will play a more active role than Israel — that they will be the first to burst forth in song. *Am Yisrael*, sensitive people that they are, will not wish to sing, feeling guilty that *"because of us"* hundreds of millions of people will suffer. Only after יאמְרוּ בַגּוֹיִם הִגְדִּיל ה' לַעֲשׂוֹת עִם אֵלֶּה — *"The nations declare: 'Hashem has done greatly with these,'"* will Israel join in, saying: הִגְדִּיל ה' לַעֲשׂוֹת עִמָּנוּ — *"Hashem has done greatly with us"* (*Tehillim* 126:2–3).

2. We can further add that, in addition to singing together with the Jewish People, the nations will sing their own song of praise, celebrating the fact that justice for Israel was carried out in such a Godly manner, the likes of which has never been seen nor heard in the history of mankind! This precise justice — as exacting as a hairsbreadth — that will be carried out against each of the nations, against every person in even the remotest village, will bring them to praise God. They will see with their own eyes that *"Their bloodshed I will not cleanse"* (*Yoel* 4:21).

   Not a drop of Jewish blood that was spilled will be forgotten, and all those who are guilty of spilling it will be brought to trial, beginning with the person who carried out the action and including all those who encouraged him, those who sheltered him, those who knew and did not hand him over. The journalists and the editor-in-chief of each and every newspaper in every city who reported the incident with even the merest hint of justifying the act, the minister and his assistants who did not feel that this incident required their involvement, all the way to the ambassador to the United Nations who knew and did nothing, as well as the "international community" who has developed expertise over the years in double talk: preaching to the Jewish People while continuing to spill innocent Jewish blood. All these will be judged — they will rub their eyes to make sure they are not dreaming — thousands of people being brought to justice for one drop of Jewish blood that was spilled!

This incredibly powerful spectacle of Divine, world-embracing, true justice will astound the entire world. How is it possible to judge countless events that have occurred over thousands of years, in each case taking into account the minutest detail? How can this be? The world will be amazed at the way Divine justice metes out a harsher sentence to a journalist who wrote out of his burning hatred while going easy on another writer who wrote identical articles, but only in order to earn a living. Amidst this maelstrom of emotions a mighty and beautiful song praising the greatness of the Creator will burst forth from their throats.

A MORE ENLIGHTENED WORLD

SOME POINTS STILL remain to be clarified. Even if the nations will be amazed by what they see, how will these same beaten nations have the physical and spiritual strength to sing such a song? To do so requires self-control that is rare among human beings, and here we are speaking of a universal occurrence. *"O nations, sing the praises of His people"* is not limited to a few righteous gentiles!

This song that will be sung in the Days to Come is in fact one of the signs foretelling the approach of this wondrous epoch. It is very difficult for us to imagine this time period, given our current limited perceptual abilities. We can compare this to a game of chess. If the players are children, the loser will cry and become upset over his loss. When the two are adults, however, the loser cannot fail to be impressed by his opponent's clever strategy. In the Messianic epoch, mankind as a whole will rise to a higher level and will reach an enlightenment it had not previously experienced, causing it to sing a song praising Divine justice, even if this comes at its own expense.

How do we know that mankind will be elevated to such a high level? So it appears from the verses themselves: *"All the trees of the forest will sing with joy — before Hashem, for He will have arrived, He will have arrived to judge the earth"* (Tehillim 96:12–13). When Hashem will appear to judge the earth, even the trees of the forest will burst into song upon seeing this dazzling spectacle of the Almighty *"judging the world with righteousness, and peoples with His truth"* (ibid.).

Not only trees (that is, the plant kingdom) will reveal their ability to praise Hashem, but even the lower class of inanimate objects: *"The sea and its fullness will roar"* (ibid.), the waves of the ocean will shout out a great and wonderful sound for Him Who has dominion in the deep waters. Certainly the animal kingdom will burst forth in song. *"The fullness of the sea"* refers to its inhabitants and they will join in this song that rises up from the sea. So too *"the field and everything in it will exult"* (ibid.). From the land will be heard the sounds of the fields and all the animals that inhabit it.

We find in the Gemara a similar phenomenon. Our Sages discuss the "enlightenment" that the wicked who are awaiting judgment in *Gehinnom* experience: עֹבְרֵי בְּעֵמֶק הַבָּכָא מַעְיָן יְשִׁיתוּהוּ גַּם בְּרָכוֹת יַעְטֶה מוֹרֶה — *"Those who pass through the Valley of the Bacha Trees, they transform it into a wellspring; also the rain will cloak it with blessings"* (Tehillim 84:7). *Chazal* interpret this *pasuk* in *Tehillim* in the following manner:

> *"Those who pass"*, עֹבְרֵי, refers to people who trespass the will of the Holy One, Blessed is He.
>
> *"The valley"*, בְּעֵמֶק, means that *Gehinnom* is deepened for them (עָמֹק — deep).
>
> *"Of bacha trees — trees of weeping"*; they weep (בּוֹכִים) and shed tears כְּמַעְיָן יְשִׁיתוּהוּ like the spring of *"sheetin"* (a spring that is constantly flowing, similar to the *"sheetin"* that existed in the *mizbe'ach*, where they would pour the wine libations).

Joy in the Execution of Divine Justice

גַּם בְּרָכוֹת יַעְטֶה מוֹרֶה — *"Also the rain cloaks it with blessings"* — despite their terrible suffering and their crying out from the depths, they still bless Hashem and say before Him: "Master of the universe, You have judged properly, You have acquitted the innocent properly, You have convicted the guilty properly, and You have properly prepared *Gehinnom* for the evildoers and *Gan Eden* for the righteous" (*Eruvin* 19a).

In other words, in the face of the ultimate truth, every level of the Creation will unleash a latent power not yet expressed in our world today. If even inanimate objects will praise Hashem, certainly the phenomenon will be revealed in full force among human beings, among those nations that will praise the justice that will be carried out against them — justice that is beyond human comprehension.

This universal "enlightenment" that will manifest itself in a public display of joy at the appearance of the Almighty, will only take place after His glory is revealed, after lessons have been learned and conclusions drawn from the events of this world of concealment we live in.

A SONG OF PRAISE BURSTS FORTH FROM THE DARKNESS

THE *TZADDIK* HAS already achieved this perspective. Even in the dark obscurity of This World, the *tzaddik* clearly sees the hand of Hashem judging and implementing all that has been said. Just as the world will sing in the future, even for its own trial, so the *tzaddik* rejoices and sings in the present — even for Divine justice against himself.

We find an example of this in the awesome scene of David fleeing from his son Avshalom. David HaMelech's body had been judged and was racked with suffering, yet his soul was happy and rejoicing at the sight of its Master, Who had now revealed another *tefach* ("handbreadth") of His mastery in this world: *"David was going up the Mount of Olives, crying as he ascended, with his* head covered, going barefoot. And all the people with him wrapped their heads and went up, crying as they ascended" (*Shemuel* II 15:30).

The hand of the Almighty came down on David with all its might. The embarrassment and shame were so immense that every moment he feared for the *chillul Hashem* that could result from this incident. People would surely say, "Look at David, composer of *Tehillim*, receiver of Divine inspiration, who so devotedly prepared materials for the construction of the *Beis HaMikdash*, who fought Hashem's wars with such self-sacrifice. And what happened to him in the end? He died an unsavory death at the hands of his own son!" What a terrible *chillul Hashem* this would cause! His mind went so far as to contemplate worshiping *avodah zarah*, to show them that he was indeed worthy of such harsh punishment. Only his advisor Chushai HaArchi prevented this, explaining that there would be no desecration of God's name, for it was well-known that Avshalom was the son of an אֵשֶׁת יְפַת תֹּאַר (literally, a woman of beautiful appearance, a gentile female prisoner brought back from the battlefield). The Torah permits a Jewish soldier to marry her after she undergoes a de-beautifying process and *Chazal* tell us that the product of such a union can only result in a בֵּן סוֹרֵר וּמוֹרֶה — "a wayward son" (see *Sanhedrin* 107a).

These terrible thoughts were coursing through David's mind during those moments, out of fear of the potential public *chillul Hashem*. Yet David knew that it was all the hand of Hashem. These *yissurim* were serving to atone for his sin (relatively speaking) with Bas-sheva. Therefore, from the depths of his great darkness emanated a song praising Hashem's judgment: מִזְמוֹר לְדָוִד בְּבָרְחוֹ מִפְּנֵי אַבְשָׁלוֹם בְּנוֹ. ה' מָה רַבּוּ צָרָי רַבִּים קָמִים עָלָי — "*A song of David, as he fled from Avshalom his son. Hashem, how numerous are my tormentors! The great rise up against me!*" (*Tehillim* 3:1–2).

The punishment was almost too heavy to bear. The onslaughts of his adversaries were like stab wounds to his heart, yet at that very juncture a song burst forth from his heart about the true Judge who had come to judge the land, about the honor of the

Joy in the Execution of Divine Justice

King of glory shining through the murkiness of This World.

Let us turn to another of David's biographical psalms. According to the Midrash, he composed this during a particularly difficult time in his life, when he was being pursued by Shaul (see *Yalkut Shimoni* 2:694). The prophet Gad directed him to flee to *"the forest of Cheres (חֶרֶת)"* (*Shemuel* I 22:5). *Chazal* ask: Why was this forest called *Cheres*? Because it was מְנֻגָּב כְּחֶרֶת — *"wiped dry as cheres"* (see *Midrash Tehillim* 23).

What is the meaning of this term חֶרֶת? There are many Hebrew words in which two of the root letters provide us with the basic definition of the word, and the third letter provides us with the specific meaning. In our case, any root that begins with the two letters חר generally has to do with creating a hole (חוֹר) — a gap, whether physical or abstract. For example: the word חָרַט means to chisel a hole. חָרַת means to engrave. Going from slavery to חֵרוּת (freedom) denotes a gap in the slavery. חָרַץ is to make a notch. חָרַשׁ is to plow, while a sword, which cuts, is called a חֶרֶב. Slits in the wall are called חֲרַכִּים. חָרַג means to go beyond, while חָרֵד, to dread, is a feeling that goes beyond the regular boundaries of man's emotions. חֵרֶם is the removal of something or someone either from the general public or from the world (as in *Yehoshua* 11:12). A hole can be made by a sharp instrument or heat: חֲרִיקַת בְּלָמִים refers to the screeching of brakes which involves friction, generating heat and thus wear. חָרוֹן refers to burning with anger.

There are other roots and nouns in this group that are related to heat. We find three different meanings for the root חרס in the Torah, all of which are heat-related:

1. Earthenware, which is made from clay that is heated in a kiln
2. The burning sun (see *Iyov* 9:7)
3. An illness that is a dry form of boils (see *Devarim* 28:27)

There are many more examples we could find.

That same *Ya'ar Cheres*, therefore, was truly a "hole" — as we colloquially refer to a far-off, deserted place. It had no water and no fruits; it was "wiped dry" from any possible good. According to the Midrash, it was precisely here, when David was alone and hounded in the heart of a parched forest, that his well-known psalm of Divine Providence burst forth: מִזְמוֹר לְדָוִד ה' רֹעִי לֹא אֶחְסָר — *"A psalm by David: Hashem is my shepherd, I shall not lack" (Tehillim 23:1)*. I lack nothing. Why? Because *"Though I walk in the valley overshadowed by death, I will fear no evil, for You are with me"* (ibid. 4). When Hashem is with me, I do not fear anything in the world. It is for this reason that שִׁבְטְךָ וּמִשְׁעַנְתֶּךָ הֵמָּה יְנַחֲמֻנִי — *"Your rod and Your staff, they comfort me"* (ibid.). The source of my comfort is not only מִשְׁעַנְתֶּךָ, "Your staff that I can lean on for support" (*Chazal* tell us this refers to "Your Torah"), but also שִׁבְטְךָ — "Your rod" — the rod of affliction that hits and hurts me. It is the combination of the two together that "comfort me." For David HaMelech there is no difference — they are both from the hand of God. Just as the Torah is something I can lean on for comfort and consolation, so too the rod of affliction provides my soul with comfort — from my continual yearning for the One Who holds the rod, as David says: *"But as for me, God's nearness is my good" (Tehillim 73:28)*.

The Torah and affliction are in fact two sides of the same coin; they serve to place man and the world on the right path — the path of Hashem. In the words of David HaMelech, just as *"I will raise the cup of salvations and the Name of Hashem I will invoke" (Tehillim 116:13)*, so too *"Distress and grief I would find, then I would invoke the Name of Hashem"* (ibid. 13:3–4).

Indeed, it is from this source that we derive the *halachah* that one is obligated to bless Hashem for the bad as well as for the good (see *Berachos* 60b).

THE TZADDIK REJOICES AT BEING CLOSE TO HIS CREATOR

UP UNTIL THIS point we have discussed the unique ability each level of creation will attain at the End of Days — to be elevated to a point where it will view everything in a more "mature" fashion, coming to the realization that being close to Hashem is the only true good in the world, even if this entails standing before Him in judgment. We also mentioned that the righteous are already able to discern this in This World. In the midst of dark clouds and Divine concealment, the *tzaddik* identifies his Creator and rejoices at being close to Him, despite physical afflictions and despite the fact that the cloud which conceals the glory of the Almighty scorches his eyes.

THE TELESCOPE OF YOM KIPPUR

OF WHAT RELEVANCE is all this to us? We have not yet reached the End of Days and, unfortunately, we are not yet counted among those righteous who already draw their spiritual nourishment from the higher source of the World of the End of Days. Is there a lesson that we can nevertheless learn from all this on the eve of the Day of Judgment? Perhaps we can say that Yom Kippur brings us closer to that mature outlook that characterizes the End of Days and the world of the *tzaddik*. In the Time to Come, all of Creation will view the world through these mature eyes. For the *tzaddik*, this is his constant outlook. We, on the other hand, can at least achieve this maturity for a few days or hours. We can pause for a moment and look out at this world and the next through that long-distance telescope known as Yom Kippur: a day whose unique light provides us with a more authentic power of observation.

And so man sits and reviews his life with introspection: What have I accomplished during my life in this world? What merits have I gathered to bring into the Next World, the eternal world? The *pasuk* says: *"Performance of justice is a joy to the righteous and destruction to workers of iniquity"* (*Mishlei* 21:15). During these moments, mankind can be divided into two groups:

1. For one who toiled in the past year to fill his spiritual world, the carrying out of justice on the Day of Judgment

is certainly a source of joy. The summary of the whole year provides him with satisfaction.
2. The workers of iniquity, on the other hand, whose entire world focuses on the present and on passing fancies, their lot as this day approaches is one of "destruction" and a broken heart.

If we look carefully at the words of *Chazal*, though, we will be astonished to discover that this is not a totally accurate representation of man. Mankind simply cannot be divided into two such extreme groups. We generally view *Gan Eden* and *Gehinnom* as two completely different worlds — in the one all is good and in the other all is bad. It appears from *Chazal*, however, that even within *Gan Eden* there are islands of *Gehinnom*! How can this be?

CANOPIES IN GAN EDEN

THE GEMARA IN *Bava Basra* (75a) brings a fascinating description of the End of Days, citing the verse in *Yeshayahu* (4:5), *"And Hashem will create over every structure of Mount Zion and over those who assemble in it a cloud by day and smoke and a glow of flaming fire by night, for this will be a canopy over all the honor."* The Talmud derives from this *pasuk* the idea that *"the Holy One, Blessed is He, will make a canopy for each and every person according to his honor."* Firstly, it must be clear that within *Gan Eden* not all *chuppos* are equal. There will be smaller canopies and larger ones, each in accordance with a person's acts in This World.

WHY SMOKE AND FIRE?

OUR SAGES WERE amazed, however, at the words "smoke" and "fire" regarding a canopy of glory! The Gemara asks:

For what purpose will there be smoke in the canopy? R' Chanina said: "Because whoever had a stingy eye with regard to Torah scholars in this world, his eyes become filled with smoke in the

> World to Come." For what purpose will there be fire in the canopy? R' Chanina said: "This teaches that each and every one will be burned by his fellow's canopy — woe for such a shame! Woe for such a disgrace!"
>
> (ibid.)

The smoke is designated for those righteous people who, despite the many good deeds they have to their merit, were too stingy in this world to support *talmidei chachamim*, who could never bear to see *talmidei chachamim* in total fulfillment. "Narrow" eyes such as these, will be unable to "see" total spiritual abundance in the Days to Come, since their ability to see was never developed. Just as smoke burns the eyes and blinds them, so, too, these *tzaddikim* will be unable to see the glory of Hashem that rests above their friends like a *chuppah*.

This explains the smoke. What is the role of fire in the *tzaddik*'s canopy? To teach you, says the Gemara, that each one will be burned by the canopy of his neighbor. The fire will cause burns to those around him. Even regarding those *tzaddikim* who are destined to sit in *Gan Eden*, those same righteous people for whom Hashem has promised seven *chuppos* each — behold! At that long-awaited moment in which their lifelong yearning is realized, they are judged with fire and smoke! What is the profound meaning behind these words of *Chazal*?

Each person has his own *chuppah* — particular mitzvos that he keeps in accordance with the strictest dictates of the Halachah, and through them the *Shechinah* will be revealed to him in the future. The canopy that Hashem creates for him will be made up of those same spiritual components that he gathered in this world. When a particular *tzaddik* stands under his canopy of mitzvos and looks at the neighboring *chuppah*, he will be "burned" by that *chuppah*. He will feel himself inferior and lacking in comparison to the perfection that the person next to him attained through his meticulousness in his observance of mitzvos.

The same will happen with that neighbor: as he views the *chuppah* next to him, he will suddenly see how beautiful his friend's canopy is. The neighbor's *chuppah* will be woven from beautiful, long strands of uninterrupted Torah learning, not like the strings of his own *chuppah* that are made of short threads that are joined together, full of many knots. Another *tzaddik* will be amazed at his friend's *gemillus chassadim*, at his consideration for others — his *chuppah* will be made of materials that he is lacking and this will "burn" him.

This is the meaning of *"everyone will be burned by his fellow's* chuppah" — it does not imply a physical fire. Rather, the mitzvos comprised in a particular *chuppah* will cause the person standing next to it to feel a spiritual "burning". He will be filled with remorse. Why did I not utilize my time the way he did? How many *tefillos* could I have *daven*ed with *kavanah*? What a beautiful *chuppah* he has built from honoring his parents!

In the future, the righteous person will experience joy through "the performance of justice," at the revelation of how close he was to the truth. Hashem's justice will provide joy to the *tzaddik*, because it brings proof as to how correct he was in the way he led his life. On the other hand, there will be "destruction to workers of iniquity," for those to whom Divine Justice will painfully reveal how far they were from the truth all those years. Worst of all, they will discover that they have reached the end — it is too late to make amends! This is the terrible grief that will burn in the future and everyone will experience it to some degree, from the workers of iniquity to the supremely righteous in *Gan Eden*.

It is incumbent upon us to keep this penetrating thought in our minds on the eve of Yom Kippur. Superficially, the Day of Judgment may appear to be like any other day, yet we know that it is the Day of Truth. On this day, more than any other, we feel the absolute truth, and in its light each person can take pride and rejoice over the *chuppos* he has built for himself. He can rejoice in his achievements in learning, in his observance of the mitzvos between man and his fellow man, in his self-discipline in attempting to better his *middos*. On the other hand, this day of truth can also lead to "destruction" when one remembers all his flaws.

THERE IS STILL TIME!

THERE IS ONE major difference between the present and the future — in the present the situation can still be remedied! A person can add to and renovate his *chuppah*. The fire burning inside me when I compare my *chuppah* to that of my neighbor is not one of hopeless despair, but one that ignites in me a will to better myself, to correct whatever needs correcting, to elevate myself!

There are many ways in which this correction can be accomplished. One way is to remember that Yom Kippur only atones for those who repent (Rambam, *Hilchos Teshuvah* 1:2). We must not be so engrossed and entranced by the beautiful melodies in the *daven*ing that we forget to have *kavanah* to repent! Sukkos is approaching; we have many opportunities to add to our *chuppah*. For one thing, when we purchase the Four Species, we can at least ensure that they be kosher. If not, it would be better to borrow a set from another person (a מַתָּנָה עַל מְנָת לְהַחֲזִיר — "a gift with the intention to return"), rather than make a purchase of questionable *kashrus*, just to be able to boast that "I have a set, too." (Regarding this, Rabba said to his disciples, *"I beg of you — do not inherit two Gehinnoms"* [*Yoma* 72b] — *"by both wasting your money in this world and disqualifying yourself from* Olam HaBa" [Rashi].)

What joy we should feel when we realize all the possibilities open to us! We can even sleep and fulfill a mitzvah! Sleeping in the *sukkah* is a greater obligation than eating there. אֲכִילַת עֲרַאי, "eating something in the nature of a snack" (even bread up to the size of a כְּבֵיצָה) is permitted outside the *sukkah*, while שֵׁינַת עֲרַאי, "sleeping even for a few moments," is forbidden outside the *sukkah* (See *Shulchan Aruch, Orach Chaim* 639:2). There is an entire world waiting for us to take advantage of it, to transform it into a *chuppah* of glory. How wonderful it is that we have learned about it while there is still time! This truly epitomizes: *"Performance of justice is a joy to the righteous."*

SICHAH EIGHT
A GOOD CHARACTER — THE KEY TO HEAVEN (AND EARTH)

THE RAMBAM'S PATH TO *TESHUVAH*

WE ARE NOW in the midst of the *Aseres Yemei Teshuvah*, those special days between Rosh Hashanah and Yom Kippur, of which it is written: *"'Seek Hashem when He can be found; call upon Him when He is near' (Yeshayahu 55:6) — these are the ten days between Rosh Hashanah and Yom Kippur"* (*Rosh Hashanah* 18a).

A grandson of R' Chaim Brisker *zt"l* related how on each day of the *Aseres Yemei Teshuvah*, it was his grandfather's custom to study one of the ten chapters of Rambam's *Hilchos Teshuvah*. This fact can serve as a wonderful guide for those seeking to do *teshuvah*. A person standing at a crossroad, wondering which path to take, who suddenly meets a reliable person of experience, would surely be happy to follow in his footsteps. Once a person of immense stature has traveled this road, it is already smoothed for those destined to traverse it in the future. Let us, therefore, go down this path together and study some of Rambam's laws of *teshuvah*.

As an introduction, let us emphasize that these are *halachos* according to the simple meaning of the word. Rambam included them in his book of *halachos*, not in his more philosophical works such as *Moreh Nevuchim*. As in his codification of other areas of Halachah, such as the laws of *Birkas HaMazon* and Shabbos, the *halachos* of *teshuvah* presented here are based on *Talmud Bavli*, *Yerushalmi*, *midrashim*, and other components of the Oral Torah. The laws of *teshuvah* are therefore as binding upon us as are the other *halachos*.

Let us begin by analyzing the structure of these ten chapters, which can be broken down into three sections:

1. The first four chapters provide us with the details of *teshuvah* and its essence. Among the topics included are: how to repent, for which sins *teshuvah* atones, the relative severity of mitzvos and transgressions as well as their associated punishments, and factors that prevent *teshuvah* from having any effect.
2. In chapters 5 and 6, Rambam lays the foundations of the concept of free choice.
3. The remaining four chapters are dedicated to describing the greatness of one who repents, the reward awaiting one who repents, the good awaiting the righteous during the days of the *Mashiach* and in the Next World, and the need to serve Hashem with love.

RAMBAM'S *CHIDDUSH*

CONSIDERING THIS DIVISION of Rambam's laws of *teshuvah*, it is quite surprising to come across chapter 7, *halachah* 3. As we mentioned above, at this point Rambam has already discussed the detailed *halachos* of *teshuvah*, which are concentrated in the first four chapters, while the seventh chapter deals mainly with general concepts of *teshuvah*. This includes an exposition discussing the great advantages of repenting and how it brings one closer to the Divine Presence, as well as the need for us to repent each and every day of the year in order to properly prepare ourselves for life in the Next World. (A description of the World to Come is found in chapters 8 and 9.) At this point the Rambam suddenly returns to what, on the surface, appears to be a halachic detail concerning *teshuvah*, which, based on what we have said above, ought to have appeared in one of the first four chapters.

These are Rambam's words in chapter 7, *halachah* 3:

A Good Character

> *Do not say that* teshuvah *only applies to sins involving action, such as illicit relations, theft, and robbery. Rather, just as one must repent for these sins, one must also search his thoughts and repent over such negative character traits as anger, animosity, jealousy, and mockery, from pursuing money and honor, and being obsessed with food. One must repent for everything. Penance for these sins is more difficult than for actions... as it says: "Let the wicked one forsake his way and the iniquitous man his thoughts, let him return to Hashem."* (*Yeshayahu* 55:7)

First and foremost, Rambam's words are undoubtedly an incredible *chiddush* — an innovation. Who would have thought that one need also repent for bad *middos* — there is not even an allusion to this in the Torah! Secondly, as we asked before, why did he not record this *halachah* of repenting for bad character traits together with the laws pertaining to repentance for improper actions outlined in chapters 1–4?

As is known, many of the commentaries on Rambam focus on his structuring of the *halachos* — such as why he chose to include a particular *halachah* in conjunction with another one, even though topically it may seem to belong elsewhere. As these commentaries point out, Rambam's structure is not haphazard, but rather, it reflects underlying concepts of great importance. We must therefore conclude that here, too, Rambam is alluding to a very fundamental precept of Judaism.

BAD *MIDDOS* ARE LIKE DEFECTIVE VESSELS

BY INCLUDING THE topic of *middos* specifically in the latter chapters of *Hilchos Teshuvah* — the section dealing with life in the Next World — Rambam is emphasizing how essential and necessary it is to correct one's *middos*. Rambam is stressing here that *tikkun ha-middos* has implications beyond the obligation to correct an action. The first four chapters have already detailed how one can make a *tikkun* for actions, but now Rambam turns to a subject that is man's ultimate aim — life in the Next World, the great pleasure awaiting the righteous, the good that *"cannot be evaluated nor imagined"* (Rambam, *Hilchos Teshuvah* 8:6), for which we have been striving throughout our lives. You must therefore realize, Rambam says, that if your *middos* are not in order, you will not merit life in the Next World. This third and final part of *Hilchos Teshuvah* is the section that discusses the wondrous life in the Next World awaiting those who serve Hashem. Rambam begins this chapter:

> *The choice is in man's hands, as we have explained (in chapters 5–6), therefore each person must endeavor to repent and to confess his sins. By doing so, he will die a* ba'al teshuvah *and merit life in the Next World.*
>
> (*Hilchos Teshuvah* 7:1)

One may wonder, "What does death have to do with me? I am young and healthy, and *baruch Hashem*, I have my entire life ahead of me." To counter this conviction, Rambam states in the second *halachah*: *"A person must always view himself as if he is about to die. He should not say 'when I grow old I will repent,' for he may die before he grows old"* (ibid. 7:2). Suffice it to mention what has become today's "plague" — traffic accidents — to understand how true this is!

The third *halachah*, which we have quoted above, comes to warn man:

> *If you do not correct this sin, this negative act, your portion in the Next World will be smaller, inferior in quality. If you do not correct your* middos, *however, you will have no portion whatsoever in the Next World! The World to Come is the world of souls; if the soul departs this world in a defective state, how can you expect to attain paradise with a defective vessel?*

Perhaps we can use the following example cited by Rambam to clarify the difference between a person whose actions are blemished and one whose soul is defective:

One who merits entry into the Next World can be compared to one who sits down to an elegant banquet (ibid. 8:4). If one of his actions is flawed by sin, he can be likened to one who is sensitive to certain types of foods, precluding his enjoyment of some of the delicacies available at the banquet. If his soul nonetheless merited other mitzvos, he will be able to partake of the many other foods offered at this lavish dinner. If, however, his middos *are corrupt, the "organs" of his soul are defective and he can be compared to one who does not have sensitivities to foods — his problem is "only" that his mouth and teeth do not function! What will such an unfortunate person do at the banquet?*

We can now understand the *chiddush* of Rambam, healer of body and soul, and why he placed such importance on *tikkun ha-middos*.

BAD CHARACTER TRAITS LEAD TO BAD ACTIONS

AS OUR BAD *middos* have a critical influence on us when we arrive in the Next World, so too they cause extensive damage in this world. While bad character traits are not themselves prohibited by the Torah, they can lead to the violation of many Torah prohibitions.

For example, anger is not distinctly forbidden anywhere in the Torah, yet Rambam informs us that this is precisely what the prophet meant when he said, וְאִישׁ אָוֶן מַחְשְׁבוֹתָיו — *"and the iniquitous man his thoughts"* (*Yeshayahu* 55:7). Some people tend to react with anger at anyone or anything that does not please them. Those who choose to follow such a path should not be surprised if they find themselves violating many Torah prohibitions that are in fact explicitly stated: these include speaking *lashon ha-ra*, embarrassing one's fellow man in public, etc. How does such a person come to violate these severe transgressions? It all begins with his anger, which although not expressly forbidden, eventually leads to these terrible offenses.

Jealousy is also in the realm of thought rather than action: A jealous person does not necessarily covet something that belongs to another, nor does he necessarily have a craving for immense wealth. When it comes to himself, he may even be a shining example of one who is satisfied with little; however, regarding others — it really hurts him when they have more than he!

Shlomo HaMelech teaches: *"Sweet is the sleep of the laborer, whether he eats little or much; the satiety of the rich man does not let him sleep"* (*Koheles* 5:11). One explanation for the latter part of this *pasuk* is that it refers to the rich: A rich man is so concerned with the safety of his money that he cannot sleep. An alternative explanation is that the subject here is the poor man. *"Sweet is the sleep of the laborer"* — the poor man works hard and, as a result, he should sleep soundly, yet *"the satiety of the rich man does not let him sleep"* — he cannot fall asleep because he is constantly thinking of how good the wealthy man has it!

The story is told of a non-Jew who was plagued with jealousy. He had a dream one night in which he was told: "All your wishes will be fulfilled — on one condition. Whatever you ask for yourself, your neighbor will receive the same, only double!" The man pondered for a long while. He thought and thought and, finally, he responded: "All right. Please poke out one of my eyes!"

The Torah does not expressly forbid jealousy. Yet this type of thought, this endless jealousy, in time will cause man to fail and to transgress explicit prohibitions, such as revenge, bearing a grudge, senseless hatred, not fulfilling the commandment to love Hashem, etc.

This can even happen to men of stature. The Torah tells us regarding Yosef's brothers: וַיְקַנְאוּ בוֹ אֶחָיו — *"His brothers were jealous of him"* (*Bereishis* 37:11). Once their jealousy was aroused — even by something as insignificant as a striped coat — it had no limits, eventually leading to hatred of their brother, which in turn brought grief to their father, as well as causing other severe transgressions.

We can conclude from this that when the prophet spoke of *machshevosav*, he was referring not only to improper thoughts and ideas, but also to character traits and tendencies, whose roots are buried deep in each man's soul.

"SEEK OUT HASHEM WHEN HE CAN BE FOUND"

WHAT WE HAVE said applies to the entire year, yet the most appropriate time to devote to *tikkun ha-middos* is during the *yamim noraim*. Why? The prophet Yeshayahu said: *"Seek out Hashem when He can be found, call upon Him when He is near."* *Chazal* explain that this refers to the *Aseres Yemei Teshuvah*. If this is correct, it would seem appropriate for the prophet to outline for us how to seek out Hashem during these days — we have so much that requires improvement! A further look at the next *pasuk*, in fact, reveals that not only does he do that, but it is the same *pasuk* that Rambam quotes in *Hilchos Teshuvah*: *"Let the wicked one forsake his way and the iniquitous man his thoughts, let him return to Hashem."* The prophet, therefore, is pointing to the strong connection between these days and *tikkun ha-middos*, the correction of one's character traits. He is telling us that the way to *"seek out Hashem when He can be found"* is first and foremost, *"Let the wicked one forsake his way."*

During these special days, while the *Shechinah* is hovering above, we are presented with a unique opportunity to deal with our greatest challenge — those sins that are buried deep in our souls. It is these sins that "are more difficult to repent for than ones of action." This is true not only because of their severity, as we have mentioned earlier, but because it is very difficult to identify precisely where the fault lies. Actions are visible and open to inspection, which is not the case regarding character traits.

This principle, that making a *tikkun* for something hidden is more difficult than for a sin that is manifest, applies not only to the private individual, but to the Jewish nation as well. The Gemara tells us:

> *The earlier ones whose iniquity was revealed had their end revealed, the later ones whose iniquity was not revealed, their end was not revealed. R' Yochanan said: "The fingernail of the earlier generations was better than the entire abdomen of the later ones."*
>
> (*Yoma* 9b)

The sins that led to the destruction of the first *Beis HaMikdash* were clear and known to all (the three cardinal sins: idolatry, illicit relations, and murder), and it was therefore much easier to locate the problem and deal with it. It is for this reason that the exile decreed upon them was for a specified period of time — seventy years. The sin of *sinas chinam*, senseless hatred, which led to the destruction of the second *Beis HaMikdash*, was buried in the depths of their souls, and for that reason we have still not succeeded in correcting it, despite this long and bitter exile whose end is hidden from us.

Based on this, the Gemara goes on to explain the words of R' Yochanan — he purposely chose the comparison between a fingernail and a stomach, because these are two signs that can render an animal not kosher. The first is in the nail of its foot (does it have split hooves?); the second is related to its stomach (does it chew its cud?). The sins of the earlier generations, which were visible like the nail of the foot, are better than the *sinas chinam* buried deep "in the stomach" of the people who lived during the period of the second *Beis HaMikdash* (see *Michtav M'Eliyahu* vol. 4, p. 4).

This is something we all know very well. We can make an extra effort to correct negative actions, to change our ways from here on (e.g. "*Beli neder*, from now on I will only travel on Sukkos to a place that has a *sukkah*"). *Middos*, on the other hand, are very hard to completely transform. I can decide that from now on I will not act in a haughty manner, but this does not alter my feelings. Inside, my haughtiness can continue to bubble up, and it will have to flow out sooner or later, like boiling lava erupting from a volcano.

The story is told of a very gifted young man who had many

shidduchim suggested to him, but without any success. His problem was that he was extremely conceited and he felt no *shidduch* was ever good enough for him. As the years passed, his father, afraid that his son would miss his chance at marriage, decided to send him to a yeshiva that placed great emphasis on *mussar* and excelled in instilling humility in its students. The son acquiesced to his father's directive. He traveled to the yeshiva and, much to his surprise, even managed to integrate into his surroundings and learn a great deal. After a lengthy period of time, the father instructed his son to return. When the *shadchanim* heard from the father about his son's change (even the neighbors testified that his manner had so dramatically changed that it was not recognizable), they suggested a wonderful *shidduch* to him, one of the young women he had rejected in the past. When the young man heard who they had suggested, he was incensed. He said to his father: "I don't understand what they want from me! If this *shidduch* was not good enough for me two years ago, how can it be fitting now that I have added humility to my other good traits?" Changing one's character requires more than just reaching the right conclusions and making resolutions.

HASHEM SEES INTO THE HEART

IN THE BOOK of *Shemuel*, we find a striking example illustrating the importance of hidden character traits — tendencies that have not even come to the surface or been put into practice. Shemuel went to Beis Lechem, following Hashem's commandment to anoint a new king for Israel from the sons of Yishai. The moment Yishai presented his eldest son, Eliav, to Shemuel, Shemuel responded: אַךְ נֶגֶד ה' מְשִׁיחוֹ — *"Surely before Hashem is His anointed one"* (*Shemuel* I 16:6). This must be the man Hashem has chosen as king! But Hashem corrects Shemuel, saying: *"Do not look at his appearance or at his tall stature, for I have rejected him. For it is not as man sees — man sees what his eyes behold, but Hashem sees into the heart"* (ibid. 16:7).

First and foremost, we must remember a fundamental principle when studying the *Tanach*. Did Shemuel really think that the king of Israel would be chosen based on his impressive height and handsome appearance, and did Hashem have to come and inform him of his error? Certainly this is not what Shemuel had in mind, God forbid. If Ari HaKadosh was able to read on someone's face which sins he was guilty of, certainly Shemuel's depth and insight were at least on that level. Ari HaKadosh might have had *ruach ha-kodesh*, yet Shemuel was a prophet, and not just any prophet — *Chazal* tell us that he was equal to Moshe and Aharon! (See *Berachos* 31b.[5]) Shemuel did indeed look at Eliav's internal state and he immediately saw that he was free of sin. If so, he reasoned, he must be the one chosen to rule over the nation of Hashem, just as Shaul, when he was chosen, was as pure from sin as a one-year-old child (see *Yoma* 22b).

Yet Hashem stopped his prophet in his tracks: *"Do not look at his appearance or at his tall stature, for I have rejected him!"* You, Shemuel, are correct; Eliav was once worthy of kingship, but he is no longer. What happened? Eliav sinned — he was angry with David on the day of the war with Golias (see *Shemuel* I, 17:28). *Chazal* tell us: *"Whoever becomes angry, even if they are in the midst of conferring greatness upon him from Heaven, they will bring him down"* (*Pesachim* 66b).

FOR WANT OF A *MIDDAH*, THE KINGDOM WAS LOST

ONE WHO TAKES a look at the chronology of these events will feel troubled by the above explanation. Was it not prior to the war with Golias that Shemuel arrived at the house of Yishai? If Eliav had not yet become angry when Shemuel arrived, why do *Chazal* tell us that it was his anger that lost him the kingdom?

---

5. Of course this comparison is not all-inclusive, for no prophet can be compared fully to Moshe, but from certain perspectives he was comparable to Moshe and Aharon.

From here we see the severity of *"the iniquitous man his thoughts."* Eliav did not need to be actively angry in order to be deemed unworthy of the kingdom. It was enough that he possessed this tendency to anger — a trait that can eventually lead to actual anger. Shemuel was correct when he said that he did not see any sin in Eliav, for the sin had not yet occurred. He Who understands what is in our hearts, however, could tell that this anger that Eliav had buried in his heart was of such a degree that at any moment it could erupt in an unseemly manner, and for this reason he forfeited the kingdom.

See how many wonderful things this one small stain in his character prevented Eliav from receiving: the kingdom of Israel that was destined to descend from the tribe of Yehudah, being the builder of the *Beis HaMikdash* and forefather of the *Mashiach*! In fact it meant forfeiting תִּקוּן עוֹלָם בְּמַלְכוּת שַׁקַּי — *"the perfection of the universe through the Almighty's sovereignty."* In his stead, David was anointed. (This also shows us the greatness of David — even a small stain like this was not found in his character).

ANGER

THE TENDENCY TO anger is extremely destructive. Besides Rambam's warning us to totally distance ourselves from it (see *Hilchos De'os* 2:3), *Chazal* state, *"One who becomes angry is as if he worshiped avodah zarah"* (*Zohar* 1:27b). As residents of the Old City of Jerusalem, we need look no further to see how right *Chazal* were. Here in the Jewish Quarter is a monument to the treacherousness of this trait. Immediately adjacent to the Ramban Shul, we find... a mosque! What is a mosque doing in the heart of the Jewish Quarter? Legend has it that the land belonged to a Jewish man. One day he got into an argument with his mother over some issue. In a fit of anger, in order to spite her, he went and gave his land over to the Muslims, who consequently built the mosque there. Is this not a clear example of how *"one who becomes angry is as if he worshiped avodah zarah"*?

MISERLINESS

THE RAMBAM THAT we quoted above (p. 123) also tells us that we must desist from *"pursuing money and honor."* Miserliness, too, can lead to the violation of Torah prohibitions and neglecting to fulfill Torah commandments. For example, one may decide to search for a cheap *esrog* (which may not really be kosher). In such a case, not only has he not fulfilled the mitzvah of *Arba'ah Minim* ("taking of the Four Species" on Sukkos), but in addition, his *berachos* were in vain and he may even have caused others to transgress by lending them his *esrog*. Miserliness can also lead a person to not giving enough *tzedakah* or to purchasing a cheap pair of *tefillin,* classifying him as קָרְקַפְתָּא דְלָא מַנַּח תְּפִילִין — *"a head that did not wear tefillin"* (*Rosh Hashanah* 17a), and causing thousands of his *berachos* to be *levatalah*, because he "trusted" that the *tefillin* sold in the market were presumably kosher.

You should be aware, by the way, that there are many pairs of *tefillin* sold that were written by women and are thus invalid. Furthermore, it is known that there are Arab students who also write *tefillin* and *mezuzos*! These are then sold via agents to stores whose owners are also "men of faith and belief," who "rely" on the word of some stranger who comes into their store that they are thoroughly kosher. We must realize that even the most meticulous *magihah* (proofreader) or computer program employed to check the parchments can never reveal who actually wrote the *tefillin*!

It is therefore imperative that we only buy *tefillin* from a well-known, God-fearing individual, who can be relied upon to only purchase *tefillin* from a trustworthy source. Of course, to do this we must overcome any tendency to stinginess, for the forgeries obviously cost less.

PURSUING HONOR

THE SAME MAY be said of the pursuit of honor. The Halachah certainly does not negate the importance of man's self-respect.

There are even prohibitions that one is permitted to transgress in order to avoid embarrassment (see *Berachos* 19b, *Shabbos* 81b, 94b, etc.). One who is overly concerned with his own honor, however, is liable to neglect mitzvos that should not be cast aside for the sake of his dignity. This, in fact, was the great test Yehudah faced in the incident involving Tamar (see *Bereishis* 38:26): Would he forego his honor and admit his guilt or not? Had he been insistent on maintaining his dignity at that time, he would have forfeited the entire kingdom of David! It is precisely because he overcame the temptation to lie and decided to forego his own dignity that he merited all that he did. We see once again that in order to be worthy of ruling over others, one is first required to rule over his own personal character!

LAZINESS

IT IS OBVIOUS that we are not only obligated to rectify our tendency to anger — listed first by Rambam because it so obviously corrupts — as well as jealousy and other traits, but we are even obligated regarding the "less threatening" characteristics, such as laziness. There is no specific prohibition against laziness; it can, however, lead to many transgressions.

One who allows indolence to overtake him will ruin his entire routine. In the morning he will not get up early enough to recite *Kerias Shema* in its proper time. He will then arrive late at shul and not *daven* with a *minyan*. He will then be late for work, thus stealing from his employer's time, or if he is self-employed, this late start will cause him to have to remain late at work, so that he definitely "will not manage" to arrive on time to his evening *shiur*. Even when he does finally sit down to learn, it is in a laggardly fashion; one day he learns, the next day he fritters away the time — any excuse to close the book! Even when he does learn, he does not go to the trouble of clarifying the *sugya* thoroughly: what precisely was the question, how did the response answer the question, and what is the practical *halachah* one may derive from this *sugya*?

We have emphasized many times in the past that it is not enough to know what is written in the works of the *poskim*, but we must constantly ask, How does this *halachah* apply in our day and age? It is true that the Torah does not change, but the circumstances do. We must be alert to this and understand that what the *Mishnah Berurah* wrote based on the horizons of Radin may not apply in Yerushalayim. A person who learns without achieving a deep understanding can end up making mistakes in his observance of the *halachah*, even if he practices exactly what is written in the book!

This applies not only to the *Mishnah Berurah*, but even to more recent works, such as *Shemiras Shabbos KeHilchasa*. Not only are new appliances constantly entering the market since the book was published, such that what may have been permitted or forbidden regarding one appliance would have to be reevaluated regarding new appliances, but in addition, many of the same appliances are now constructed differently. There is no other choice. We must constantly keep up to date regarding any changes in circumstances and reanalyze the application of the *halachah* accordingly. Only once we uncover the reasoning behind the *halachah* and arrive at the root of the matter, can we apply the *halachah* to a new appliance with confidence. Laziness, of course, precludes achieving this.

Laziness … I know from personal experience how this works. You go to purchase the *Arba'ah Minim* for Sukkos and are suddenly overcome with laziness. After examining two or three *lulavim*, you get tired of checking whether or not the *teyomes* is whole, if the *lulav* is bent, and whether it has forty centimeters of length until the end of the spine. If you get through that, then come the *hadassim*! You have to check them up and down to see if they truly are *meshulashim*. Finally you find one that meets the requirements — now go and find two more like it! And what about the *esrog* — laziness turns the whole effort into too much to handle.

HASHEM SEES AND REMEMBERS

ON ROSH HASHANAH, during *Mussaf*, we recite the *berachah* of *zichronos*. We say that Hashem remembers: מַעֲשֵׂה אִישׁ וּפְקֻדָּתוֹ — וַעֲלִילוֹת מִצְעֲדֵי גֶבֶר, מַחְשְׁבוֹת אָדָם וְתַחְבֻּלֹתָיו וְיִצְרֵי מַעַלְלֵי אִישׁ — *"everyone's deed and mission, the accomplishments of man's activity, man's thoughts and schemes, and the motives behind man's deeds."* Four expressions are used in this sentence, which seem redundant. It occurred to me that we could analyze them in the following manner:

1. מַעֲשֵׂה אִישׁ וּפְקֻדָּתוֹ — *"Everyone's deed and mission"* refers to actions that the person carried out from beginning to end.

2. וַעֲלִילוֹת מִצְעֲדֵי גֶבֶר — *"The accomplishments of man's activity"* refers to the steps and actions man took en route to accomplishing something, although for one reason or another he was unable to complete his mission. When a person is judged, these steps are taken into consideration as well.

3. מַחְשְׁבוֹת אָדָם וְתַחְבֻּלֹתָיו — *"Man's thoughts and schemes"* refers to ideas that man only considered doing. He may have had detailed strategies for how to carry out his wish. Hashem also judges these plans, for better and for worse. A positive thought is judged as if he had actually carried out the intent. For example, plans to do battle against the *yetzer ha-ra* are also remembered for good by the One Who remembers all, as it says, *"For through wise strategies, you can wage war for your benefit"* (*Mishlei* 24:6) (see also *Metzudas David* there). In the case of *avodah zarah*, this applies to negative intent as well (see *Kiddushin* 40a).

4. Buried deep beneath these three lie יִצְרֵי מַעַלְלֵי אִישׁ — *"the motives behind man's deeds,"* man's innate tendencies, his latent desires and instincts that have not yet risen from the depths of his psyche or even entered the planning

stage. These include tendencies towards lying or anger, and certainly positive tendencies such as the desire to assist others and perform mitzvos. In all these, even if I have not yet thought of acting upon them, owing to extenuating circumstances for example, since this is what I really wish, Hashem sees and remembers.

We see how deep and penetrating Divine judgment really is.

TAKING BITTER MEDICINE

WE HAVE SAID that correcting one's *middos* is a very difficult task — what, then, can we do about so crucial an issue? Our life in the Next World hangs in the balance! Rambam tells us that one who is aware of his negative traits and does not approach a wise man to help heal him is nothing but a fool, as Shlomo HaMelech said: *"Foolish ones scorn wisdom and discipline"* (*Mishlei* 1:7, *Hilchos De'os* 2:1). Rambam then instructs us (in *halachah* 2) that in order to heal negative traits, one must go to the opposite extreme. For example, one who has an insatiable need to be honored should dress in the clothing of the poor and degrade himself, bringing humiliation upon himself until he achieves an average level of self-respect. From then on, he should work hard to remain on that middle path. The same applies to all other negative traits. The Vilna Gaon adds that even the most stubborn person can succeed in accepting strict resolutions upon himself. From experience, however, I can tell you that for the vast majority of our generation, this type of approach is difficult, if not virtually impossible.

HEALING IN STAGES

IT SEEMS TO me that one who knows for sure that he has the emotional strength to do so, should follow the above suggestion of the *gedolim*. This method of switching to the opposite extreme does at times make it easier to realize our goal. (Perhaps an example we can relate to is the removal of a band-aid. Removing it in a single, quick motion reduces the duration of the pain, yet requires greater inner strength.)

For most people, though, I would advise that they heal themselves in stages. We have all witnessed people who thought they had the ability to achieve a total transformation, but who broke down at a certain point and, in some cases, lost everything. A slower, yet steadier method is therefore more realistic. To do this we must combine two types of "medication" — learning and action. We must set aside fixed "doses" of both studying the foundations of our belief and correcting our actions. According to the principle of the *Sefer HaChinuch*: *"The heart will follow the actions"* (*mitzvah* 16). This suggestion, in fact, is in accordance with the view of Rambam. The only difference is that he suggests extreme action.

We, recognizing the weakness of our generation, are attempting to adapt the words of that "great eagle" to the fragile souls of our time. This was the holy method of the *mussar* giants: Each Yom Kippur they would accept upon themselves new resolutions as a continuation of the healing process in the upcoming new year.

Therefore, for example, a person who feels that he is too tight-fisted should do the following:

1. Study all the great advantages there are to giving *tzedakah*. For example, we are told, וּצְדָקָה תַּצִּיל מִמָּוֶת — *"Charity rescues from death"* (*Mishlei* 10:2). He should also learn that giving to charity grants one longevity and brings him into the Next World (*Tanna d'vei Eliyahu Zuta* 1).

2. He should give a bit more to charity than he was formerly accustomed to and should set aside a little more money for purchasing items required for performing mitzvos than he did previously. (Of course, these resolutions should be *beli neder*.)

WHEN PRIDE COMES TO PREVENT A FALL

ON THE SUBJECT of modifying negative traits, I would like to add something important. Because we are addressing *b'nei Torah*, there is one particular trait we must be careful not to reduce: that is the trait of *ga'avah* — haughtiness. You heard correctly! At times it is dangerous for *b'nei Torah* to break this trait. On the contrary, one must search for ways to destroy one's humility! Why is this so? Is humility not a very precious and important *middah* that our holy forefathers and all the *gedolim* were praised for? Pride, on the other hand, is known to be a terrible *middah*, as Shlomo HaMelech testifies: *"Every haughty heart is the abomination of Hashem"* (*Mishlei* 16:5).

The explanation of this is that the *yetzer ha-ra* succeeds in recruiting humility for its own nefarious purposes, easily causing this precious trait to become destructive among yeshiva students. How? If you take a look at all the vocations in the world, you will see that any professional believes he is the best there is. A doctor is convinced that he is tops in the land (or at least among the best), a lawyer will explain to you why he is better than all the rest, so too, thinks the carpenter, with total self-assurance. Take a look at the newspaper advertisements: "the best carpet there is," "the greatest washing machine in the world." How can this particular washing machine be the best one when the very next advertisement boasts the same about the competitor's machine?! That is the way it is; they are all outstanding and crown themselves with the *"crown of a good name"* (*Pirkei Avos* 4:13).

But for some reason, among those whose occupation is Torah study, the situation is radically different — there humility rules! The student is convinced that he is not "cut out" for learning Torah — nothing good will come from his stay in yeshiva. He claims he does not understand the *shiurim*, does not catch on so quickly, etc. To combat this weakness, the *ben Torah* has to develop his *ga'avah*. He must compare and see how far he has advanced in learning in general and in understanding this *sugya* in particular (perhaps the reason he feels lacking in knowledge is because he did not review the Gemara according to the directive of *Chazal* — see *Ta'anis* 8a). He should sit calmly and calculate how much this year has added to his knowledge of essential *halachos, yiras Shamayim,* and Jewish philosophy, and ask himself when he will ever again have the time to involve himself in these precious pursuits.

Even if he does not feel progress, one thing is for sure — and this he must reiterate to himself — his spiritual merits have grown tremendously! Each moment in the yeshiva raises him even higher — just being in the company of those who try to amass spiritual wealth makes him into a better Jew. This is true even if he does not feel it and cannot measure it at this moment.

To what can we compare this? To a diligent construction worker who stands on the scaffolding, very much involved in his building. Because he does not take a break from his work and get down off the scaffolding, he has no opportunity to see how tall the building has grown. What is most interesting is that people who are not involved in the construction and who stand a distance away can see very clearly all the building that is taking place. As the year passes, however, one day he takes a look down and sees how far away and how small are those who have elected to stand on the sidelines, and he suddenly realizes what an immense building he has constructed!

It is here that we witness a recurring phenomenon. People who have left their yeshivos after years of learning will admit to themselves in a moment of truth that their leaving the yeshiva was premature. The fast pace of their current life does not leave them any time for learning — not even in order to clarify an urgent halachic matter. Their pain at having left the sheltering walls of the *beis midrash* is great and cannot be relieved.

The *ben Torah* who sits and evaluates his learning with this in mind will suddenly realize how successful he actually is, and he will feel satisfaction. If not, he will be like one who approaches any task without believing either in his ability to perform or in the importance of what he is doing, in which case he is destined to fail.

This psychological principle is spelled out clearly in the Talmud (see *Eruvin* 54b). The Gemara relates how R' Preida had a student with whom he had to review the *shiur* 400 times until it was properly understood (either R' Preida's *shiurim* were incredibly deep or the student did not catch on so quickly). In any event, the story is told that R' Preida was once invited to a mitzvah function. Before leaving, he sat with his student and learned with him 400 times as he did every day, yet he realized that the student did not understand a single word. R' Preida asked, "How is it that today you were unable to understand anything, even after 400 reviews?" The student answered that the moment he had heard that the Rav was invited to the function, he assumed his *rebbe* would be in a rush and would not have time to review 400 times with him. Since he knew that reviewing the *sugya* less than 400 times would make it impossible for him to understand, he gave up before he even began and could no longer concentrate. R' Preida faced him squarely and said, "Listen now carefully, for I will not go until you understand." R' Preida then proceeded to review the material an additional 400 times.

There are two main lessons that we can derive from this story:

1. If a person has decided that he will never understand, even reviewing the material 400 times will be useless.
2. Once he has decided that he cannot understand — the 400 times that he learns are worth less than even one time! We see that it was not enough for Rav Preida to review the *shiur* an additional 399 times, he had to start again and repeat the lesson another 400 times, as if he had not even said it at all!

As the new year begins, let us strengthen our *ga'avah*, our "pride", *l'shem Shamayim* — the type of pride used to describe Yehoshafat, king of Yehudah: *"His heart was elevated in the ways of Hashem*" (*Divrei HaYamim* II 17:6). We must boastfully advertise what we have merited to give to ourselves and the Jewish nation — an item that is truly "the best in the world," that is "better than thousands of gold and silver" — the Torah. Let us strengthen that pride, whose ultimate purpose is to push ourselves to accomplish more in Torah and *gemilus chassadim*, with Hashem's help.

SICHAH NINE
"CHATASI LAHASHEM"

VIDUY — WHAT AND WHY

AS PART OF his Yom Kippur service, the Torah commands the *kohen gadol*: *"Aharon shall lean his two hands upon the head of the living he-goat and confess upon it all the iniquities of the Children of Israel"* (*Vayikra* 16:21). It is imperative that the *kohen gadol* place his hands upon the goat destined for *Azazel*, and while doing so, confess the sins of the Jewish People. In this way he will *"place them upon the head of the he-goat"* (ibid.); i.e. then the sins will be transferred onto the head of the goat, after which he is commanded to *"send it with a designated man to the desert"* (ibid.).

The *Tanna'im* dispute what would be if the *kohen gadol* were to neglect to recite the *viduy* before sending the goat to *Azazel*. Would the atonement still take effect or not? (See *Yoma* 40a.) We believe that were this to happen, the *kohen gadol* clearly would have been negligent in fulfilling one of the Torah's mitzvos.

This obligation to recite *viduy* and explicitly mention the sins of the nation requires further analysis. Throughout Yom Kippur, in the introductory portion of the *viduy*, we repeatedly say: *"You know the secrets of the universe, and the hidden-most mysteries of all the living. Nothing is hidden from You and nothing is concealed from Your eyes."* Hashem is more aware of our sins than we are! For what purpose, then, must we enumerate them before Him? Of what benefit is the *kohen gadol's* listing עֲוֹנוֹת בְּנֵי יִשְׂרָאֵל וְאֶת כָּל פִּשְׁעֵיהֶם לְכָל חַטֹּאתָם — *"The iniquities of the Children of Israel, and all their rebellious deeds among all their sins"* (*Vayikra* 16:21)?

Furthermore, it is known that *viduy* is one of the basic elements of *teshuvah*, without which *teshuvah* cannot take place. *Viduy* is not a mere introduction and preparatory stage for *teshuvah*, it is one of its three pillars, along with *charatah*, regret, and *azivas ha-cheit*, determination not to repeat the sin. *Teshuvah* can only take effect when composed of all three of these elements. Moreover, one who analyzes Rambam's language will notice that he elaborates much more on the obligation of *viduy*, confessing one's sins, than on the obligation to repent. Rambam never speaks of a positive commandment to repent, he simply says:

> When one returns from his sin, he must confess before Hashem, Blessed is He, as it says: "They shall confess their sin that they committed" (Bemidbar 5:7), this viduy *is a positive commandment.*
>
> (*Hilchos Teshuvah* 1:1)

Many commentaries explain that Rambam is of the opinion that *teshuvah* is not a commandment in and of itself; it is simply an *eitzah tovah*, a commendable thing to do. Once one makes the decision to repent, he is commanded to recite *viduy*. Based on what we have just said, our question is reinforced: Why is *viduy* so basic an element of *teshuvah* that the Torah saw fit to explicitly command it?

There is a further difficulty. The Mishnah details the words of the *kohen gadol*'s confession on the head of the goat: עָווּ פָּשְׁעוּ חָטְאוּ לְפָנֶיךָ עַמְּךָ בֵּית יִשְׂרָאֵל — "*Your nation, the House of Israel, has sinned inadvertently, sinned willfully, and sinned rebelliously before You*" (*Yoma* 66a). I noticed that the *Yerushalmi* quotes the opinion of Bar Kapara that the words, עַמְּךָ בֵּית יִשְׂרָאֵל — "*Your nation, the House of Israel,*" are not mentioned. Why not? In order not to publicly disgrace the Jewish People, the *kohen gadol* does not utter an obvious accusation against them (see *Korban HaEidah* and *Mareh Panim* there). Rambam rules, however, that the *kohen gadol* mentions the words עַמְּךָ בֵּית יִשְׂרָאֵל (*Hilchos Avodas Yom HaKippurim* 4:2), and we, in fact, recite them in our *davening*. It is possible that even according to Bar Kapara, the *kohen gadol* recites these words and that Bar Kapara simply questioned whether they appear in the Mishnah.

In any event, we must examine this. Jewish tradition elucidates many instances in which we go out of our way to avoid making any reference to sin or to events which disgrace the Jewish nation. Why, of all times, on this Day of Judgment, must we point out our faults? Our goal, on this pivotal day, is to search out any tiny scrap of merit that we can find in our favor. We therefore take extreme care not to even mention sin. The *kohen gadol* is forbidden to enter the *Kodesh HaKodashim* in gold-colored clothing, lest the color serve as a reminder of the sin of the Golden Calf, God forbid (*Rosh Hashanah* 26a). Can it be that at that very same moment, while the Jewish nation is still standing on the scales of judgment, the *kohen gadol* utters such a sharp accusation against the Jewish nation?

There is one answer to all these questions: From the very moment of his creation, man tends to look for ways to justify his actions. This not only gives him a more positive image in the eyes of others, it also serves to give him a better impression of himself. There are times when this is essential; we have elaborated on this elsewhere (see *Sichah* 33 in the Hebrew *Sichos LeSefer Bereishis*). There is no room for justification, however, regarding *viduy*. The *viduy* is supposed to bring about sweeping changes in one's life. How can a person be expected to accomplish that if he keeps attempting to convince himself that his actions are justifiable? As long as a person dreams up explanations and reasons, whose very purpose is to assuage his guilt, he will be unable to change. The Torah, therefore, commanded us to enunciate the *viduy* until our sins ring in our ears! There must be no doubt in our mind that we need to begin anew.

The Mishnah, therefore, did not wish to leave any uncertainty as to the intent of the *kohen gadol's viduy*. Bar Kapara's version could lead a person to convince himself that the words, חָטְאוּ עָווּ פָּשְׁעוּ לְפָנֶיךָ — "they have sinned inadvertently, sinned willfully, and *sinned rebelliously before You,"* refer to others — the other nations, those evil *goyim* — the Russians, the Syrians, and other peoples who bring forth Hashem's anger. As for us, the Jewish nation? *Baruch Hashem*, we do not sin, all our actions are praiseworthy! The way to prevent even the smallest misconception is for the text of the *viduy* to elucidate in no uncertain terms that the guilty party is *"Amcha Beis Yisrael."*

If the *viduy* is so clear and unambiguous, there is a chance that the *teshuvah* will be so, too. A generalized and ambiguous *viduy* will lead to an ambiguous *teshuvah* that carries with it no obligation. A somewhat forced answer may perhaps resolve a difficult *Tosafos*; it is not sufficient, however, for *viduy*, whose very purpose is to bring about a metamorphosis in our lives. The Gemara therefore tells us that one must explicitly spell out the sins that he has committed (see *Yoma* 86b). The *Shulchan Aruch* rules that one who confesses silently must still enumerate his sins. It is customary to spell out additional transgressions one may have committed, even beyond those specified in our *machzorim*. The purpose is to cause further shame to the person confessing, inducing him to repent (*Orach Chaim* 607:7, *Mishnah Berurah* 8).[6]

There is a principle taught to every new medical student — a proper diagnosis is half the cure. This applies to afflictions of the soul as well as those of the body.

SHAUL AND DAVID

THIS IDEA ALSO explains the distinction *Chazal* made between Shaul HaMelech and David HaMelech: *"Shaul erred in one sin and it was reckoned against him, David erred in two sins and it was not reckoned against him"* (*Yoma* 22b). Shaul sinned once in his failure

---

6. It was unclear to me whether one also needs to elaborate on every instance in which he transgressed a particular sin. I consulted with the Rav (HaGaon HaRav Shlomo Zalman Auerbach *zt"l*), who ruled that while one need not do so, one should still say: "I have stumbled and sinned in this area many times."

to totally destroy Amalek. David, on the other hand, sinned on two occasions — in the incident involving the killing of Uriah and in the episode when he counted the Jewish People. Shaul's lone sin was sufficient reason for him to have to forfeit the kingship, whereas David's two sins did not lose him the kingship.

Why is this the case? The answer is found in *Chazal*'s explanation of the *pasuk* in *Mishlei* (28:13): מְכַסֶּה פְשָׁעָיו לֹא יַצְלִיחַ וּמוֹדֶה וְעוֹזֵב יְרֻחָם — *"One who conceals his sins will not succeed, but he who confesses and forsakes them will be granted mercy."*

Chazal tell us that the beginning of the verse, *"One who conceals his sins will not succeed,"* refers to Shaul, while the words, *"He who confesses and forsakes them will be granted mercy,"* refer to David.

When Shemuel comes to chastise Shaul for not having fully obeyed Hashem's commandment, Shaul joyfully comes out to greet him, proclaiming: *"Blessed are you to Hashem! I have fulfilled the word of Hashem"* (*Shemuel* I 15:13). *Baruch Hashem*, I have fulfilled the mitzvah of wiping out Amalek as I was required to do.

Shemuel then proceeds to hint to Shaul his displeasure: *"And what is this sound of sheep in my ears?"* (ibid. 15:14). Shaul does not understand Shemuel and responds that, in addition to destroying the people of Amalek, he had some of their choice sheep sacrificed to Hashem.

Shemuel then spells it out more clearly: *"Desist, and I shall tell you what Hashem spoke to me last night ... why did you not obey the voice of Hashem? You rushed after the spoils and you did what was evil in the eyes of Hashem"* (ibid. 15:16, 19).

Yet Shaul continues to argue on his own behalf: *"But I did heed the voice of Hashem and I did walk the path on which Hashem sent me!"* (ibid. 15:20).

Shemuel persists in his rebuke, emphasizing, *"Behold, to obey is better than a choice offering, to be attentive than the fat of rams, for rebelliousness is like the sin of sorcery, and verbosity is like the iniquity of idolatry. Because you have rejected the word of God, He has rejected you as king"* (ibid. 15:22–23).

Only then does Shaul respond, *"I have sinned, for I have transgressed the word of Hashem and your word"* (ibid. 15:24).

Even so, Shaul adds justification for his actions: *"For I feared the people and I hearkened to their voice"* (ibid.). A *viduy* that is accompanied by excuses and justifications cannot be classified as a true *viduy*. Repeated rationalizations make it clear that the regret is not wholehearted. Had Shaul's first reaction been *"I have sinned,"* perhaps Hashem would have rescinded His decree of confiscating the kingdom from him. Shaul, however, repeatedly tried to show how he had actually fulfilled the commandment. This spelled the end of his reign.

It is very difficult for us to speak this way of Shaul, whom a heavenly voice declared to be בְּחִיר ה' — *"the chosen one of Hashem"* (*Shemuel* II 21:6). When discussing the giants of the world, we must keep in mind that we are not judging their actual deeds. Rather, we are attempting to learn lessons that are appropriate for our own status. From the minor infractions of our great ancestors, we can extract lessons that we can apply to our much greater failings.

One may be tempted to ask, if these were indeed minor infractions, why does the *Tanach* relate to them in such strong language? The reason is that commensurate with the high spiritual status of the particular person, his minor failing is magnified until it equals a much more serious one in the average person.

Shaul's error in the incident involving Amalek was in actuality relatively minor. In fact, the head of the Sanhedrin instructed him not to destroy Amalek's sheep, as Rashi interprets the *pasuk*, *"For I have feared the people"* (*Shemuel* I, 15:24), as referring to *"Doeg the Edomite, who was equal to all in importance."* With this information, we view Shaul's action in an entirely different light. On the contrary, what would we have said of a king who did not follow the directive of the head of the Sanhedrin? This was the highest halachic authority in the nation!

There was, however, an error in the way Shaul followed Doeg's directive. Shaul was given a very clear prophecy instructing him to destroy Amalek: *"Ox and sheep alike, camel and donkey alike"* (ibid. 15:3). Had he truly felt there was a contradiction between this prophecy and the ruling of the Sanhedrin, he should have gone to the prophet Shemuel to consult on how to respond. We see that his argument, therefore, was not on such solid ground. Shaul believed in his heart that it was the people who were guilty, or maybe Doeg the Edomite, but not himself! It is clear from his conversation with Shemuel that this attitude prevented him from achieving total regret and repentance. It is based on this that *Chazal* tell us: *"Shaul erred in one sin and it was reckoned against him."*

"CHATASI LAHASHEM"

WHEN IT CAME to David, however, the situation was totally different. When the prophet Nasan rebuked David for the killing of Uriah, David listened intently to these harsh words and the severe punishment meted out to him and his descendants (David HaMelech was judged very severely for this sin, according to his own level). At the conclusion of Nasan's words, David responded with just two words: חָטָאתִי לַה' — *" I have sinned to Hashem"* (*Shemuel* II 12:13).

His declaration was not followed by any "buts". David does not claim: *"Bas-sheva the daughter of Eliam was suited to David since the Six Days of Creation"* (*Sanhedrin* 107a), nor does he make mention of: *"Whoever said that David sinned is simply mistaken"* (*Shabbos* 56a), nor does he allude to the other justifications *Chazal* give for David's action. His words are clear, simple, and direct: *"Chatasi laHashem"*. He sinned and he now must concentrate all his efforts on correction.

The Vilna Gaon adds his personal touch to the incident. In his commentary on the *pasuk* in *Tehillim*: חַטָּאתִי אוֹדִיעֲךָ וַעֲוֹנִי לֹא כִסִּיתִי, אָמַרְתִּי אוֹדֶה עֲלֵי פְשָׁעַי לַה' — *"My sin I make known to You, my iniquity I do not hide; I said, 'I will confess my transgression to Hashem'"* (*Tehillim* 32:5), the Vilna Gaon explains that David is hinting at his desire to confess to the prophet Nasan using all three expressions of *viduy* — 'חָטָאתִי עָוִיתִי פָּשַׁעְתִּי לַה — *"I have sinned inadvertently, I have sinned willfully, and I have sinned rebelliously before Hashem."* Here (in *Sefer Shemuel*), the prophet stopped him after *"chatasi laHashem"*, because his action was only a *cheit*, implying that it was unintentional. There was no intentional *avon* or *pesha* here (see *Yoma* 36b).

David's sincere regret and *teshuvah* produced immediate results. The moment he uttered the words *chatasi laHashem*, the message came from Hashem to the prophet Nasan to tell him: *"So too Hashem has commuted your sin; you will not die"* (*Shemuel* II, 12:13). The punishment of death that David had decreed upon *"the rich man, who stole the sheep of the poor person,"* was rescinded. This is alluded to at the conclusion of the *pasuk* we quoted earlier from *Tehillim*: וְאַתָּה נָשָׂאתָ עֲוֹן חַטָּאתִי — *"You have forgiven the* עָוֹן *of my sin"* (*Tehillim* 32:5) (see Rashi there).

We have mentioned on numerous occasions that the term עָוֹן often connotes the punishment that occurs as a result of the sin.[7] If so, we can understand the *pasuk* thus: *"You have forgiven the* עָוֹן *of my sin"* — the result of David's total *viduy* was that Hashem rescinded the punishment.

We see David HaMelech immediately express regret regarding his other sin as well — counting the Jewish People. Even before the prophet came, David regretted his action: *"David's heart smote him after having counted the people and David said to Hashem, 'I have sinned greatly in what I have done.... for I have acted very foolishly.'"*

Following the words of the prophet and the beginning of the plague, David repeats: *"Behold, I have sinned and I have transgressed ... let your hand be against me and my father's family"*

---

7. An example of this is found in Ibn Ezra's commentary on Kayin's statement: גָּדוֹל עֲוֹנִי מִנְּשֹׂא — *"My* עָוֹן *is too great to bear."* The *pasuk* then goes on to detail the punishment: ...הֵן גֵּרַשְׁתָּ אֹתִי... וּמִפָּנֶיךָ אֶסָּתֵר... וְהָיִיתִי נָע וָנָד.. — *"You have banished me...can I be hidden from Your presence?...I must become a wanderer and an exile"* (*Bereishis* 4:13–14).

(*Shemuel* II, 24:10, 17). David takes sole responsibility upon his shoulders. Here, too, forgiveness from Hashem was not long in coming. The plague that was to continue for three days, according to Hashem's words (ibid. 24:13), in fact lasted only one day or, according to some opinions, only one hour (*Berachos* 62b).

THE THIRTY-FIVE MERITS OF AM YISRAEL

THE TALMUD ASKS, In whose merit did the plague come to an early end? The Gemara provides several possible answers: in the merit of Yaakov Avinu, due to the ashes of Yitzchak, because of the *Beis HaMikdash*, etc. The *Midrash Shochar Tov* brings a very interesting calculation. The plague was destined to last for thirty-six hours — the "three days" promised by Hashem (not including the nights). Thirty-five merits of Israel presented themselves before Hashem, pleading for mercy for the Jewish People. They were: the Ten Commandments, the two Tablets, the three forefathers, the five books of the Torah, the seven days of the week, and the eight days of the *bris milah*. Each of the thirty-five merits managed to erase one hour of the plague, so that out of the original thirty-six hours, only one remained.

These merits of Israel are always present. Why was it only now, to annul the punishment of this particular plague, that they stood up in support of the Jewish People? While these merits are always present, they need to be activated. Since David's admission was complete and sincere, and its accompanying *teshuvah* was also unequivocal, the path was then opened for these merits to aid the Jewish People by bringing about Hashem's forgiveness.

What distinguished David from Shaul, therefore, was a clear and sweeping admission. The word *viduy* is from the root of *levadeh*, meaning to admit, here speaking about guilt. *Viduy* comes to declare a genuine and sincere admission of one's guilt. The admission must be true, sincere, and from the heart. Again we must emphasize, we are not trying to present a true understanding of the sin of Shaul, who is destined to be one of the future leaders of Israel (see *Sukkah* 52b). We have merely attempted to extract whatever lessons we could, keeping in mind that only נְבוּאָה שֶׁהוּצְרַךְ לְדוֹרוֹת נִכְתְּבָה — *"a prophecy needed for future generations was recorded"* (*Megillah* 14a).

Now you may ask, does this mean that there is never any allowance for coming to the defense of *Am Yisrael*? Did R' Levi Yitzchak of Berdichev not spend his life defending the nation? Did *Chazal* not tell us that it is the *yetzer ha-ra* and the oppression at the hands of foreign kings that cause the Jewish nation to be remiss in following Hashem's will (*Berachos* 17a)? We know that Moshe Rabbeinu was the *"father of all advocates"* — he maintained that the sin of the Golden Calf came about because of the massive amount of gold the Jewish nation amassed and took out with them from Egypt (*Berachos* 32a). What, then, is wrong with defending or justifying our actions?

The answer is very simple: Moshe Rabbeinu, as well as any other person, can and must be *melamed zechus* on behalf of others who sinned, in order that Hashem forgive them. The violator himself, however, cannot be *melamed zechus* on himself until he first recognizes his wrongdoings. Only after he acknowledges and admits his guilt can he claim that he is mere flesh and blood, and thus arouse Hashem's mercy for one who already realizes the error of his ways.

THE CONCEPT OF FREE WILL

IF WE WISH to strengthen this foundation and to undertake a total *viduy* before Hashem, if we wish to reach a true understanding that despite all our excuses, there is no justification for the sin we have committed, we must begin by understanding the concept of free choice. Rambam (*Hilchos Teshuvah* 5:1–2) emphasizes that there is nothing that can compel a person to be evil or righteous, for each individual is in complete control of his own actions. A person is not "programmed" at birth to be good or bad, therefore each and every one of us has the potential to become a Moshe Rabbeinu (except regarding his level of prophecy).

In order to clarify what we have just said, let us analyze these words of Rambam. Is a person really not influenced by his surroundings? There are many people who did not merit growing up in a religious household, while many more did not have the opportunity to study in a yeshiva and experience a taste of the Torah. Can we rightfully say that a Jew born in a small town in Siberia, who has never heard of Judaism, has the same potential for spiritual growth as one born and raised in a chareidi neighborhood? Does a young man who grew up in Meah She'arim have to deal with the same temptation to smoke on Shabbos as a young man who grew up in a *Shomer HaTza'ir* kibbutz? (As an aside, I would like to say that smoking on weekdays is not so great either — in fact, it is a dying habit). The social pressure in Meah She'arim would make it extremely difficult to transgress Shabbos, while the *kibbutznik* has no reason in the world not to light up then.

PERSONAL CROSSROADS

MY ESTEEMED TEACHER, HaRav Dessler *zt"l*, explains that for our entire lives we are in constant movement across a long axis extending, as it were, between heaven and earth. Along the entire path are points of decision. At each of these points, one can choose between good and bad. From the moment a person is born, he is positioned at one of these points of decision. The choice made at each one will determine the character and level of the next choice. If he chooses good, he will move up one notch; if he chooses bad, he will descend to a lower level. Each and every person, without any exception, has the ability to rise higher or, God forbid, to move downward. If a person consistently chooses good, after a period of time he will climb higher and higher until he reaches the level of Moshe Rabbeinu — so

Rambam promises us. The opposite holds true as well: if one is on a constant descent, his decision points will drop lower and lower until he falls to the level of Yeravam ben Nevat. No matter what, a person cannot remain stagnant; the movement must be either up or down at all times. *Chaim* — life — implies movement on this axis of choices.

What distinguishes one person from another is his point of origin. One's starting point is determined by the spiritual standards he inherits from his parents. Of course, the child can lose the high level he was born with, or he can ascend much higher — it all depends on his own will.

Free choice means man has the ability to rise one rung above his current level or to descend by one rung. It is impossible for man to reach the top or bottom rung instantly (barring rare exceptions).

Let us now apply these principles to the examples we gave before. The young man brought up in a chareidi neighborhood is not faced with the dilemma of whether or not to smoke on Shabbos — he is above such a decision. In addition, imagine the uproar if he were caught! He would be thrown out (and in the confusion, someone might accidentally extinguish the cigarette!). The *kibbutznik* does not have this dilemma either, for he is well below this level.

Each one's point of decision is relative to where he is currently standing: a *yeshivah bachur*'s decision could be whether to improve his *daven*ing over his performance the day before, or whether to be satisfied with where he was yesterday. In the field of *bein adam le-chavero*, he can decide whether to attempt more *chesed* or to be content with the status quo. The same may be said regarding *middos*, learning, etc. Not for a moment would he consider turning on a light in the room while his friend is sleeping; he is well beyond that point of decision. But if he decides not to improve his *daven*ing today, tomorrow he may very well find himself debating whether to turn on the light and risk waking his roommate or to make do with the light from the hallway. If he makes a wrong decision here and he does turn on the light, he will start to deteriorate. The level of his choices will become lower and lower, eventually descending to the spiritual plateau of the *Shomer HaTza'ir kibbutznik*. If he slides further down the line, he may eventually reach the level of Yeravam ben Nevat.

The *kibbutznik's* choice is also commensurate with the level he is on. His decision might entail whether to strengthen his level of *ahavas Yisrael*, love for his fellow Jew, or not, whether he should he act more morally, or show more respect for his wife and friends (obviously, all this applies to the religious person as well). As time passes, after many positive decisions, this *kibbutznik* might reach the critical decision of whether or not to consider an alternative, more authentic lifestyle than that of the kibbutz. If he continues to make correct decisions in all his struggles, he will have the opportunity to ascend to the level of Moshe Rabbeinu.

What about the cannibal in Africa? Does a person who has sunk so low still have free choice? Certainly! His decisions might entail, perhaps, whether to kill his victim and then cook him, or cook him while he is still alive! If he makes a positive decision here, the path towards the next level of selection will be open before him: Should he kill people at all or should he be satisfied with animal meat — a choice that is not available to him at his current level.

In our quest to fulfill the requirements of *viduy* in the optimal manner, without any excuses or justifications, we must carefully contemplate these words of Rambam: that each one of us has the potential to become a Moshe Rabbeinu. We must understand that if we really want to, we have the ability to climb higher and surmount any obstacles.

If we really want to — this is the key phrase! We have mentioned in the past the words of the *Chovos HaLevavos* (*Sha'ar Avodas HaElokim* 8), that the essential element in man's free choice is not in the action alone, but in the desire to act. Translating this desire into deed, the action is in Hashem's hands. It is true that in general, בְּדֶרֶךְ שֶׁאָדָם רוֹצֶה לֵילֵךְ, בָּהּ מוֹלִיכִין אוֹתוֹ — *"In the way that a man wishes to go, in that way he is led"* (Makkos 10b), but sometimes, for a variety of reasons, Hashem may decide not to allow someone to realize his wishes. The main requirement of man is that he desire to choose good. Choice is exclusively in man's domain.

WE CANNOT REMAIN STAGNANT

DURING THESE DAYS, when our fate is being inscribed and sealed in the heavenly tomes, it must be emphasized that what is demanded of us is our resolution — our desire to do good. Our task is to want to advance in Torah learning and to grow in *yiras Shamayim*. We must strive to raise our level of *chesed*. We must wish that our acts of *chesed* be on a higher level. In most cases, when Hashem sees what a person's true desire is, He will assist him in realizing his wishes. According to Rav Dessler *zt"l*, this means new challenges. Rising to higher levels of mitzvah observance entails climbing to a higher level on the axis of choices. We can, therefore, anticipate for ourselves in the coming year more difficult struggles, more delicate points of choice, but these will serve to bring us closer to our ultimate goal. If we can win the battle, we can become holier and closer to Hashem than we were in the past year.

Sometimes man may think to himself, "It is true that this year I did not elevate myself spiritually, but thank God I did not fall either." There is no such thing! It is impossible to remain stagnant! The *pasuk* tells us: *"A path of life waits above for the intelligent one, so that his soul will turn away from the grave below"* (Mishlei 15:24).

It is incumbent upon us to choose a lifestyle of upward striving; this is the only way to avoid plummeting to the depths. This battle takes place each and every moment, without any cease-fire. Once we have successfully passed one trial, we find ourselves at the next crossroad and must make another decision: Should we climb up His holy mountain or shall we allow ourselves to slide down the slippery slopes into that yawning abyss?

One cannot avoid making decisions. Life is made up of choices and each movement upward or downward is the consequence of a decision. As long as we are alive, we are moving along this pole. (It may be possible that one's ascent in *mitzvos bein adam laMakom* is offset by his fall in *mitzvos bein adam lechavero*, or vice versa, thus leaving him on the same general level he was on before. In each area individually, however, there has to be movement — either upward or downward).

HOW TO ACHIEVE AUTHENTIC VIDUY

ON THE BASIS of this understanding, let us return to our discussion of *viduy*. We can now explain that just as a person's actions must be in accordance with his level of choice, so too must his confession be commensurate with the level he is on. If we desire authentic *viduy* which will inspire us to *teshuvah*, we must confess to our failures on the level we are on, based on the choices we have now, and not for decisions on levels far above us.

To what am I referring? *Chayei Adam* is of the opinion that we should confess even for sins we are certain we did not commit, lest we transgressed them in our soul's previous incarnation (*gilgul*). I would think that this type of *viduy* is appropriate for someone on the level of the *Chayei Adam*. He was unable to find sins he had committed in this *gilgul* and thus felt the need to confess those he might have transgressed in a previous lifetime! The great *tzaddikim* strive to totally purify their souls from all faults, including those in the distant past.

I suspect that for us, though, this type of *viduy* is the antithesis of the truth. I cannot speak for others, but for myself I can think of more than enough sins I have committed in this *gilgul*, so that I see no need to search for sins in previous incarnations. There is no reason for us to recite *viduy* for sins that we have not committed. By so doing, one would turn the *viduy* into a big farce. Rather than concentrating on areas where it is clear that we have failed, we would occupy our thoughts with our previous *gilgulim*. We would spend our time wondering whether or not we ate sacrificial offerings outside the walls of Yerushalayim or whether we mistakenly placed the *choshen* above the *ephod*! By occupying our minds with such things, we might forget to confess to and correct the sins that are within our reach — the mitzvos that are on our own "crossroads of choice." What would be the point of our saying: "Hashem, please forgive me for not having reached the level of Ari HaKadosh"! Is this is a *viduy*? That level is far beyond anything we can even hope to attain; thus this type of *viduy* is mere lip service.

Let us concentrate on the level we are on, on the choices we should have made. We need not confess for not having studied all the hidden secrets of the upper worlds, but rather that we did not properly learn Gemara with Rashi, for of this we are truly guilty. We know that לֹא בַשָּׁמַיִם הִיא — "*it is not in heaven*" (*Devarim* 30:12). We have the ability to correct our ways, and with Hashem's help may we be on a higher level next year. Otherwise, in addition to everything else, we will have to confess: עַל חֵטְא שֶׁחָטָאנוּ לְפָנֶיךָ בְּוִדּוּי פֶּה — "*For the sin that we have sinned before You through insincere confession*"! (One way of explaining this confession is that only the mouth participated in the *viduy*; it was all lip service.) The process of *teshuvah* cannot begin without an authentic and appropriate *viduy*.

This brings us to the ultimate question: How do we reach this level of profound and total regret? How can man elevate himself to a level where he is capable of reciting *viduy* by totally revealing his heart to his Creator, without the barriers of excuses and rationalizations at all?

One way we can accomplish this is by raising our personal awareness of the importance of the mitzvos we are observing. Torah scholars, those who set aside time for learning, as well as those who study *Daf Yomi*, must all realize the importance of what they are doing. The same is true for those involved in *chesed*, promoting *shalom bayis*, ensuring that Jewish children receive a Torah education, and similar endeavors. We must all revitalize that feeling that may have worn away with time — that what we are doing is of the utmost importance. Its reward in the eternal world is unlimited, and very often in this world as well. We must study the words of *Chazal* as they relate to the importance of the mitzvah. We must strengthen ourselves in understanding that we are building spiritual worlds and bringing the redemption of the Jewish People that much closer.

Then, when a person understands that each minute he is involved in a mitzvah he is gathering precious pearls, he will feel tremendous regret about valuable time that is not properly utilized — for wasting time and certainly for the time spent not in gathering precious pearls, but in scratching his hands on thorns! If he feels true joy from what he has gained and profited, then surely he will feel pain at unnecessary loss.

As we approach this Day of Judgment, we must strengthen ourselves and feel pride that we merited for ourselves, as well as for the Jewish nation, an eternity of redemption and salvation. This feeling will have a twofold effect:

1. It will mark a change in our future — it will cause us to become more involved in Torah and acts of *chesed*, to the best of our ability.
2. It can effect a change in the past — he who understands the great value of each word of *Talmud Torah*, the joy achieved through fulfillment of the Torah, will naturally experience heartfelt regret over not having utilized his time properly. He will now feel regret for the lost opportunities of the past. (How could I have wasted my time on trivialities?) When this regret is sincere, the *viduy* will also be sincere — a confession free of empty excuses.

We will then be able to admit with a full heart, חָטָאתִי לה'. When the confession and regret are strong and solid, they will necessarily serve to bring about such a profound and inner *teshuvah* that *"the One Who knows the deep secrets will testify about him that he will never again return to this sin"* (Rambam, *Hilchos Teshuvah* 2:2).

SICHAH TEN
TAKING ADVANTAGE OF HEAVENLY GIFTS

THE DAY ITSELF ATONES

כִּי בַיּוֹם הַזֶּה יְכַפֵּר עֲלֵיכֶם לְטַהֵר אֶתְכֶם מִכֹּל חַטֹּאתֵיכֶם.

For on this day he shall provide atonement for you to cleanse you from all your sins.

(*Vayikra* 16:30)

The Torah does not specify who will provide this atonement. Ibn Ezra points out that from the context of the *pasuk*, one may conclude that this is referring to the *kohen gadol*. A few *pesukim* earlier, it is stated: *"Aharon shall place his hands"* (ibid. 16:21) and *"Aharon shall come"* (ibid. 16:23).

Shortly thereafter, the Torah refers to the *kohen gadol* who will replace Aharon (see ibid. 32). The subject of our *pasuk*, too, appears to be the *kohen gadol*, and it is he is who offers the atonement while it is Hashem Who does the forgiving.

In that case כִּי בַיּוֹם הַזֶּה — *"for on this day"* — denotes the time frame for the atonement. When does the *kohen gadol* provide the atonement? On the tenth day of Tishrei. This is the *peshat* (the simple understanding of the *pasuk*).

Chazal, however, tell us: *"Yom Kippur atones"* (*Yoma* 86a). In other words, the phrase כִּי בַיּוֹם הַזֶּה does more than inform us of the calendar date this atonement takes effect. It stresses that the day itself is the vehicle for carrying out the atonement (כִּי בַיּוֹם הַזֶּה — *"with this day"*). *"He shall provide atonement"* is therefore referring not to the *kohen gadol*, but rather to Hashem. Similarly we find: הִנֵּה אָנֹכִי מַכֶּה בַּמַּטֶּה אֲשֶׁר בְּיָדִי — *"and behold I am hitting with the staff that is in my hand"* (Shemos 7:17). Moshe Rabbeinu is performing the action with his staff, but it is Hashem Who is performing the miracle.

According to this interpretation, Hashem provides the atonement with the instrument of Yom Kippur — man shall "attain atonement" simply by virtue of being alive on Yom Kippur.

YOM KIPPUR ONLY ATONES FOR THOSE WHO REPENT

THIS LATTER EXPLANATION poses a difficulty. In *Parashas Emor*, the section dealing with Yom Kippur opens with these words: אַךְ בֶּעָשׂוֹר לַחֹדֶשׁ הַשְּׁבִיעִי הַזֶּה יוֹם הַכִּפּוּרִים הוּא — *"But on the tenth day of this month it is the Day of Atonement"* (Vayikra 23:27).

Whenever the Torah uses the word אַךְ, it denotes exclusion. If so, before the Torah even begins teaching about the subject, its very first word already poses certain restrictions. (In fact, in the cantillations, the word אַךְ appears here with a *pazer*, which serves to emphasize it still further.) What is the word אַךְ coming to exclude?

If up until this point we were under the impression that *"for on this day He shall provide atonement"* — using this day as a medium, atonement is granted under all circumstances — we should be aware that there are those who are excluded from this atonement. אַךְ teaches us that Yom Kippur only offers atonement for those who repent, and not for those who have not repented (*Shevuos* 13a). (The *halachah* does not follow the opinion of Rebbi, who states that Yom Kippur atones, even for those who do not repent).

FOUR LEVELS OF REPENTANCE

THIS LEADS US to a fundamental question. If *teshuvah* is a prerequisite for the atonement of Yom Kippur, in what way is the uniqueness of this day manifested? On the one hand, without

Taking Advantage of Heavenly Gifts

teshuvah atonement is not granted, on the other hand, if we have already repented, what need do we have for Yom Kippur? One can do *teshuvah* any day of the year. What special benefit, then, does this day hold for us?

The Gemara explains that there are four levels of repentance, each commensurate with the level of the infraction (see *Yoma* 85b–86a):

1. *Teshuvah* on its own atones only for מִצְוֹת קַלּוֹת — light sins, i.e. neglecting to fulfill a positive commandment (such as reciting *Birkas HaMazon*), or violating a לָאו הַנִּתָּק לַעֲשֵׂה (such as the mitzvah of *shiluach ha-kein*. The Torah commands us, *"You shall not take the mother with the young,"* yet if one transgressed and took the offspring with the mother still present, he will not be punished with lashes, because the prohibition is detached [*nitak*] from the punishment of *malkos* and can be corrected via fulfillment of the positive commandment, *"You shall surely send away the mother."*).

2. For violating negative prohibitions (excluding לָאו הַנִּתָּק לַעֲשֵׂה mentioned above and those transgressions punishable by death or *kareis*), תְּשׁוּבָה תּוֹלָה — repentance leaves atonement suspended until the final atonement is granted on Yom Kippur.

3. For the more severe negative prohibitions (those punishable by *kareis* or death at the hands of a *beis din* — e.g. one who ate on Yom Kippur or intentionally violated Shabbos), in addition to *teshuvah* and Yom Kippur, one must undergo *yisurim*, afflictions, in order to reach full atonement.

4. For *chillul Hashem*: *teshuvah*, Yom Kippur, and *yisurim* are not sufficient. One is not granted full atonement until one dies.

These four levels of atonement are also quoted by Rambam (*Hilchos Teshuvah* 1:4).

MEIRI'S CHIDDUSH

MEIRI, IN HIS commentary on the Gemara, provides us with a different understanding of *Chazal*'s words, *"Yom Kippur atones."* The very fact of the sun rising on Yom Kippur is sufficient to atone. There is no need for the special sacrifices associated with the day, nor for the service led by the *kohen gadol*. How can this be? Do we not know that Hashem does not forgive sins without sufficient reason (*Bava Kamma* 50a)? In what way, then, does this atonement take effect? Even if one were to answer that Yom Kippur alone is not what brings about atonement, but that it must be accompanied by *teshuvah*, we still need to explain the unique role of the day in facilitating the atonement which *teshuvah* alone is unable to accomplish.

We now return full circle to our initial question: If *teshuvah* alone is not sufficient to effect total atonement — perhaps because the person did not have the requisite remorse — then how will Yom Kippur "aid" a person in erasing his improper deeds?

Meiri explains that for all levels of sin, there is one sole factor which brings about atonement: *teshuvah*! *Teshuvah* and *teshuvah* alone — there can be no atonement without it. According to this view, the four categories outlined in the Gemara, some of which assign roles to Yom Kippur, *yisurim*, and death in the atonement process, do not imply that these factors grant the atonement. Rather, their role is to facilitate a person's attaining the appropriate level of *teshuvah* required to atone for the particular sin.

Let us now outline Meiri's understanding of the four levels of atonement:

1. For the קַלּוֹת, the light transgressions (neglecting to fulfill a positive commandment or violating a לָאו הַנִּתָּק לַעֲשֵׂה), one can attain the requisite level of *teshuvah* without assistance. Once one has achieved that level, *"he does not move from there until he is forgiven"* (*Yoma* 86a).

2. For violation of negative commandments (with the exception of those punishable by *kareis* and death), a higher level of *teshuvah* is required. The Torah understands that man is incapable of reaching this level without some means of assistance. The greater the sin, the greater the awakening needed — and man can only achieve this type of awakening on Yom Kippur. The day itself provides a sort of illumination that opens up one's heart to *teshuvah*, purifies the soul, and imbues man with the power to succeed in reaching the level of *teshuvah* required to atone for these negative commandments.

3. Transgressions punishable by *kareis* or death are deemed so severe that one cannot achieve sufficient regret without the awakening provided by Yom Kippur along with the addition of *yisurim*.

4. For the terrible sin of *chillul Hashem*, nothing short of death can arouse the proper feelings of *teshuvah*. Therefore, only during the final hours of one's life can one achieve atonement for this sin.

According to Meiri, the Gemara's intention was not to say that there are factors other than *teshuvah* that atone. Indeed, if a person were to feel a sudden internal urge that would arouse him to proper repentance any other day of the year, he would truly have no need for Yom Kippur! *Teshuvah*, deep regret, is what atones. Anything else only provides assistance in reaching that level.

Do we not enlist any means at our disposal in our quest to create and maintain an atmosphere conducive to opening our hearts? Do our *rabbanim* not awaken us with their inspiring words of wisdom and *mussar*? Does each community not have its own special *niggunim* meant for just that purpose? Not one of us would entertain the notion that the *derashos* or the beautiful *niggunim* in themselves atone. These are only aids to facilitate our attaining authentic *teshuvah*.

"TUNING IN" TO CHANNELS WITH GOOD RECEPTION

ACCORDING TO MEIRI, therefore, the purpose and uniqueness of Yom Kippur is to awaken in our hearts a feeling of renewal. There are many unique advantages to this special day: It was on this day that Hashem forgave the Jewish People for the חֵטְא הָעֵגֶל — the sin of the Golden Calf, and Moshe received the second Tablets (see *Midrash Tanchuma, Ki Sisa* 31). The Midrash tells that it was on Yom Kippur that Avraham Avinu's *bris milah* took place (see *Pirkei d'Rabi Eliezer* 29). In addition, there is an opinion that the binding of Yitzchak took place on this tenth day of Tishrei. The סְגֻלּוֹת — the special virtues that are associated with this day, of course, are not what truly determine matters for the individual Jew. The main work of *teshuvah* man must do himself, within his own soul.

The Creator is ready to forgive us at each and every moment. The problem is that man is not always receptive to Hashem's wishes. It is only at certain times of the year, such as Shabbos and festivals, when we refrain from the physical labor that tends to weaken us spiritually, that the outer seal surrounding our hearts is removed and we become receptive. It is in this way that Yom Kippur has more power than the other festivals, for on Yom Kippur not only do we refrain from using our hands to do certain things, but our internal organs (e.g. our digestive system and blood vessels — the center of man's desires) slow down as well. Without these distractions, it is much easier for us to attain the appropriate level of *teshuvah*.

Yom Kippur is the most auspicious day of the year for repentance. We must realize, however, that Hashem is always calling us: festival or not, day or night. It all depends on our willingness to absorb Hashem's great light. We can compare this to a radio station: There may be some times when the reception is better than others — inclement weather may account for poor reception — yet the broadcast is "on the air" at all times. One who puts in that extra effort, one who works at getting the clearest reception, can hear Hashem's words even under difficult conditions. By the same token, one who "tunes out" cannot receive broadcasts, even under the most favorable conditions.

The above applies not only to times of sanctity (Yom Kippur, festivals, etc.) but to places of sanctity as well. The Torah tells us: וְזָנָה אַחֲרֵי אֱלֹהֵי נֵכַר הָאָרֶץ — *"The people will stray after the gods of the foreigners of the Land"* (*Devarim* 31:16). Do you think that, God forbid, there is a separate god for *chutz la'aretz* (places outside the Holy Land)?

Ibn Ezra, in his own inimitable style, tells us, "We all know that Hashem is One — the difference will come from those who receive His word." It is quite obvious that Hashem is also God in *chutz la'aretz*; in the Land of Israel, however, the heart is more open to absorb Hashem's light. Is Hashem any different in *Eretz Yisrael* than in *chutz la'aretz*? No, it is we who are different! It is easier for us feel sanctity in *Eretz Yisrael*. Similarly, we are more receptive in Yerushalayim than in the rest of *Eretz Yisrael*, and more so in proximity to the Kotel than in the rest of Yerushalayim. Speedily in our day, the best reception for this holiness will be on the wavelength of *Har HaBayis*.

The above, however, is only the means to help us absorb this sanctity. One who seals off his heart will not be reached by means of any sanctified times or places. The wicked Titus stood in the *Kodesh HaKodashim*, while Rav and Shemuel stood in distant Bavel. Which of them achieved a higher level of sanctity? Certainly Rav and Shemuel! They may have been a great distance away, yet their hearts were *kodesh kodashim*. Sages throughout the generations were able to receive the word of Hashem, even while living in Bavel, Vilna, Morocco, and Japan. Had they moved to Israel, they would have absorbed still more as their hearts opened up to the holy environment. Titus, even while standing in the *Kodesh HaKodashim*, remained a Roman through and through, and the awesome ground on which he stood was unable to affect him in the slightest.

TAKING ADVANTAGE OF HEAVENLY GIFTS

WE HAVE JUST presented Meiri's opinion regarding the role of Yom Kippur in attaining *teshuvah*. In addition, there is another explanation that we have discussed elsewhere — that Yom Kippur has its own unique ability to bring about atonement when accompanied by *teshuvah* (see *Michtav MeEliyahu*, vol. II, p. 96 for Rav Dessler's profound understanding of Maharal; see also p. 101 for his explanation of the dispute between Rebbi and the Sages regarding whether Yom Kippur atones even without *teshuvah*). No matter which approach we take, whether we say Yom Kippur has the unique power to effect *teshuvah* or whether Yom Kippur only aids one in opening his heart to *teshuvah*, we must keep in mind a fundamental axiom in our relationship with Hashem: The more means and assistance a person is given to absorb Hashem's holiness (e.g. sacred places and times), the more this will count against him in the event that he neglects to take advantage of it.

The Creator of the world gave you a golden opportunity for spiritual elevation, and yet *"You have cast Me behind your back!"* (*Melachim* I, 14:9). Imagine! You were given this incredible gift and you did not utilize it! It would be understandable if you were living in a faraway place where holy books were unavailable and you had nothing from which to learn. What could we expect from you? But someone living in *Yerushalayim*, surrounded by sanctity and holiness? A person with such opportunities will have a lot to answer for!

We were given *Eretz Yisrael* to facilitate our *avodas Hashem*, we were given *Yerushalayim* to inspire us, and we were given Yom Kippur in order to open our hearts to *teshuvah*, to penetrating *teshuvah*, to *teshuvah* which we hope will permanently alter our lives. One who does not repent on this holy day, God forbid, has taken the tools of his defense and transformed them into evidence for the prosecution to use against him! If the Divine Spirit has come down from Heaven and has not been absorbed, it will return from whence it came and become a tool in the hands of the accuser. You have merited concluding the year (something thousands were unable to do); you have reached this awesome day during which the heart trembles — how could you not even absorb any of this light? How could you emerge from Yom Kippur as empty as you entered? Hashem made Himself available to you during these days — He opened up a "branch" right in your vicinity and instructed His prophet to post a sign that boldly displays the words:

> "Seek Hashem when He can be found."
> (*Yeshayahu* 55:6)

Under this sign, *Chazal*'s explanation is displayed for the benefit of all who did not understand the prophet's words: *"During the* Aseres Yemei *Teshuvah, I receive everyone"* (*Rosh Hashanah* 18a). How can you pass by such a sign in total apathy?

ERETZ YISRAEL IS A DIVINE GIFT

THIS IDEA THAT wasted spiritual energy becomes a weapon for the prosecution is not merely an abstract concept, but takes place in actuality. Ramban tells us that the Heavenly Tribunal takes this into account. According to Ramban, Sodom was no worse than many other cities of the world. The one difference that led to Sodom's destruction and not to the destruction of the other cities was its location. Sodom is in the Land of Israel. It is here, in the Land of Hashem, where there exists a greater ability to reach the Almighty, where Hashem's reaction to not availing oneself of this opportunity is immediate. Even though the people of Sodom were not Jewish (what did they know of the sanctity of the Land of Israel?), we see that more is expected from anyone who resides in the Holy Land. Even a non-Jew has the ability, and in fact the obligation, to absorb something from its sanctity.

If we stop for a moment to reflect on the sin of the דּוֹר הַפְּלָגָה — the Generation of the Dispersal — we can understand it in a profound way. It appears that the Divine plan was for all the descendants of Noach to become unified as one nation. Following the flood, all the nations were to go to *Eretz Yisrael* and there be transformed into the nation of Hashem. From *Eretz Yisrael*, they were to spread out and populate the entire world, "drawing along" with them the sanctity of the Land. The entire world would thus be "conquered" and imbued with the holiness of *Eretz Yisrael*. The first sin that generation committed was that they settled in Bavel, rather than in Israel. The only person who rejected this choice and made the journey to *Eretz Yisrael* was Avraham Avinu. We see from here that even a non-Jew is endowed with the ability to absorb holiness from the Land of Israel.

Ramban (commentary on *Vayikra* 18:25) continues in this manner to explain what happened to the Kuttim whom Sancheriv brought with him to *Eretz Yisrael*. Upon arrival, they continued to worship *avodah zarah* as was the custom in their own country, until lions suddenly emerged and began to kill them. Sancheriv's "advisors on Kutti affairs" then informed him of what was happening to the Kuttim that he had exiled to Shomron, adding that this phenomenon occurred because: לֹא יָדְעוּ אֶת מִשְׁפַּט אֱלֹקֵי הָאָרֶץ — *"they do not know the law of the God of the Land"* (Melachim II 17:26).

To us it is clear that the God of the Land is also the God of *chutz la'aretz*. The prophet, however, used this expression because in *Eretz Yisrael*, Hashem is revealed in far greater force. Although *avodah zarah* is one of the seven Noachide Laws forbidden to all peoples at all times, even in Kutta, they were not punished until they arrived in *Eretz Yisrael*. In the Holy Land, they were punished immediately, because the Land cannot tolerate those who worship *avodah zarah*. You may ask, What does it mean that the Land cannot tolerate it? Is the Land not mere earth? Yes, it is nothing but earth, but one who stands on this ground has the ability to absorb the Godly light. One who does not take advantage of this opportunity is guilty of an offense severe enough to bring about a plague of lions.

Therefore we, as residents of the Land of Hashem, must act with extra caution and take advantage of the great opportunity we were given to cleave to the Almighty. On Yom Kippur at *Minchah* we read the section of the Torah dealing with illicit relationships. Many reasons have already been given for this particular reading; perhaps we can offer an additional explanation. The *parashah* ends with the *pasuk*: וְלֹא תָקִיא הָאָרֶץ אֶתְכֶם בְּטַמַּאֲכֶם אֹתָהּ — *"Let not the Land disgorge you for having contaminated it"* (*Vayikra* 18:28). As we read these words in shul, Yom Kippur is nearing its end, and we are faced with our last opportunity to do *teshuvah* under the ideal conditions this holy day affords. Therefore, in order to awaken man before his judgment is finally sealed, this *pasuk* — one of the harshest in the Torah — is read at this juncture. In addition to the threat of exile — a very severe punishment in its own right, it contains an allusion to what we have just discussed — our obligation to take advantage of all the spiritual gifts Hashem has given us, including our residence in the Holy Land!

TORAH — THE GREATEST GIFT OF ALL

SINCE WE ARE on the subject of not neglecting gifts from Hashem, we cannot but be reminded of that most precious gift of all — the Torah! Can one possibly think of a greater gift? We have come to the understanding that a great gift that is not taken advantage of is transformed, God forbid, into an accusation against us. This is the *Baraisa's* meaning when it says:

> *Every day a Heavenly Voice goes forth from Mount Chorev, proclaiming and saying: "Woe to mankind for their disdain of the Torah," for he who does not occupy himself with the Torah is called "rebuked," as it is written: "As a golden ring in the snout of a swine, so is a fair woman without discretion"* (*Mishlei* 11:22).
>
> (*Avos* 6:2)

The *pasuk* quoted in the *Baraisa* falls exactly in line with what we have just been saying. It is comparable to one who takes a precious piece of pure gold jewelry and, rather than use it to adorn royalty, places it on the nose of a creature who will without doubt make it filthy with garbage. *Chazal* continue by comparing the Torah to a *"Beautiful woman, one who is lovely and gracious, but in our eyes she is* saras ta'am — *distasteful."* In our eyes she is so ugly that everyone distances himself from her and has no desire to marry her.

No one takes the trouble to derive any benefit from the precious life's treasure found in the Torah. The piece of jewelry and the beautiful woman are good analogies for that which is lost by *bittul Torah*. Rather than taking advantage of the gift of Torah to glorify countless worlds, it is neglected, left on the bookshelf, until such a day when it shall fall into the hands of those who would destroy it with their distorted commentaries.

This heavenly accusation is perpetual and never-ending: *"Every day the Heavenly Voice goes forth"* — just as the gift is infinite, so too the potential claim against us is never-ceasing. When *Chazal* said *"every day"*, they must surely have included *bein ha-zemanim*! The awesome day of Yom Kippur is immediately followed by the *bein ha-zemanim* vacation. It is true that we need to regain our strength, but we must realize that even the most *machmir* opinions permit learning at this time — in fact it is highly recommended! How can it be that we conclude our use of the precious gift of Yom Kippur with plans for wasting the gift of Torah during the next twenty days?

In addition to these gifts that we have mentioned — Yom Kippur, *Eretz Yisrael*, and the Torah — there is another gift that Hashem has given us, one that unfortunately too few merit — that is the yeshiva. Compared to the rest of the world, the yeshiva is a place where we are more receptive to holiness. Absorbing sanctity is made easier in a place where everyone is learning and *daven*ing, where the very atmosphere is imbued with fear of Heaven and striving for spiritual growth. One who does not take advantage of the opportunity to learn in a yeshiva will never know what it means to rise above the trivialities of this world.

Unfortunately, even with all the yeshiva has to offer, heaven and earth can testify that it is possible to waste one's time there as well! One who seals his heart from absorbing its holiness, such that רֹאשׁוֹ וְרֻבּוֹ — his head and most of his body — are outside the yeshiva, will certainly not derive any benefit from this wonderful, heavenly gift. In general, however, it is very difficult not to be positively influenced by a yeshiva; no matter how one views it, the atmosphere inside it is far, far better than that on the outside.

YOM KIPPUR — MICROCOSM OF THE WORLD TO COME

WE ONCE MENTIONED that if we analyze *Chazal*'s definition of the Next World, we will be able to see in it the essence of Yom Kippur.

> *The Next World is not like this world. In the Next World there is no eating, nor drinking, nor propagation, nor business, nor jealousy, nor hatred, nor competition, but the righteous sit with their crowns on their heads, feasting on the brightness of the Divine Presence.*
>
> (*Berachos* 17a)

The tenth of Tishrei is מֵעֵין עוֹלָם הַבָּא — a microcosm of the Next World! In order to feel this, however, we are required to alter an attitude we have possessed since childhood. We need to move our center of gravity from the prohibition against eating and drinking to *"feasting on the brightness of the Divine Presence."* The affliction we undergo on Yom Kippur shall in itself become our rejoicing on this day. We must feel how good it is not to need to ask "What's for dinner?" and to be able to distance ourselves from our physical needs, instead concentrating on the spiritual concerns of devotion to Hashem. At the end of this great day, during those few moments of purity when we feel enveloped in spiritual majesty, we must keep in mind the pain of our soul, that princess within us, whose "freedom" is coming to an abrupt end.

YESHIVA — MICROCOSM OF THE DAYS OF THE *MASHIACH*

THERE IS, HOWEVER, a small consolation that we can offer our soul. There is a place that may not be a microcosm of the Next World, but it certainly is a model of the days of the *Mashiach* — the yeshiva! This similarity is true of every day of the year. Rambam (*Hilchos Melachim* 12:4) writes that the righteous desire the days of *Mashiach* only to be able to live in peace and serve Hashem. Hashem has created the yeshivos in order that there be a place in this world that perpetually demonstrates the days of *Mashiach*, serving as a sort of "permanent exhibition". The yeshiva is that place where one has no financial or material worries, a place where one is always free to bask in the light of Torah and mitzvos — the very embodiment of the days of the *Mashiach*!

Although there are differing opinions as to the specific nature of יְמוֹת הַמָּשִׁיחַ, the days of *Mashiach*, all agree that there will no longer be the constant mad pursuit of money nor the rush to hear a news update every hour. Someone who has difficulty understanding how it can be called a "perfect world" if there are no stock market reports or news flashes should perhaps be a little worried about the days of the *Mashiach*, because during that period there will be no other way to spend time — that precious gift from Hashem — except by being involved in Torah and mitzvos!

Blessed is he who has the merit of spending Yom Kippur in our yeshiva, which is as close as Jews can get to the site of the *Beis HaMikdash*. Such a person receives a double taste of the Next World.

The twenty-five hours of this Divine gift are a wonderful opportunity to remove ourselves from the burdens of our physical bodies and to drill into our hearts: שִׁוִּיתִי ה' לְנֶגְדִּי תָמִיד — "*I have set Hashem before me always*" (*Tehillim* 16:8). With this quote,

Rama begins his work on the *Shulchan Aruch* and adds: *"This is a great rule of the Torah and of the positive attributes of the righteous who always walk before Hashem."*

Those who strive to make use of the heavenly gifts and to be counted among the *"righteous who always walk before Hashem"* will certainly benefit כִּי בַיּוֹם הַזֶּה יְכַפֵּר עֲלֵיכֶם לְטַהֵר אֶתְכֶם מִכֹּל חַטֹּאתֵיכֶם לִפְנֵי ה' תִּטְהָרוּ — *"For on this day He shall provide atonement for you to cleanse you; from all your sins before Hashem you shall be purified."* Amen.

SICHAH ELEVEN
CHUKKAS OLAM
(TURNING BACK THE CLOCK)

WHAT IS THE MEANING OF *CHUKKAS OLAM*?

PARASHAS ACHAREI MOS describes the Yom Kippur service. At its conclusion the Torah presents a précis of sorts: וְהָיְתָה זֹּאת לָכֶם לְחֻקַּת עוֹלָם לְכַפֵּר עַל בְּנֵי יִשְׂרָאֵל מִכָּל חַטֹּאתָם אַחַת בַּשָּׁנָה — *"This shall be to you an eternal decree to bring atonement upon the Children of Israel for all their sins once a year"* (*Vayikra* 16:34).

The entire Yom Kippur service, including the offerings of the bull, the two goats, and the *Ketores* that is brought in the *Kodesh HaKodashim*, as well as the sprinkling of the blood within the *Heichal*, is described by the Torah as *chukkas olam*, an eternal decree or statute. The term *chukkim*, as opposed to *mishpatim*, implies mitzvos whose reasoning lies beyond the grasp of our limited human intellect. Let us attempt to clarify what specific part of this service is indeed beyond our grasp.

From the expression *chukkas olam*, *Chazal* learn that if a single detail is omitted, atonement is not achieved. *Chok*, by definition, implies that every detail must be carried out exactly as commanded. We know, for example, that two goats are required, and a lottery determines which one is chosen for Hashem and which goes to *Azazel*. Had there not been a stipulation requiring adherence to each detail, we might have thought that if only one goat was available, a lottery could be held to determine if the lone goat were to be for Hashem or for *Azazel*. The *halachah*, however, is that without that second goat, the entire service is invalidated, for the Torah mandates the presence of two goats. (There is a dispute in the Gemara regarding precisely which details, if omitted, invalidate the entire service).

This explanation clarifies for us the term *chukkas olam* as it relates to the Yom Kippur service. The question that remains, however, is why the Torah saw fit to repeat this expression another three times. In addition to the *pasuk* quoted above, we read: *"This shall remain for you a* chukkas olam: *In the seventh month on the tenth of the month, you shall afflict yourselves"* (Vayikra 16:29). Two *pesukim* later the Torah tells us: *"It is a Shabbos of complete rest for you, and you shall afflict yourselves,* chukkas olam,*"* followed by: *"You shall not do any work; it is a* chukkas olam *throughout your generations in all your dwelling places"* (Vayikra 23:31).

What is this phrase trying to teach us?

DOES THE CHOK REFER TO THE SA'IR LA'AZAZEL?

AT FIRST GLANCE we might think that it is the *sa'ir la'Azazel* that is the *chok* aspect of Yom Kippur — for this bears the least resemblance to any of the other sacrificial offerings. In the beginning of *Parashas Chukkas*, Rashi tells us that the *sa'ir la'Azazel* is one of the mitzvos for which the Satan and the nations of the world mock the Jewish People, calling them "illogical". How is it possible, they ask, that this goat atones for and purifies the Jewish People, yet the person who accompanies it to the desert, who assists in this purification process, becomes impure? Just as the *parah adumah* is referred to as a *chukkas haTorah* because those involved in the purification process become impure, so too the *sa'ir la'Azazel* is referred to as *chukkas olam*.

There are many aspects of this ceremony that are beyond our comprehension: Why is the goat sent to the desert and thrown from the top of the cliff? How can it atone for all who repent — for transgressions both severe and not so severe, both those transgressed intentionally and not intentionally? There is one answer to all these questions: This is the way Hashem determined things! The Almighty, in His infinite kindness, has given us this opportunity for atonement. We follow His commandments and believe in their effect — even if we do not fully understand how they work.

Our Sages allude to this idea that the goats constitute the *chok* aspect of Yom Kippur in their discussion of the *sa'ir la'Azazel*: *"Now perhaps you will say that they are empty acts."* On this, Rashi explains, *"You may wonder what atonement can there be by sending it away, what [attribute] does this cliff have that will help."* The Gemara responds: *"'I am Hashem'* (*Vayikra* 18:4)*, I, Hashem, have decreed it and you have no right to ponder them"* (*Yoma* 67b).

I have always had difficulty understanding why *Chazal* find the *sa'ir* and the *parah adumah* more difficult to comprehend than other sacrifices. Do we really understand how other *korbanos* atone for transgressions? The Torah decreed: *"For it is the blood that atones for the soul"* (*Vayikra* 17:11), meaning that the moment the blood is sprinkled upon the *mizbe'ach*, atonement is achieved. Is a *chatas* or an *asham* therefore more logical to us? Just as the Creator decreed that sprinkling blood upon the *mizbe'ach* of the *Mikdash* atones, He decreed that the sprinkling of the ashes of the *parah adumah* purifies and the sending of the *sa'ir la'Azazel* atones. Are any of us able to comprehend the *sa'ir la'Hashem*? Can we grasp why the *kohen gadol* specifically sprinkles once on top and seven times down below (as described in *Yoma* 85b), and why not ten times?

The Kabbalists may have fathomed the way in which atonement is achieved. Ibn Ezra wrote to a certain individual who inquired as to the meaning of the *sair la'Azazel* that he would reveal to him part of the secret behind the name *Azazel* and its implications when he reached the age of thirty-three. Most of you here have not yet reached that age and maybe still have a chance, but for those who have not merited understanding the hidden worlds, the reason is quite simple: The rationale for the *sa'ir la'Azazel* is because Hashem commanded it to us!

It therefore seems unclear why the *sa'ir la'Azazel* is considered more difficult to comprehend than other *korbanos*. Ramban was bothered by this difficulty and he explained that the mockery of the nations stems from the unique method of this offering. The *sa'ir* is sent from the top of a cliff in the desert — outside of the *Beis HaMikdash*. The *parah adumah*, too, is slaughtered and burned outside the *Chatzer*. From the perspective of the gentiles, this is not so unusual — for their sacrifices are offered: עַל הֶהָרִים הֶהָרִים וְעַל הַגְּבָעוֹת וְתַחַת כָּל עֵץ רַעֲנָן — *"on the high mountains and on the hills and under every leafy tree"* (*Devarim* 12:2), and they therefore conclude that since Jewish law strictly forbids any sacrifice outside the confines of the *Beis HaMikdash*, *Am Yisrael* is now following in the ways of the non-Jews, and, according to Ramban, this is the reason for their mockery.

This may explain why the nations of the world find this practice peculiar, but why should we have trouble understanding it? We know that everything is a decree from the King. We know that the *sa'ir la'Azazel* and the *parah adumah* are not any more of a *chok* than other offerings. It cannot be, as we attempted to explain, that the *chukkas olam* emphasized on this Day of Judgment is the *sa'ir la'Azazel*. If so, our original question remains: Why does the Torah emphasize that Yom Kippur is a *chok*; what part of it classifies it as a *chok*?

YOM KIPPUR IS BEYOND HUMAN COMPREHENSION

IT IS THE whole concept of Yom Kippur that is beyond our understanding! There can be no greater *chok* than a day that atones, a day that contradicts everything that we are accustomed to during the rest of the year.

First and foremost, we must keep in mind that the distinction between a *chok* and a *mishpat* (a *mishpat* being something that we understand, whereas a *chok* is something we cannot) only exists as a byproduct of our limited intellectual capacities. For Avraham Avinu, for example, all the mitzvos were clear and easily understood, whereas we do not even have a sufficient understanding of the *mishpatim*. The Torah testifies that Yom Kippur is deserving of the description *chukkah*, for the spiritual value of the day is something that is beyond human comprehension.

The concept of *teshuvah* contradicts the regular order of the world. Anything a person does affects either the present or the future. For example, a criminal can be imprisoned from today onwards; money can be collected from someone now or later. Legally, a house can be sold and the sale will take effect some time in the future, but in no way can our actions of today have any influence on the past. A marriage, for example, cannot take effect retroactively. Is there anything we can do now that will retroactively affect what has already taken place?

Teshuvah is capable of doing just that! When we repent out of love (*teshuvah me'ahavah*), we are moving backwards in time and transforming our past sin into a mitzvah. Even one who repents out of fear of God (*teshuvah me'yirah*) retroactively transforms his intentional sin, even one which is punishable by *kareis*, into an unintentional sin in the eyes of Heaven (see *Yoma* 6b).

YOM KIPPUR — THE ULTIMATE CHOK

THE DAY SET aside for this amazing, incredible phenomenon is Yom Kippur. Rambam tells us, *"Yom Kippur is the time for everyone to repent...therefore all are obligated to repent and confess their sins on Yom Kippur"* (Hilchos Teshuvah 2:7). Two conditions are required in order to effect these changes to our past, he says:

1. Repentance
2. Being alive during Yom Kippur

Even sincere *teshuvah* on its own cannot atone unless one experiences some moments of this great day (with the exception of one who is guilty of not performing positive commandments). The moment Yom Kippur begins, the *teshuvah* goes into effect. During that moment, the inexplicable happens — the past is rewritten!

We have discussed elsewhere the relationship between the size of a gift and the greatness of the charge against one who neglects to take advantage of it. Yom Kippur is an auspicious time of forgiveness that has been bestowed upon us as a gift. Meiri (in *Rosh Hashanah* 16b) goes so far as to say that one who is negligent and does not repent during this day has no share in Hashem, the God of Israel.

While the entire world is run within a framework of time (the Torah even opens with a point in time — "*Bereishis* — in the beginning"), *teshuvah* hovers above time. While time moves forward, *teshuvah* works against this forward tide. This is one reason why *Chazal* tell us that *teshuvah* was one of seven things that were created prior to the creation of the world (*Pesachim* 54a), because *teshuvah* cannot have a place within the time framework of this world as we know it.

Yom Kippur is the source of the wellspring of *teshuvah*. Our ability to repent throughout the year stems from the power of Yom Kippur. From this perspective, Yom Kippur is the *chok* of all *chukkim*. Hashem took a limited period of time within the dimension of time — the tenth day of Tishrei — and gave it the power to work against the framework of time, of which it is a part. Can there be a greater *chok* than this? Is this not a *chukkas olam*, the ultimate *chok* in the *olam*, the world?

YOM KIPPUR — SPECIAL DAY OF HASHEM

יָמִים יֻצָּרוּ וְלֹא (וְלוֹ – קרי) אֶחָד בָּהֶם.

Though they will be fashioned through many days, to Him they are one.

(*Tehillim* 139:16)

Our Sages explain this verse in *Tehillim* as referring to the Yom Kippur of the Jewish People (*Tanna d'vei Eliyahu Rabbah*). The One Who created everything, created many *yamim*, days in the year, yet He chose וְלוֹ אֶחָד — one for Him, from among them.

Chukkas Olam (Turning Back the Clock)

That day is Yom Kippur for the Jewish People (for the other nations it is no different than any other day — the sun sets and rises as usual, the birds go on chirping, and to all appearances the day follows the course of nature). But for Hashem this day on which His children draw close to Him is a greater source of satisfaction than all the other days that He created.

The word *ve'lo* in this *pasuk* is read as if it were spelled וְלוֹ, meaning "and for him" – referring to Hashem. It is written, however, וְלֹא אֶחָד בָּהֶם — "and not one of them." This can be interpreted as referring to the perspective of the Jewish People. The fact is, if a person really wishes to do *teshuvah*, there is no distinction between Yom Kippur and any other day of the year. In all the days He created, the Almighty waits for man, וְלֹא — and He does not lock the door of repentance on אֶחָד בָּהֶם — any one of them. On Yom Kippur, however, the loving Father created a simplified way for his children to return. This idea that Yom Kippur has capabilities beyond the boundaries of the laws of time is what the Torah is emphasizing with the repeated expression *chukkas olam*.

In order that our discussion not seem like a *chukkah* that we are incapable of understanding(!), let us try to explain how this incredible wonder takes effect. (In fact, it is incumbent upon us to comprehend to the best of our abilities all the *chukkim* of the Torah).

When all is said and done, Yom Kippur exists within the framework of time — it is not a spiritual concept that hovers above the days of the year. Yom Kippur is one unit within the 365 established units of the year: *"On the tenth day of this month it is the Day of Atonement"* (*Vayikra* 23:27). It is a day within a clearly delineated block of time — it occurs after the ninth of Tishrei and before the eleventh. Our Sages have taught: *"Hashem has nothing in His world but the four amos of Halachah"* (*Berachos* 8a). We must, therefore, attempt to understand what area of Halachah is ascribed to the tenth of Tishrei. What is the source of the great power of this day?

UPROOTING A VOW

THE BASIS FOR all this is the concept of feeling regret for the past. This is not a new concept, but one that we are already familiar with from laws pertaining to vows. Let us assume that a person took upon himself a particular vow, only to discover that fulfillment of his vow causes pain and anguish to his wife. In order to annul this vow, he is obligated to go to a *chacham* or to create his own *beis din* of three people (see *Shulchan Aruch* 228:1), who will then search for an opening (a *petach*) in order to nullify his vow. One of the questions he may be asked is: Had you known that this would cause anguish to your wife, would you still have taken this vow? If he answers in the negative, the three then tell him *mutar lach* — it is permitted to you, and the vow is annulled. In other words, it became clear that the person, when he made the vow, did not sufficiently consider the situation from all its different perspectives. Now that he sees it more clearly, he regrets what he did in the past. This regret has the halachic power to turn the clock back to the moment he made the vow and to uproot the basis upon which the vow stands.

EXPERIENCING TRUE REMORSE

THIS IDEA OF regret, of uprooting what was done in the past, is the basis for *teshuvah*. It is not sufficient to declare that I will not sin in the future; I must have total regret for what I have done in the past. I am announcing today that my sin was a total error. If it was committed unintentionally then it certainly was in error, but even regarding sins committed intentionally, it is now clear to me that I was totally mistaken in my behavior. I did not sufficiently appraise the situation, with all its many facets. I did not properly understand the holiness of the Torah and the holiness of the mitzvos; I did not sufficiently understand Hashem and I was lax in my obligation to totally surrender myself to Him. Perhaps if I had been asked then, I would have said that this was not an error and that I truly possessed the intent to commit this sin. Nevertheless, in light of the knowledge that I have gained today and based on my reflections and the feelings that have awakened within me, it is clear to me that had I been on the spiritual level I am on now, I would not have sinned.

The new knowledge I have acquired serves as an opening to uproot my sinful action; it shakes the very foundations from which the sin sprouts. And furthermore, because it is due to this sin in particular that I have now come to realize the greatness of the Creator, the sin itself is transformed retroactively into something praiseworthy, and then it is transferred over to the side of merit.

In truth, although we have attempted to make Yom Kippur more understandable to us, it still remains a *chok*. It still remains a unique and incredible *chesed* that Hashem has given us. The sin we committed has disappeared and in its place there now stands a beautiful mitzvah! The more intentional our sin was, the more *hiddurim* this new mitzvah has.

In earthly law, *teshuvah* has no practical application. If one testified while having the status of a *gazlan* (a robber, whose testimony is invalid) and he then repents, his testimony is not then retroactively accepted, because in human terms, time is significant — one cannot change what has occurred in the past. In the heavenly courts, however, this man is viewed as if he had never stolen!

People may whisper and speak behind the back of a person who was found guilty of embezzling public funds, yet *"Hashem sees into the heart"* (*Shemuel* I, 16:7) and knows that he repented out of love (*teshuvah me'ahavah*). Hashem thus views him as a totally righteous person — as one who is pure from all sin, who has been very careful not to touch anything that did not belong to him!

SIN DOES NOT PAY

TO REACH THIS level of *teshuvah* requires a very profound and deep regret. This requires that we truly experience remorse. It is the need to feel intensely contrite that makes it necessary for us to recite in our *viduy*: סַרְנוּ מִמִּצְוֹתֶיךָ וּמִמִּשְׁפָּטֶיךָ הַטּוֹבִים וְלֹא שָׁוָה לָנוּ — *"We have turned away from Your commandments and from Your good laws, but to no avail."*

In order to fully understand the implication of our *viduy*, it is essential that we understand each and every word of this sentence. *"To no avail"* means that nothing whatsoever was gained by our sinning. There are times when a person feels that what he did was not right, but that at least from a certain perspective, there was some advantage to it. If this is how we recite our *viduy*, we must come to a total halt immediately! We may not proceed until it is clear to us beyond any shadow of a doubt that anything we perceived as a gain was nothing but a figment of our imagination. In reality, all that was "gained" was trouble.

As long as the person does not recognize this, as long as his regret does not shake the very ground on which the sin is standing, the past cannot be affected. The sin will continue to sit there as it did yesterday and the day before. As long as a person feels that he stands to gain from his corrupt ways, yet he has no choice but to repent, he does not demonstrate sufficient regret and has not done *teshuvah*. *"To no avail"* means that even if there appears to be a gain from the sin, we must realize that it will be canceled out by losses that will occur in the future — or vice versa, if I "lost out" by doing a mitzvah, it will all balance out with the reward that is awaiting me (*Avos* 2:1). There will never be any gain from sin or from neglecting to perform a mitzvah that we are required to do. The future will prove this, either in this world or the next.

Without this basic understanding, all the *viduy* and *selichos* of the ten days of *teshuvah* and Yom Kippur have no value. They are simply a waste of time. Rather than beating the heart, we must first "beat out" the misunderstandings and misconceptions in our heads!

A TRAITOR IN THE TEMPLE

OUR SAGES BRING a *midrash* (*Bereishis Rabbah* 65:18) that beautifully illustrates man's sudden insight when he perceives with his entire being that it was all *"to no avail"*:

> *When the enemies of the Jewish nation wished to enter the* Beis HaMikdash, *they had greatly feared the sanctity of the place.*
>
> *They knew that even a* kohen *was forbidden to enter if not for the express purpose of performing his duties. They therefore announced that the courageous person who would be the first to enter and desecrate this holy site would be allowed to keep a vessel of his choice for himself. A traitor named Yossi Meshita got wind of this declaration and decided that this was the realization of his life's dream! He proceeded to enter the* Beis HaMikdash *and remove the golden Menorah from the* Heichal, *imagining how this solid chunk of gold would provide him with livelihood for many years to come. When the enemies saw what he had done, they stopped him, saying they had not intended that such a precious vessel be allowed to fall into the hands of a Jew. However, since he had already "volunteered" to do so, he could enter again and this time whatever he removed would truly be his.*
>
> *Try as they could to persuade him, first by offering him rewards and then by inflicting pain and torture upon him, Yossi Meshita could not be induced to repeat the same sin.*

Why had he suddenly changed his mind? It was very simple. He had suddenly realized that it was all *"to no avail."* The moment they took the Menorah away from him, the moment the glittering gold that blinded him was removed from his hands, a complete metamorphosis took place in his thinking. Something broke down in his view of the world. It was not the holy books that convinced him, not even inspiring *mussar* lectures. With his own eyes he saw that nothing at all is to be gained from sin, even in This World!

As the enemies inflicted pain upon him, he shouted: "Woe, I have angered my Creator!" During those moments anything associated with This World, even pain and suffering, did not affect him at all; he was totally absorbed in the absolute truth he had suddenly discovered. Sin does not pay! The realization that he had erred his whole life by running after the trivialities of This World caused more pain and suffering to him than anything his enemies could do. Since nothing was to be gained from sin, for what had he angered his Creator?

Based on this incident, *Chazal* elucidate the *pasuk*: וַיָּרַח אֶת רֵיחַ בְּגָדָיו — *"He smelled the fragrance of his garments"* (Bereishis 27:27). *"Do not read it as* בְּגָדָיו — *'his clothes', but rather as* בּוֹגְדָיו — *'his traitors'"* (Sanhedrin 37a). Even the traitors among the Jewish People emit a pleasant fragrance when they fully repent by opening their eyes and discovering the falsehoods of this world!

This is the level of regret that a person must reach. If one can come to the realization that there is nothing to be gained by sin, then perhaps the next time he is tempted by a sparkling piece of gold to defile the holiness of his soul, he will overcome his temptation. He has already "been there" — and walked away emptyhanded. Even if someone should try to convince him that although he did not profit the last time, this time he surely will — he should remember Yossi Meshita, the man who knew how to derive a lesson of truth from his life's experience!

THE CHOICE AT THE CROSSROADS

AS WE STAND today before this Day of Judgment, we need to realize that there are two paths before us. One is the *chukkah* aspect of Yom Kippur and repentance. This *chukkah* is lofty, wondrous and beyond our understanding, yet it is firmly entrenched in reality, in that it affects the past, present, and future. This *chukkah* and all that adhere to it are eternal.

The other path, on the other hand, is clear, immediate, and concrete. It tries to entice us with a handful of gold, yet any potential gains are only short-lived. A good look at this path will reveal how limited the gain from sin really is. The sincere regret that comes from this realization will place us firmly on the path to eternity.

SICHAH TWELVE
"SELACH NA AL KAL VA'CHOMER"

WHAT IS WRONG WITH BEING MACHMIR?

ABOUT ONE THOUSAND years ago, in North Africa, there lived a man named Rabbeinu Nissim Gaon, a student of Rav Hai Gaon and one of the *rebbeim* of Rif. A prolific writer, he authored the well-known commentary on the Gemara, *Mafte'ach Man'ulei HaTalmud* — *Key to the Locks of the Talmud* (available in many editions of *Massechtos Berachos*, *Shabbos*, and *Eruvin*). Rabbeinu Nissim is also widely accepted as the author of the *viduy* recited on *Yom Kippur Katan* (which according to Sephardic custom is also included in the repetition of the *Shemoneh Esrei* on Yom Kippur morning).[8]

The latter section of this *viduy* begins:

> *How can I approach You, Hashem my God, what healing can I request of You? I was like the wayward son always doing wrong in Your eyes, as a slave rebelling against his master, and as a student in conflict with his Rav.*

It then goes on to specify a number of transgressions:

> *What You have declared pure, I have declared impure, and what You have declared impure, I have declared pure. What You permitted, I have forbidden, and that which You have forbidden I have permitted.*

---

8. In the *siddur* of Rav Amram Gaon as well as certain *machzorim*, authorship is credited to Rabbeinu Nissim, *rosh yeshivah* of Bavel, probably the grandfather of the Rabbeinu Nissim Gaon referred to above.

It concludes with:

Where you were lenient, I was stringent, and where You were stringent I was lenient.

This last passage requires clarification. Obviously a person who was lenient when he should have been strict needs to confess, but why would being stringent in a circumstance demanding leniency connote an offense? Does the *Shulchan Aruch* not often quote a lenient view yet conclude with the remark that whoever follows the stricter view will be blessed? Why should this necessitate confession?

One possible explanation is that Rabbeinu Nissim was referring to his own world as a *posek*. Perhaps the Rabbi issued a strict halachic ruling when leniency was called for? Although a Rav may encourage people to follow the stricter view when there are two opinions, in a case where the Halachah rules leniently, there is no place for the Rav to impose stringency. He could be causing the person unnecessary hardship, such as additional financial burden or needless physical or emotional suffering, and for this a *posek* must confess and ask for forgiveness.

WHOEVER ADDS, SUBTRACTS

IT WOULD SEEM to me, however, that being unnecessarily *machmir* is more than an offense between man and his fellow man (in the above example, between the Rav and the one seeking counsel); it is a transgression between man and God as well. We must take great care not to distort Hashem's Torah. If the Halachah dictates that something is permitted, we have no right to rule that it is not. Distorting the Torah by being excessively *machmir* is no less an offense than being overly *meikel*. Although *Chazal* tell us that the *pasuk*, *"You shall be holy"* (*Vayikra* 19:2), means we are to sanctify ourselves by refraining from that which is really permitted, Ramban tells us that the application of this mitzvah is limited to specific areas. When there is no reason for creating an additional fence around the Torah, ruling in this manner is a violation of *bal tosif*. In the very same *pasuk* where we are commanded not to detract from the teachings of the Torah, we are also forbidden to add to them: לֹא תֹסִפוּ עַל הַדָּבָר אֲשֶׁר אָנֹכִי מְצַוֶּה אֶתְכֶם וְלֹא תִגְרְעוּ מִמֶּנּוּ — *"You shall not add to the word that I command you, nor shall you subtract from it..."* (Devarim 4:2). Shortly thereafter the Torah repeats this prohibition: אֵת כָּל הַדָּבָר אֲשֶׁר אָנֹכִי מְצַוֶּה אֶתְכֶם אֹתוֹ תִשְׁמְרוּ לַעֲשׂוֹת לֹא תֹסֵף עָלָיו וְלֹא תִגְרַע מִמֶּנּוּ — *"The entire word that I command you, that shall you observe to do, you shall not add to it and you shall not subtract from it"* (Devarim 13:1).

The Vilna Gaon addresses the apparently superfluous repetition of this verse in the following manner: The prohibition in the first *pasuk* is about adding to the 613 mitzvos, while the second *pasuk* forbids adding a specific detail to an already existing mitzvah (for example, if one wishes to take a fifth species on Sukkos).

What would be wrong with demonstrating our gratitude to Hashem by holding a beautiful and rare flower alongside our lulav? From the story of Chavah and the Tree of Knowledge, *Chazal* derive the principle, כָּל הַמּוֹסִיף גּוֹרֵעַ — *"Anyone who adds, subtracts"* (Sanhedrin 29a).

Hashem's commandment was to refrain from eating from the tree. Chavah, out of her own volition, added a prohibition against touching the tree. As we know, the serpent then pushed her into the tree, knowing that when she touched the tree and was not punished, she would then doubt the veracity of the prohibition against eating from it. From this, we see that adding to a mitzvah of the Torah (e.g. prohibiting touching the tree when it was in fact permitted) can actually lead one to violate the Torah (subtracting from the Torah).

In addition, the words *"anyone who adds, subtracts,"* can be understood to mean that if one grows accustomed to adding to the Torah, with time he will begin to feel that he is not obligated to fulfill the Torah's commands in a precise manner. This attitude will eventually lead to his violating precepts of the Torah by subtracting from the mitzvos. This prohibition against distorting the words of the Torah formed the basis of a halachic ruling of far-reaching historical consequence:

> *Bar Kamtza was bringing a sacrifice from the Caesar to be offered on the* mizbe'ach.[9] *In order to provoke trouble, en route to the* Beis HaMikdash, *Bar Kamtza intentionally blemished the animal, knowing that the Rabbis would not permit it to be offered and this way it would look like the Jews were unwilling to accept the Caesar's sacrifice. R' Zechariah ben Abkulas refused to permit the offering, explaining: "People will then say that blemished animals may be offered on the* mizbe'ach" (Gittin 56a).

This decision at the time was deemed very controversial. Did R' Zechariah not realize that this pronouncement was likely a matter of pikuach nefesh? Was he unaware that Bar Kamtza was planning to report to the Caesar that the Jewish People were insulting him by rejecting his sacrifice? Certainly, preserving Jewish lives would take precedence over the sacrificial laws!

AVOIDING DISTORTION OF THE TORAH SUPERCEDES *PIKUACH NEFESH*

HARAV CHAIM SHMUELEVITZ *zt"l* explained the incident as follows: R' Zechariah's concern was not that people would infer from this incident that it is permitted, in a case of danger to life, to offer animals with blemishes, because *pikuach nefesh* would indeed take precedence in such a case. He was concerned that conclusions would be drawn that the Torah permitted the offering of an animal with a blemish (even if there was no *pikuach nefesh* involved). From here on, the *beis midrash* would reverberate with discussions and analyses of the details of permitting the sacrifice of a blemished animal, and thus the Torah would be distorted

---

9. Bar Kamtza was angry at *Klal Yisrael* and the Rabbis of his generation who, in his opinion, had not reacted fittingly to his being publicly shamed. He therefore set out to get revenge by turning the Caesar against them.

forever! According to R' Zechariah's ruling, avoiding such an everlasting perversion of the Torah supercedes even *pikuach nefesh* (see Hebrew edition of *Sichos leSefer Bereishis*, p. 20, for a discussion of where R' Zechariah erred).

We have learned that the Torah preceded the creation of the world and that all events in history are mentioned or alluded to in the Torah — the Torah is the "map" for all future events. Where, then, does the Torah hint that Bar Kamtza's offering should have been accepted? This event, which, after all, had major repercussions for the Jewish People, as well as the entire world, surely should be alluded to in the Torah.

The logical place to begin our search is in the section dealing with laws regarding offering animals with blemishes (see *Vayikra* 22). The concluding *pasuk* of this section refers to the very subject before us — how we should handle a blemished animal offered by a non-Jew: וּמִיַּד בֶּן נֵכָר לֹא תַקְרִיבוּ אֶת לֶחֶם אֱלֹקֵיכֶם מִכָּל אֵלֶּה — *"From the hand of a stranger you may not offer the food of your God from any of these"* (*Vayikra* 22:25). This means that although during the period of the *bamos* (when altars outside the *Beis HaMikdash* were permitted), a non-Jew was permitted to offer a blemished offering, in the *Mishkan* and in the *Beis HaMikdash* this was forbidden.

The case we are looking for lies in the expression, וּמִיַּד בֶּן נֵכָר — *"and from the hand of a stranger."* מִיַּד, from the hand, implies something that is passed directly from hand to hand. We see this in the phrase, וְכִי תִמְכְּרוּ מִמְכָּר לַעֲמִיתֶךָ אוֹ קָנֹה מִיַּד עֲמִיתֶךָ — *"and when you make a sale to your fellow or acquire from the hand of your fellow"* (*Vayikra* 25:14).

The Gemara tells us: *"The verse refers to something that is acquired by passing it from hand to hand"* (movable, as opposed to immovable, property — *Kiddushin* 26a). In addition we are told, *"He plundered the spear* מִיַּד*, from the hand of the Egyptian"* (*Shemuel* II 23:21). The Gemara derives from this that one is guilty of *gezel*, robbery, only if the item was taken directly from the hand of the owner (*Bava Kamma* 79b).

Would it not, therefore, have been more appropriate in the above case for the Torah to use the expression, וּמֵאֵת בֶּן נֵכָר — from a stranger, meaning that such an offering is forbidden, whether brought directly by the non-Jew or via a messenger? Similarly, וּמֵאֵת עֲדַת בְּנֵי יִשְׂרָאֵל יִקַּח שְׁנֵי שְׂעִירֵי עִזִּים — *"From the assembly of the Children of Israel he shall take two he-goats"* (*Vayikra* 16:5). This teaches us that the *kohen gadol* need not take these two goats directly from the hands of the Jewish People; he may receive them from the people by any available means. By using the expression וּמִיַּד בֶּן נֵכָר, the Torah is hinting to us how to rule in a case that was destined to take place in the future — that involving Bar Kamtza. We are told here that the prohibition against accepting a blemished animal from a non-Jew only applies to one that is personally delivered by the non-Jew. When delivered via a messenger, however, (for this is not מִיַּד בֶּן נֵכָר), we are permitted to receive such an animal — thus Bar Kamtza's offering should have been accepted.

A THIRD EXPLANATION

WE HAVE DISCUSSED some of the pitfalls of acting stringently when one should be lenient. These interpretations, however, would perhaps more appropriately explain the declaration אֶת אֲשֶׁר הִתַּרְתָּ הֶאֱסַרְתִּי — *"That which You have permitted, I have forbidden."*

There is actually a third explanation that would probably shed a more accurate light on the words, *"Where You were lenient, I was stringent."* Being *machmir* when we should not is not only an offense committed by a Rav in his ruling, as suggested in the first explanation above, but even the person being *machmir* on himself has erred. In the second idea that we expanded on above, we said that forbidding that which is permitted is tantamount to creating a new mitzvah that did not previously exist. Being stringent in a case where leniency is called for, on the other hand, does not refer to adding another mitzvah, but to ascribing greater weight to one mitzvah over another. What we will see is that one guilty of such practice has not only erred regarding the mitzvah in question, but in his view of the entire Torah!

KEEPING THINGS IN PROPORTION

MAN IS IMBUED with limited strength. One who is unnecessarily *machmir* in one particular area does so at the expense of another mitzvah. Practically speaking, placing additional physical, mental, or emotional energy or financial resources in an area where it is not called for leaves one with less to use for another mitzvah where it is needed. The Creator gave us a specific amount of strength with which to serve Him. Unnecessary use of these resources in one area detracts from their availability elsewhere, disturbing the relative balance between the components that make up man. We can use a simple example to illustrate this point.

THE KETORES

DURING *SHACHARIS* AND *Minchah*, it is customary to recite the *parashah* dealing with the *Ketores*, the eleven spices which make up the incense offering. The *Baraisa* states: *"If one omits one of all the ingredients, he is liable for the penalty of death"* (*Kerisus* 6a). One who has added sixty-nine *maneh* of *tzarri* instead of seventy has clearly violated this prohibition. But what if instead of seventy *maneh*, seventy-one were used — would this constitute a violation of the precept? From a simple reading of the words of *Chazal*, it would seem that there is nothing wrong with this, since the one making the mixture has not "omitted" anything.

Yet the answer is simple: Adding to the amount of a particular ingredient is just as much forbidden as subtracting from it. The reason is that when one adds to an ingredient, he is altering the proportion of all of the ingredients — he is, in effect, detracting from the other ten components. Had the *Ketores* been made up of a single ingredient and an individual wanted to offer more than what was called for, perhaps the mitzvah would still be fulfilled.

The *Ketores*, however, is composed of eleven ingredients, where each one is relative to the others and affects the entire mixture in a specific manner. The fragrance commanded by the Torah can only result from the synthesis derived from the prescribed amount of each ingredient.

Another example is the singing of the *leviyim* in the *Beis HaMikdash*. Rambam lists the specific number of each musical instrument that accompanied them (see *Hilchos Klei HaMikdash* 3:4). If one were to add more instruments than specified, it would be at the expense of the balance of sound produced by the entire orchestra. The overall sound of the music would be altered.

Similarly, what was Miriam the prophetess guilty of when she claimed, *"Was it only to Moshe that Hashem spoke? Did He not speak to us, as well?"* (*Bemidbar* 12:2). She did not intend to detract from Moshe's worth. However, the statement *"Did He not speak to us as well?"* implies that she presumed herself to be on the level of Moshe. Not to perceive the difference between Moshe Rabbeinu's level and that of all the other prophets is in itself a lessening of his honor!

It is clear, therefore, that one who adds to an ingredient of the *Ketores* will pay for it with his life. This same rule is applicable to other laws of the Torah. The Torah is composed of hundreds of mitzvos which, when combined together, form a unique blend known as *avodas Hashem*, service of the Almighty. Any disturbance to the equilibrium of these mitzvos by being strict where one should have been lenient will result de facto in being lenient where one should have been strict. The terms *chumrah* and *kulah* are relative, and by giving more weight to something with less significance, you will come to view an issue that the Torah regards with stringency as less binding than the *chumrah* that you made up on your own! This idea that being strict where we should be lenient will surely result in being lenient in a situation that requires strictness is an axiom to be applied to our daily lives, because we know that one cannot be stringent in everything. Let us cite a few examples.

LEARNING TORAH

THERE IS NO doubt that the study of Torah is of paramount importance. The Chafetz Chaim calculated that every minute one spends learning is a fulfillment of 200 positive commandments! When one sits down to learn, he is confronted with a wide range of subjects calling for his attention — *Tanach*, Gemara *b'iyun*, Gemara *bekius*, Halachah — these are but a few examples. The number of hours we can devote to this most important mitzvah is limited; our time, therefore, must be properly divided among these many subjects. Spending more time in one area will necessarily be at the expense of time spent in another area. We need to contemplate seriously how to properly prioritize and apportion our time: Should we try to amass as much Talmudic knowledge as possible even at the expense of gaining mastery over *Tanach* — or should we, perhaps, do the opposite? Since every person is unique, it is worthwhile for each individual to discuss his own case with a *talmid chacham*.

CHARITY

WE SEE THE same thing regarding the laws of charity — we are obligated to give *tzedakah*, yet the Gemara cautions us: *"One who lavishes money on charity should not lavish more than a fifth of his assets"* (*Kesubos* 67b). If one is too scrupulous in heeding this warning not to give away too much, he may end up not giving enough. On the other hand, one who gives *tzedakah* with no regard for his financial situation may inadvertently violate other areas of Halachah as a consequence. I know of a family that is very careful to give *ma'aser kesafim* regardless of their monetary situation, but their bank account is in constant overdraft — which may be a violation of the Torah's usury laws because of the interest payments it entails. This is an example of how being extra careful with respect to *tzedakah* (which in and of itself is very praiseworthy) can result in being *meikel* in other mitzvos.

SETTLING THE HOLY LAND

SETTLING THE LAND of Israel is a very important mitzvah. Yet living in a settlement far from the central areas might necessitate leaving yeshiva. Which mitzvah takes priority? Does the mitzvah of *yishuv ha'aretz*, settling the Holy Land, justify the time lost from learning? For decisions such as this, too, one must seek the guidance of a *chacham*.

A person can find many beautiful sayings of our Sages to support his own personal bias! For example, it says *"Settling Eretz Yisrael is equal in importance to all the other mitzvos"* (Sifri, *Re'eh* 12:29). However, it also says, *"Shabbos is equal in importance to all other mitzvos"* (*Yerushalmi, Berachos* 1:5) and *"The mitzvah of tzitzis is equal in importance to all other mitzvos"* (*Nedarim* 25a). Does this mean that someone whose *tzitzis* become invalid on Shabbos may tie on new ones?

We have no right to make decisions on when to be strict or lenient based on a superficial understanding of these sayings. In any case, our personal inclinations can go a long way in influencing our decisions. Since we cannot rely on ourselves to weigh such questions objectively, we must obtain the advice of a *gadol baTorah* in order to establish what really constitutes a mitzvah of greater or lesser severity.

"STRINGENCIES" IN THE SUKKAH

THE STORY IS told of a good Jew who was found eating outside of his *sukkah* on the first night of Sukkos. His neighbors asked him, "What's this?" and he answered, "My wife brought pots into the *sukkah* by mistake, and the *halachah* states explicitly, 'It is forbidden to bring pots into the *sukkah* out of respect for the *sukkah*'" (see *Mishnah Berurah* 639:5–6).

They asked him, "Nu, so does this disqualify the whole *sukkah*?"

He replied "I took my *she'eilah* to the Rav."

"And what did the Rav say?"

"He said it does not invalidate the *sukkah*."

"Nu, so why are you eating outside?"

Answered the good Jew, his whole being suffused with modesty: "I decided to be *machmir*!"

TREATING MITZVOS TOO CASUALLY

UNTIL NOW WE have discussed the issue of being *machmir* where we should be *meikel*. Let us now view the opposite side of the coin — being *meikel* where we should be *machmir*. There are many mitzvos of great significance which are treated too casually. Refraining from *melachah* on *Chol HaMo'ed* is an example of this. *Baruch Hashem*, the situation has improved and there is greater awareness regarding this *halachah* today, yet it is still an area that needs *chizuk*. Many people think that refraining from *melachah* on *Chol HaMo'ed* is a form of piety — a *middas chassidus*, while in fact it is mandated by Halachah.

There are authorities who rule that it is a Torah prohibition, while others opine that it is Rabbinic in nature. (The *Mishnah Berurah* leans towards the former — see the first *Beur Halachah* in *siman* 530). According to the more lenient view, that washing clothes on *Chol HaMo'ed* is "only" a Rabbinic prohibition, we should ask someone who "is accustomed" to washing adult clothing on *Chol HaMo'ed* if he is also "accustomed" to spreading cheese on his chicken? "*Chas ve-shalom*!" He would tremble at the mere thought! But really, what is the difference between doing laundry on *Chol HaMo'ed* and eating chicken and milk together — are they not both Rabbinic prohibitions (*Mishnah Berurah* 534:1)?

SLEEPING AND EATING IN THE SUKKAH

IN A FEW days we will be celebrating the festival of Sukkos. In many parts of *chutz la'aretz*, particularly Northern Europe, the severe cold precludes sleeping in the *sukkah*: *"One who experiences stress is exempt from the mitzvah of* sukkah" (*Sukkah* 25b). Rama, who lived in the frosty climate of Krakow, attempts to justify this custom. Here in the Land of Israel, where the weather is more pleasant during the festival except for the rare occasions when it rains, there is no justification for not sleeping in the *sukkah*. One who feels a little cold can simply don a sweater or use an additional blanket, yet many of those born and raised in the colder climates have become accustomed to the idea that there is "no obligation" to sleep in the *sukkah*. Observing this, many people born in *Eretz Yisrael* draw the conclusion that perhaps this is not such an important mitzvah after all.

Many people (often including those same people who do not sleep in the *sukkah*) are *machmir* not to eat anything outside the *sukkah*. One who learns the *halachah* thoroughly will find that such a person has been *machmir* where he should have been *meikel* and *meikel* where he should have been *machmir*. Dozing off, even for a short nap, is forbidden outside the *sukkah*. Regarding eating, on the other hand, anything that can be classified as אֲכִילַת עֲרַאי (a quick snack — cheese, fruits, even bread less than the size of a כְּבֵיצָה, etc.) may be consumed outside the *sukkah*, while there is no such dispensation for sleeping! It is imperative that we learn the *halachos* rather than simply follow other people's "*minhagim*."

The Gemara tells us: *"Travelers are exempt from the mitzvah of* sukkah" (*Sukkah* 26b). Many people therefore assume that any outing falls under this category and that during a pleasure trip they are permitted to eat and sleep outside the *sukkah*. I heard from the Rav (HaGaon HaRav Shlomo Zalman Auerbach *zt"l*) that this ruling refers only to someone whose circumstances necessitate traveling during the festival (e.g. for a business matter that is permissible during *Chol HaMo'ed*). One who is traveling without a compelling need to do so (even if fulfilling the mitzvah of traversing four *amos* in the Land of Israel) is not exempt from anything to do with the *sukkah*. With regard to eating, it is possible to rely on fruit, meat, or cheese, which are *patur* from *sukkah*; sleeping in the *sukkah*, however, is a halachic requirement.

As a rule of thumb, we have to be vigilant not to invent our own stringencies, but also not to dismiss things too lightly. A guest might be offered food that he suspects may be forbidden — either by Torah law or Rabbinical injunction (it may contain worms, for example). On the one hand, being *machmir* in such a situation is not a simple matter — we have to be very careful not to insult the host or hurt his feelings needlessly, as it is said:

גָּדוֹל כְּבוֹד הַבְּרִיּוֹת — "*Great is [the matter of] respect for one's fellow man.*" On the other hand, food prohibitions are very serious — consuming forbidden foods has a powerful, damaging influence on a man's soul.

In order not to trip while between the two stumbling blocks of *"Where you were lenient, I was stringent,"* and *"where You were stringent I was lenient,"* there are two requirements:

1. It is imperative that we have a thorough and in-depth knowledge of the Halachah. This will aid us in deciding when being strict takes precedence over *k'vod ha-brios* and when it does not, and regarding which Rabbinic prohibitions we can be lenient about and which require stringency. When one is properly prepared, the problem becomes easier to handle.

    The best solution, of course, is to avoid the problem altogether. One who is fully aware that it is forbidden to sleep outside the *sukkah* may postpone his trip to another time, choose a route in which a *sukkah* is available, or among his many belongings pack with him a portable *sukkah* (which can result in his helping others as well). Regarding food served that is of questionable *kashrus*, one must do his utmost to avoid insulting his host. One can prepare in advance excuses and "emergency measures". It is known that when HaRav Eliyahu Lopian *zt"l* was served such food, he would claim that the doctor forbade him to eat it. (He later explained to his students that the doctor he was referring to was Rambam!)

2. Even after an in-depth analysis of the relevant *halachah*, one must be able to assess the situation facing him in order to weigh the specific factors: Does this case fit a particular *halachah* I have learned or is a different law more applicable here?

In addition to our *viduy* for the misdeeds of the previous year, let us plead with the Creator on this Day of Judgment to help us acquire the ability to make better and more reliable decisions in the upcoming year.

SICHAH THIRTEEN
"BEFORE HASHEM YOU SHALL BE PURIFIED"

TWO SPECIAL MITZVOS

IT IS *EREV Yom Kippur*; the spiritual suspense is at its peak. We have reached the culmination after many days of preparation and the day of the sealing of judgment is fast approaching. The Jewish nation tries to "grab" as many mitzvos as it can in order to enter the holy day of Yom Kippur with as much merit as possible. There are two special mitzvos associated with this day, one on the physical plane — the commandment to eat, the other of a more spiritual nature — immersion in a *mikveh*.

THE MITZVAH TO EAT ON *EREV YOM KIPPUR*

WITH RESPECT TO the commandment to eat on *Erev Yom Kippur*, the *Shulchan Aruch* (*Orach Chaim* 604:1) writes that one must eat and have a bigger *seudah* than usual. This means that in addition to partaking of the large main meal, there is a mitzvah to eat throughout the day. Rama adds that one may not even observe a *ta'anis chalom* on *Erev Yom Kippur* (this is a fast one takes upon himself in response to a bad dream, which is even permitted on Shabbos [*Shulchan Aruch, Orach Chaim* 288:4]).

A woman who, in her childhood, lived in the same building as R' Moshe Feinstein *zt"l*, recalled how R' Moshe used to give out candies to the neighborhood children on *Erev Yom Kippur* in an effort to show them the importance of this mitzvah of eating. He specifically chose sucking candies, because they last a long time, thus affording the children the opportunity to fulfill this mitzvah each and every moment the candy remained in their mouths.

EATING IN ORDER TO MERIT A REWARD

THE SOURCE FOR the mitzvah of eating on *Erev Yom Kippur* is found in the verse: וְעִנִּיתֶם אֶת נַפְשֹׁתֵיכֶם בְּתִשְׁעָה לַחֹדֶשׁ בָּעֶרֶב — *"You shall afflict yourselves on the ninth of the month in the evening"* (*Vayikra* 23:32). *Chazal* find this *pasuk* puzzling: *"Now, do we fast on the ninth? Why, we fast on the tenth! But this teaches us that if a person eats and drinks on the ninth, the Torah views it as if he has fasted on both the ninth and the tenth"* (*Berachos* 8b). Would it not have made more sense for the Torah to explicitly command us to eat on *Erev Yom Kippur*? Why the need to derive the mitzvah in such a fashion that it comes out as the equivalent of fasting for two days?

It can be understood as follows: Had the Torah simply told us that we are commanded to eat on the ninth of Tishrei, fulfillment of this mitzvah would not have brought with it such a great reward. What would be so praiseworthy about eating and rejoicing? Does not everyone wish to do so? Although Hashem desires for us to eat on *Erev Yom Kippur,* in His infinite kindness, He referred to this eating as *inuy,* affliction, and thus the reward for eating on *Erev Yom Kippur* is the equivalent to the reward for fasting. The reward for a mitzvah performed through suffering is greater than that performed through physical pleasure (see *Mishnah Berurah* 604:1 and Rashi, *Rosh Hashanah* 9a). Having eaten throughout the day, we can now approach the holy day of Yom Kippur having already "bagged" a mitzvah that carries a great reward.

This explanation would imply that it is a Torah obligation to eat on *Erev Yom Kippur* (so rules Magen Avraham, *Orach Chaim* 570; some authorities, however, claim that the commandment is Rabbinic in nature). In any event, the Torah refers to this eating as *inuy,* and this stems from the great mercy Hashem shows to

His people by seizing any potential opportunity to avail them of a greater reward.

This still does not explain, however, why He commanded us to eat on this day. Do eating and drinking not seem incongruous with the spirit of the *Yamim Nora'im*? Would we not expect to prepare for this crucial holy day by performing a mitzvah of a more serious nature? Yet this is the substance of Hashem's command for the ninth of Tishrei: to eat. We see that it is not only the way the mitzvah is phrased, in terms of affliction, but even this commandment shows us Hashem's kindness. The Creator, prior to sealing His judgment, wishes to aid His children in their effort to tip the scale to the positive side. He chooses the easiest way possible, by rewarding us for an act we would have performed without being commanded. Who would not have thought of eating an extra amount in preparation for the upcoming twenty-five hour fast?

EATING L'SHEM SHAMAYIM

I WOULD LIKE to offer an additional reason for this mitzvah. There is an opinion in the Midrash that the *Akeidas Yitzchak*, the binding of Yitzchak, occurred on Yom Kippur. If this is so, then Avraham and Yitzchak must have set out for their journey on the eighth of Tishrei, as we are told: בַּיּוֹם הַשְּׁלִישִׁי וַיִּשָּׂא אַבְרָהָם אֶת עֵינָיו וַיַּרְא אֶת הַמָּקוֹם מֵרָחוֹק — *"On the third day, Avraham raised his eyes and perceived the place from afar"* (Bereishis 22:4). Halachically, the binding of Yitzchak was parallel to an actual animal offering. Many *halachos* pertaining to *korbanos* in the *Beis HaMikdash* have *Akeidas Yitzchak* as their source (e.g. placing the wood upon the altar, tying the arm and leg of the animal, receiving the blood in the right hand, the prohibition against benefiting from the offering, etc.).

The Gemara tells us that it is a *hiddur mitzvah*, a beautification of the mitzvah, for a *korban* to be as fat as possible. In fact, this *hiddur* even takes precedence over Shabbos. If, for example, a lean animal was sacrificed for the communal offering on Shabbos, when a fatter one was available, the fatter one must now be slaughtered and offered on Shabbos — even though the *korban* was already brought (see *Menachos* 64a and Rambam, *Hilchos Shegagos* 2:15). It was in fulfillment of this mitzvah that Avraham Avinu took so many provisions for the way — in order to fatten up the *korban* (Yitzchak) prior to the *Akeidah*! It is in commemoration of this eating that was exclusively *l'shem Shamayim* that we are commanded to eat a *seudas mitzvah*. (Although Yitzchak ate on the eighth and ninth days of Tishrei, we are only commanded to spend one day commemorating this — the Torah did not wish to create an atmosphere of feasting during the days between Rosh Hashanah and Yom Kippur).

EATING TO STRENGTHEN BODY AND SOUL

RABBEINU YONAH, IN his work *Sha'arei Teshuvah* (*Sha'ar* 4:8–10), provides us with three explanations for the obligation to eat and drink on *Erev Yom Kippur*:

1. Just as other occasions are marked by festive meals, so too is Yom Kippur. Given the prohibition to eat and drink on Yom Kippur, our celebration must take place on *Erev Yom Kippur*.

2. We eat and drink in order to garner sufficient strength for the upcoming fast. Rashi (*Yoma* 81b) explains the *gemara* quoted above, *"The Torah views it as if he has fasted on both the ninth and the tenth,"* that since the eating on *Erev Yom Kippur* provides us with the necessary strength to fast, the fulfillment of the mitzvah of fasting actually begins with our eating on *Erev Yom Kippur*. If we analyze the language used by Rabbeinu Yonah, we will see that the reason he offers for eating on *Erev Yom Kippur* is, "in order that we should have sufficient strength for the vast amount of prayer and supplication of Yom Kippur, and to ponder for ourselves the way in which we must repent."

It is not only during *daven*ing that we must possess clarity of mind in order to concentrate. Yom Kippur is a day of introspection; we have many decisions to make — how we can improve ourselves, what aspect of our behavior is inappropriate, etc. To accomplish this, our concentration must be at its peak.

We fast on Yom Kippur in order to mitigate the excessive physicality of our bodies, so as to strengthen the power of our souls. On Yom Kippur, the soul is given the authority to plan and decide what changes we need to undertake at the outset of the upcoming year. We can only achieve this if we have absolute clarity of thought. Is it conceivable that we are awake and alert the entire year, and on the most crucial day of the year we are drowsy and do not have all of our wits about us? Should it be that the *"one thing I ask of Hashem"* (*Tehillim* 27:4) is "Tell me how many hours are left until the day is over"?!

"How can you sleep so soundly?" (*Yonah* 1:6), cries out the ship's captain in the Book of *Yonah* (which is read as *Haftarah* for *Minchah* on Yom Kippur). We need to hear in these words the voice of the Captain of the universe! He is willing even to descend to the bowels of our ship in an effort to awaken us from our slumber: *"Wake up! Call to your God"* (ibid.).

(There is a practical distinction between these two explanations offered by Rabbeinu Yonah. If we eat in order to celebrate the festive aspect of Yom Kippur, then it is imperative that we partake of foods that we enjoy, which taste good to us. If the purpose is to give us strength and to ease our fast the following day, we must be sure to eat foods that fortify the body.)

3. The third reason offered by Rabbeinu Yonah is related to the theme of celebration mentioned in the first explanation. We demonstrate our joy that the day has finally arrived

when we are forgiven for all our transgressions. By celebrating the forgiving of our sins, we are implicitly declaring how perturbed we are by our misdeeds. During the *seudah*, one who is cognizant of the relief and the happiness he feels that he is about to be rid of the enormous burden of sin will in time come to feel pain for his transgressions.

Yom Kippur presents a dual motif: on the one hand, pain at having sinned, on the other hand, joy at being forgiven. The pain causes us to approach Yom Kippur with a broken heart, out of immense remorse for our actions — how could we have behaved that way throughout the past year? Our contrition at having sinned means that we enter Yom Kippur with fear and trepidation.

נְהַר דִּי נוּר נָגֵד וְנָפֵק מִן קֳדָמוֹהִי אֶלֶף אַלְפִים יְשַׁמְּשׁוּנֵּהּ וְרִבּוֹ רִבְוָן קָדָמוֹהִי יְקוּמוּן.

A stream of fire was flowing forth from before Him, a thousand thousands were serving Him and myriad myriads were standing before Him.

(Daniel 7:10)

One who reads of this great stream of fire emerging from the bodies of the *chayos ha-kodesh* as a result of their awe and fear of Hashem is himself filled with fear. This fear and pain mark the path to repentance, as the prophet tells us: *"With weeping they will come and through supplications I will bring them"* (*Yirmeyahu* 31:8). (Rambam takes this *pasuk* so literally that he rules that Yom Kippur is the only day classified as a *mo'ed* on which *Tachanun* is recited [*Hilchos Tefillah*, end of chapter 5 — although *Hagahos Maimoniyos* records that our custom is not to do so]).

In addition to being a time of fear and trepidation, Yom Kippur is a time of joy — rejoicing that our sins have been erased. We look toward the future, we are overjoyed at the prospect of turning over a new leaf in our relationship with the King of kings, and we are thrilled that the Jewish nation as a whole has been forgiven for its sins. We wear white on this awesome day as a demonstration of our belief that the entire nation will emerge pure and worthy of serving Hashem — this can explain why at the onset of Yom Kippur we recite אוֹר זָרֻעַ לַצַּדִּיק וּלְיִשְׁרֵי לֵב שִׂמְחָה — *"Light is sown for the righteous, and for the upright of heart, gladness"* (*Tehillim* 97:11). Anyone whose heart is in the right place will rejoice on this day — he has achieved his *raison d'être*, that of becoming close to His Creator. Although throughout the year, *"Hashem is close to all who call upon Him"* (*Tehillim* 145:18), on Yom Kippur we are given permission to call out to Hashem five times! Five personal encounters with the Almighty, each of which serves to strengthen this closeness. What a unique opportunity!

This duality of joy and trepidation on Yom Kippur is enacted in the behavior of the *chayos ha-kodesh*: *"The chayos ran to and fro like the appearance of a flash"* (*Yechezkel* 1:14). On the one hand, they run towards the *Shechinah* in an ecstasy of cleaving to Hashem, while on the other hand, their fear causes them to retreat.

CHANNELING OUR PHYSICAL ACTS TO THE SERVICE OF HASHEM

I WOULD VENTURE to say that being commanded to eat on *Erev Yom Kippur* has an additional aspect: to teach us that even our physical needs must become tools with which to serve Hashem. Eating, in this context, symbolizes all the physical pleasures from which we abstain on Yom Kippur, and it is the most central — being the only one that man requires for survival throughout his entire life, both in his youth and in his old age.

It is specifically during this time of year that the Torah takes advantage of the lofty spiritual levels we have attained to teach us this valuable lesson. After having concluded the month of Elul, having just crowned Hashem King on Rosh Hashanah and completed a lengthy period of *selichos* and *tachanunim*, we must learn that even our physical needs must be channeled towards serving Hashem. Our lives, in fact, are a constant struggle between the need to satisfy our bodies and the obligation that every move we make be *l'shem Shamayim*. On this pivotal day, out of our extreme sense of closeness to all that is holy, we teach ourselves how not to let the means become an end. Just as on *Erev Yom Kippur*, when we are anxious about our upcoming judgment, we are not really in the mood to eat and have no appetite, yet we eat because Hashem commanded us to, so should our eating during the entire year also be viewed as a tool with which to better serve Hashem. Would it not be appropriate to recall this prior to sitting down to any meal? Having this in mind on *Erev Yom Kippur* is a good beginning.

One of the sins enumerated in our *viduy* is, "for the sin we have sinned before You with food and drink." Sinning with food and drink is not limited to eating prohibited foods. Eating and drinking simply for pleasure's sake and not for the purpose of facilitating our *avodas Hashem* falls under this category as well. When we partook of our Shabbos meal, was the food so delicious that we lost sight of the fact that this meal was our way of honoring the special day of the King of kings?

Having achieved on *Erev Yom Kippur* the proper attitude towards eating and other physical pleasures, we are now ready to enter the holy day of Yom Kippur itself — a day in which we completely remove ourselves from the physical world. Only after we have totally subjugated our physical bodies to the spiritual world are we able to contemplate the true meaning of life: there is nothing of any consequence or importance in the world, save that which is spiritual. Our soul has no need for anything physical, for our entire existence is only for the purpose of sanctifying His great name and His sovereignty in this world.

"THE MIKVEH OF ISRAEL IS HASHEM"

THE SECOND SPECIAL mitzvah associated with *Erev Yom Kippur* is immersion in a *mikveh*. The source for this mitzvah is not as clear as the commandment to eat (the *Rishonim* referred to this immersion as *tevillas zekeinim*). Although the source is unclear, there are those who are of the opinion that the immersion requires a blessing. Even though the *Tur* and *Shulchan Aruch* do not rule this way (*Orach Chaim* 606:4, *Mishnah Berurah* 17) — and thus our custom is not to say a *berachah* — the *Be'ur Halachah* states that even those who do not generally immerse in the *mikveh* should do so on *Erev Yom Kippur*. According to Shelah, this immersion is of greater importance than all immersions the entire year, while the *Sefer Chassidim* says that one should immerse himself three times — one for *cheit*, one for *avon*, and one for *pesha*, denoting three different types of sins.

Immersion in a kosher *mikveh* symbolizes a new creation — in body and soul. While one's body is under the water, it is as if his physical life has ceased, and when he takes his initial breath upon emerging from the *mikveh*, it is as if he has been given new life. He is like a new being filled with the Godly spirit and purity that permeated the entire world at the dawn of Creation, as it is written, וְרוּחַ אֱלֹקִים מְרַחֶפֶת עַל פְּנֵי הַמָּיִם — *"and the Divine Spirit hovered upon the surface of the waters"* (*Bereishis* 1:2).

R' Akiva refers to the spiritual aspect of this renewal when he says: "Fortunate are you, O Israel! Before whom do you cleanse yourselves? Who cleanses you? Your Father in heaven! As it is stated: *'I will sprinkle pure water upon you and you shall be cleansed'* (*Yechezkel* 36:25) *and it says,* 'מִקְוֵה יִשְׂרָאֵל ה' — *'The* mikveh *of Israel is Hashem'* (*Yirmeyahu* 17:13). *Just as a* mikveh *purifies the contaminated, so does the Holy One, Blessed is He, purify Israel"* (*Yoma* 85b).

Although the simple interpretation of *"mikveh Yisrael Hashem"* is that Hashem is the hope of Israel, the end of the *pasuk* seems to concur with R' Akiva's *derashah* that the Almighty is like a *mikveh*, that body of water in which Israel is purified:

מִקְוֵה יִשְׂרָאֵל ה' כָּל עֹזְבֶיךָ יֵבֹשׁוּ וְסוּרַי בָּאָרֶץ יִכָּתֵבוּ כִּי עָזְבוּ מְקוֹר מַיִם חַיִּים אֶת ה'.

The Mikveh *of Israel is Hashem, may all who forsake You be ashamed, may those who turn aside from my teachings be*

inscribed for burial in the earth, for they have forsaken Hashem, the Source of fresh water.
(*Yirmeyahu* 17:13)

The verse uses the expression *mayim chayim* — fresh water (literally: living water). This refers to a *mikveh* of the highest caliber — pure spring water, which serves to purify even such cases that a regular *mikveh* cannot (see end of the first chapter of *Masseches Mikvaos*).

"THE PEOPLE OF ISRAEL AND THE HOLY ONE, BLESSED IS HE, ARE ONE"

WHY DOES HASHEM purify the Jewish People specifically in this way and how does this purification work? The Rav (HaRav Shlomo Zalman Auerbach *zt"l*) explained as follows: A *mikveh* can only purify a person or vessel if there is total immersion. The one exception to this rule concerning purification is water — water becomes pure by a process called *hashakah*, minimal physical contact. Even if a bottle containing water is located outside the *mikveh*, so long as a single bit of the water in the bottle touches the waters of the *mikveh*, all its ritually impure contents become purified. Why is this so? Why is it sufficient for water to come in contact with the *mikveh* at one point only, whereas anything else must be fully immersed?

The impure water in the bottle in relationship to the waters of the *mikveh* can be classified as *min be'mino* — a substance that is mixed with its own kind. This forms an immediate mixture and there is no way to distinguish between that which is pure and that which is impure. In that way, the waters of the *mikveh* immediately purify the impure water.

The Rav explained that this is the manner in which Hashem purifies the Jewish People — "The people of Israel and the Holy One, Blessed is He, are one." If we can speak in such terms, we can say that Hashem's relationship with the Jewish nation is one of *min be'mino*. The Jewish People are like water — simple *hashakah* is sufficient to purify them. This *hashakah* works even if they are still surrounded by the material world and have not totally rid themselves of their past. The moment there is even the smallest amount of devotion to the Almighty, *"each has found his own kind and has been awakened"* (*Eruvin* 9b). Minimal contact is enough to cause this total purification process to take effect and to spread to the water at the very bottom of the container as well.

It may be true that the repentance of the people of Ninveh, who were not Jewish, was accepted; this, however, was only after they put on sackcloth and ashes and fasted and changed their ways. They had to first thoroughly remove the outer layers of sin from their bodies (see *Yalkut Shimoni* 550 for the extent of their repentance; see also the opinion of Shemuel in *Ta'anis* 16a).

There is one thing, however, that can prevent any sort of purification: *"A person who holds a dead* sheretz, *a vermin, in his hand: even if he immerses in all the waters of the world, his immersion is not effective"* (*Ta'anis* 16a). The *sheretz* in our case is sin: *"Your iniquities have caused a separation between you and your God"* (*Yeshayahu* 59:2). A person who continues to hold on to his sin and has no resolve to cease from doing so cannot become purified! Only one who has resolved to desist from wrongdoing can become *min be'mino* with Hashem, so to speak. Just as the Almighty is distant and distinct from all physicality like a *mikveh* which can never become impure, so must we distance ourselves on this day from any physicality. When that happens, a holy spirit will descend from above and imbue us with additional holiness — for each person in accordance with his preparation. It is not for nothing that the Jewish People on Yom Kippur are compared to angels. Our donning white garb and reciting, בָּרוּךְ שֵׁם כְּבוֹד מַלְכוּתוֹ לְעוֹלָם וָעֶד — *"Blessed is the name of His glorious kingdom for all eternity"* out loud testifies to this great closeness to Hashem.

THE ANGEL WITHIN US

PARENTHETICALLY, I WOULD like to add another idea I heard from the Rav *zt"l*. The first time we recite *"Baruch shem kevod malchuso le'olam va'ed"* out loud, in our resemblance to angels, is in *Kerias Shema* at the beginning of Yom Kippur. At this point it is difficult to see our likeness to angels: after all, we have just finished eating our festive pre-Yom Kippur meal and we are in the mood to enjoy the many beautiful melodies of the Yom Kippur *daven*ing. Despite this, like angels of Hashem we recite out loud, *"Baruch shem kevod malchuso le'olam va'ed."*

Let us take a quick preview: it is twenty-four hours later, the close of Yom Kippur. After an entire day of affliction and fasting, of holiness and purity, of very emotional *daven*ing, we recite *Kerias Shema* for the first time in the post-Yom Kippur *Ma'ariv*, and there we say *"Baruch shem..."* silently. How can this be? At the onset of Yom Kippur, while we were still digesting the delicious chicken, we considered ourselves as angels, whereas twenty-four hours later, after all that has transpired, and our condition really is similar to the angels, the comparison is no longer valid?

The answer is that man is defined by his thoughts and intentions. At the beginning of Yom Kippur, our bodies may be full of food and drink, yet our thoughts on this holy day revolve around whether or not we will succeed in *daven*ing properly. We worry about whether or not our prayers will be accepted and about what Hashem has decreed for us, as well as for the entire nation. One whose thoughts are on spiritual matters can truly be compared to an angel. At the *Ma'ariv* at the conclusion of Yom Kippur, the opposite is the case. The body may have gone through a process of affliction and purification, yet the moment we recite *"Ve-hu rachum ye'chaper avon,"* our mind is on the cake awaiting us. The angel within us seems to have disappeared!

CONTINUE CLIMBING THE MOUNTAIN!

THE ANGEL MAY have departed, but we must not allow the day's accomplishments to "fly away" as well. We have attained a much higher level and we must do our utmost to retain it. This idea is alluded to in the Torah reading for the first day of Rosh Hashanah. Hagar sighted one angel after another, yet the end result was, *"And his mother took a wife for him from the land of Egypt"* (*Bereishis* 21:21). Could the woman who was in the constant company of angels do no better for her son than find him a *shidduch* with an Egyptian, a people whose immoral, base instincts are expounded upon in the Torah? (See *Vayikra* 18:3.) We read this portion on the first of the ten days of *teshuvah* to remind us that our ascent to the level of angels should not end up the way Hagar's did.

We rejoice on *Motzaei Yom Kippur* for what we have accomplished. We must realize, however, that this is not enough. We must decide in our hearts that this upward progression has to continue. We must spiritually prepare ourselves for the upcoming year. It is at this crucial moment that we must organize our time, committing ourselves to more Torah study, to acts of *chesed*, to properly honoring our parents, so that our material occupations revolve around these spiritual tasks. We must not first find a job, work out the salary, and only then look for a bit of time to squeeze in some mitzvos. If this spiritual ascent does not continue, God forbid, then we have not achieved the goal of Yom Kippur as the Almighty intended. For the past forty days we have been strengthening ourselves by elevating the spiritual above the physical, culminating in a total immersion in the forty *se'ah* of the purity of Yom Kippur. This is the time, while we truly believe in our capabilities, to resolve that next *Erev Yom Kippur* we will be on yet a higher level than this one. One who believes he has the potential and resolves to fulfill it can withstand all obstacles and difficulties.

ALL EYES ARE UPON US!

AS STUDENTS OF the yeshiva, let us take stock. We have spent forty days purifying ourselves. We have just discussed the importance on the ninth of Tishrei of channeling our physical pleasures towards serving Hashem. The climax of all this is Yom Kippur — proof of the supremacy of the spiritual over the physical. How can we even imagine ourselves at this point leaving this holy framework the moment this day of purification ends?[10]

Bittul Torah, neglect of Torah study, in the home is, in one way, a worse offense than in the yeshiva. Regrettably, there are students who sometimes waste their time in yeshiva; but when a *yeshivah bachur* arrives home, all eyes are upon him — he represents all yeshiva students. If he does not learn and does not involve himself in Torah and mitzvos, he is guilty of a tremendous *chillul Hashem*. Other people witnessing this behavior can maintain that if he is free from any obligation to observe the Torah, then they certainly are. Even activities which, in and of themselves, are not prohibited may be a source of *chillul Hashem*. We must remember that all eyes are upon us, because we represent the Torah! (See Rambam, *Hilchos Yesodei HaTorah* 5:11; *chillul Hashem* is on the most serious of the four levels of *kaparah* [*Hilchos Teshuvah* 1:4].)

It is told of R' Yisrael Salanter that he once took ill and was forbidden by his doctors to study Torah. He obeyed the doctors' orders scrupulously, but he made sure, nevertheless, to sit next to an open book and act as if he were learning. R' Yisrael explained that he may have had a valid reason for not learning, but others were not aware of it, and this might cause a *chillul Hashem*.

We must transform these days of *bein ha-zemanim* into a period of *kiddush Hashem* and apply our incredible achievements of

---

10. Yeshivos traditionally begin the *bein ha-zemanim* break after Yom Kippur.

the past forty days to our daily lives. We must help our neighbors and our parents and we must deal honestly in business; this, after all, was the purpose of our eating on *Erev Yom Kippur* — to channel our physical activities into serving Hashem. Once we have built our *sukkah* and purchased our *Arba'ah Minim*, we must return to our learning, so that all those who see us will think, "That is how I would like my sons to act."

The younger generation often feels certain that the older generation has a clear picture of what life is all about. The widening distance from traditional Judaism, however, has caused even older people to lose their clarity. The modern world offers so many diverse lifestyles that it is difficult for people to choose. They often choose according to their assessment of the end product, by comparing the products of various educational systems. Thus, setting a good example is worth more than tens of thousands of exciting *sichos* and *derashos*. This is something we all can do!

THE UPCOMING WEDDING

THE CHASSIDIC WRITINGS tell us that the seven days between Rosh Hashanah and Yom Kippur can be compared to the *shiv'ah neki'im* — the seven clean days of purification the "bride," the Jewish nation, must undergo in preparation for her upcoming "wedding" on Yom Kippur (see *Pri Tzaddik* 8). It is on this day that the great union takes place and all obstacles and barriers between the loving couple are removed.

Following the wedding are seven days of celebration in the "*chuppah*" of the *sukkah*. The seventy nations, Hashem's creatures, are invited as guests, and it is in their honor that we offer seventy bulls on Sukkos. At the conclusion of the seven days, the guests take their leave and on Shemini Atzeres, the *chasan* and *kallah* enter their permanent home alone together (this is symbolized by bringing only one bull on Shemini Atzeres). The *chut hameshulash*, the three-ply cord (*Koheles* 4:12) that ties it all together is the rejoicing over the Torah. On Simchas Torah: The Holy One, Blessed is He, the Torah, and the people of Israel literally become one. May it be the will of Hashem that we merit acting in a way commensurate with the tremendous awakening we are now experiencing. Amen.

GLOSSARY

The following glossary provides a partial explanation of some of the Hebrew and Yiddish (Y.) words and phrases used in this book. The spellings and explanations reflect the way the specific word is used herein. Often, there are alternative spellings and meanings for the words.

AM YISRAEL: the Jewish People.

AMORA: a Talmudic Sage.

AMOS: cubits; arm's lengths.

ARBA'AH MINIM: the Four Species taken on the holiday of Sukkos.

ASHAM: a guilt-offering, a type of sacrifice brought in Temple times.

AVINU: "our father"; referring to the Almighty or title of a patriarch.

AVODAH ZARAH: idol worship.

AVODAS HASHEM: service of God.

BA'AL TESHUVAH: a penitent; a formerly non-observant Jew who returns to Jewish practice and tradition.

BAL TOSIF: "Do not add", the prohibition of adding extraneous elements to a Torah commandment.

BARUCH HASHEM: "Blessed be God!" "Thank God!"

BE'EZRAS HASHEM: "With God's help"; "God willing."

BEIN ADAM LA-MAKOM: between man and God.

BEIN ADAM LE-CHAVERO: between man and his fellow.

BEIN HA-ZEMANIM: a yeshiva vacation period.

BEINONI'IM: average people, between righteous and wicked.

BEN TORAH: a person devoted to a Torah way of life.

BEIS DIN: a court of Jewish law.

BEIS HAMIKDASH: the Holy Temple.

BEKIUS: [Torah] study which is aimed at covering a lot of material, rather than going into depth.

BERACHAH: a blessing.

BIRKAS HAMAZON: the Grace after Meals.

BITTUL TORAH: neglect of Torah study.

B'IYUN: [Torah] study in depth, in close detail.

B'LI NEDER: "without a vow," said when making a commitment, in order to avoid being guilty of a transgression if unable to fulfill it.

BRIS MILAH: the ritual of circumcision.

CHACHAM: a wise, learned person; a Torah authority.

CHASAN: a bridegroom.

CHATAS: a sin-offering, a type of sacrifice brought in Temple times.

CHAYOS HAKODESH: a group of angels that surround God's Throne of Glory.

CHAZAL: the Hebrew acronym for "our Sages, of blessed memory."

CHESED: lovingkindness; acts of kindness.

CHIDDUSH: a new, original explanation of a Torah topic.

CHILLUL HASHEM: desecration of God's Name.

CHOL HAMO'ED: the intermediate days of Pesach and Sukkos.

CHOSHEN: the breastplate, one of the special garments of the High Priest, worn for the Temple service.

CHUMRAH: stringency in interpretation or observance of a Torah commandment.

CHUPPAH: the wedding canopy; the wedding ceremony.

CHUTZ LA'ARETZ: the Diaspora, all countries outside the Holy Land.

DAF YOMI: "a daily page," a program of studying one leaf of Talmud per day.

DAVEN: (Y.) pray.

DERASHAH: a lecture or sermon in which a Torah topic is elucidated.

DIVREI TORAH: words of Torah.

EMUNAH: faith in God.

EPHOD: one of the special garments of the High Priest, worn for the Temple service.

ERETZ YISRAEL: the Land of Israel.

EREV YOM KIPPUR: the day preceding Yom Kippur.

ESROG: the citron, one of the Four Species taken on Sukkos.

GADOL BATORAH: a great Torah scholar.

GAZLAN: one guilty of robbery.

GEMILLUS CHASSADIM: acts of kindness.

HADASSIM: myrtle branches, one of the Four Species taken on the holiday of Sukkos.

HALACHAH: the entire body of Jewish law; a specific law.

HAMELECH: "the King" — God.

HIDDURIM: "beautifications", that is, enhancements to mitzvos.

IM YIRTZEH HASHEM: "God willing."

INUY: affliction.

KALLAH: a bride.

KAREIS: "cutting off of the soul," a Divine punishment for violating certain prohibitions.

KAVANAH: intent and concentration on one's prayers.

KETORES: the incense used in the Temple service.

KIDDUSH HASHEM: sanctification of God's Name.

KODESH HAKODASHIM: the Holy of Holies.

KOHEN: a member of the priestly clan, a direct descendant of Aharon.

KOHEN GADOL: the High Priest.

KORBAN: an offering brought in the Holy Temple.

KULAH: a leniency in interpretation or observance of a Torah commandment.

K'VOD HA-BRIOS: treating one's fellow man with respect.

LASHON HA-RA: derogatory or harmful speech, forbidden by the Torah.

LEHAVDIL: "to differentiate," an expression used to emphasize contrast between the sacred and the profane.

LEVATALAH: in vain, said of a blessing recited with no valid reason.

LEVIYIM: Levites, members of the tribe of Levi.

L'SHEM SHAMAYIM: lit., "for the sake of Heaven," said of an act dedicated to the service of God.

LULAV: a palm branch, one of the Four Species taken on the holiday of Sukkos.

MA'ARIV: the evening prayer service.

MA'ASER KESAFIM: a tithe taken from one's money to be used for charity or another mitzvah.

MACHMIR: to follow a stringent opinion in observance or in ruling on a halachic issue.

MACHZOR: a Holiday prayerbook.

MALKOS: [a punishment of] 39 lashes.

MANEH: a unit of measure.

MASHIACH: the Messiah.

MEIKEL: to follow a lenient opinion in observance or in ruling on a halachic issue.

MELACHAH: a labor forbidden by the Torah on the Sabbath and Festivals.

MELAMED ZECHUS: to judge favorably, to give one the benefit of the doubt.

MESHULASHIM: "triple," the requirement that leaves of myrtle branches taken on Sukkos grow in groups of three (see *hadassim*).

MIDDOS: attributes; character traits.

MIKVEH: a special pool of water for spiritual purification.

MINCHAH: the afternoon prayer service.

MINHAGIM: Jewish customs.

MINYAN: a quorum of ten men required for public prayer service.

MITZVAH: a Torah commandment.

MO'ED: a Jewish holiday.

MOHEL: one who performs ritual circumcision.

MOTZA'EI YOM KIPPUR: the night following Yom Kippur.

MUSSAR: ethical teachings.

NE'ILAH: the closing prayer of the Yom Kippur service recited towards evening.

NIGGUNIM: melodies.

PARAH ADUMAH: the Red Heifer (see *Bemidbar* 19).

PARASHAH: the weekly Torah portion.

PASUK: a Scriptural verse.

PATUR: exempt.

PIKUACH NEFESH: saving a human life.

PIYUT: a liturgical poem.

POSEK: a rabbi qualified to deliver rulings in Halachah.

RABBEINU: our teacher; our master.

RAMBAM: a Hebrew acronym for Rabbi Moshe ben Maimon (Maimonides).

RASHA: a wicked person.

REBBEIM: teachers.

RUACH HAKODESH: Divine inspiration.

SA'IR LA'AZAZEL: the scapegoat chosen by lots on Yom Kippur.

SEFER TORAH: a Torah scroll.

SELICHOS: special penitential prayers.

SEUDAH: a festive meal.

SEUDAS MITZVAH: a festive meal held in honor of particular special occasions.

SHACHARIS: the morning prayer service.

SHADCHAN: a matchmaker.

SHALOM BAYIS: marital harmony.

SHECHINAH: the Divine Presence.

SHE'EILAH: a question on a halachic issue posed to a Torah scholar.

SHEMA: the verse, "Hear, O Israel...," the opening words of the fundamental Jewish prayer which proclaims the unity of God, recited by Jews morning and evening.

SHIDDUCH: a marital match.

SHILUACH HA-KEIN: the commandment to send away a mother bird before taking her young or her eggs.

SHIUR: a lecture on a Torah topic.

SHEMONEH ESREI: lit., "eighteen"; the eighteen blessings of the silent prayer said standing.

SHOFAR: a ram's horn, blown on Rosh Hashanah.

SICHAH: a Torah lecture whose aim is spiritual inspiration.

SUGYA: a specific topic of Talmudic discussion.

SUKKAH: a temporary dwelling erected for the Festival of Sukkos, in which Jews are commanded to spend the Festival.

TACHANUN: prayers of petition, requesting Divine mercy.

TALMID CHACHAM: a Torah scholar.

TANACH: a Hebrew acronym for the Holy Scriptures: Torah, *Nevi'im* (Prophets), and *Kesuvim* (Writings).

TANNA'IM: the Sages of the Mishnah.

TEFILLAH: prayer.

TEFILLIN: boxes of leather encasing specific verses from the Torah written on parchment, worn by Jewish men on the head and the arm during morning prayers.

TESHUVAH: repentance and return to the way of life prescribed by the Torah.

TIKKUN: rectification.

TEYOMES: the central leaves of the palm branch taken on Sukkos.

TZADDIK: a righteous, holy person.

TZADDIK GAMUR: a completely righteous person.

TZARA'AS: a disease of the skin, resembling leprosy.

TZARRI: one of the ingredients of the incense which was burned in the Temple.

TZEDAKAH: charity; righteousness.

TZITZIS: knotted fringes attached to four-cornered garments worn by Jewish males to remind them of God and His commandments.

VIDUY: the confession of sins.

YAMIM NORA'IM: the Days of Awe, Rosh Hashanah and Yom Kippur.

YETZER HA-RA: the evil inclination.

YIDDISHKEIT: (Y.) Judaism.

YOM KIPPUR KATAN: "little" Yom Kippur, a day of repentance observed monthly by pious Jews on the eve of Rosh Chodesh.

ZICHRONOS: "Remembrances," part of the *Mussaf* prayer of Rosh Hashanah detailing God's fulfillment of His promises to the Jewish People.

ZT"L: a Hebrew acronym for "May the memory of the righteous be for a blessing."